Money Method & Mindset

A Simplified Approach to Trading Stocks, Commodities & Forex using Technical Analysis

BHARAT JHUNJHUNWALA

notionpress.com
INDIA · SINGAPORE · MALAYSIA

ISBN 979-8-89363-286-6

Acknowledgements

First and foremost, I extend my deepest gratitude to the Almighty for guiding me and providing me with the opportunity to create this work.

This book would not have been possible without the guidance and inspiration of countless individuals. First and foremost, I extend my deepest gratitude to all the teachers who have shaped my understanding of the markets and fueled my passion for this field. Your knowledge and dedication ignited a fire within me that continues to drive my work.

To my students, past and present, thank you. Your insightful questions, unwavering enthusiasm, and genuine curiosity have pushed me to be a better teacher and a more thoughtful trader.

My journey as a writer and educator would never have begun without the steadfast support of my mother. Your unwavering belief in my abilities has always been my greatest source of strength. To my wife - Ritu, thank you for your love, patience, and the countless cups of tea that fueled the writing process. Your encouragement and sacrifices made this book a reality.

For clear and insightful analysis, all charts in this book utilize the industry-leading TradingView charting platform. (www.tradingview.com)

Finally, I'd like to acknowledge the broader trading community. The camaraderie, the shared experiences, and the endless opportunities for learning have been invaluable along this journey.

About Me

With a career spanning over two decades in the heart of the financial markets, I'm a passionate technical analyst, trader, and mentor. My journey began as the Founder of Opulence Capital Inc., followed by 15+ years as a Prop Trader & Mentor at https://www.prorsi.com. I thrive on translating complex market dynamics into actionable trading strategies across global equities, commodities, equity derivatives, and foreign exchange.

My dedication to continuous learning has led me to earn esteemed certifications such as MFTA, CMT, CFTe and MSTA. These credentials reflect my deep understanding of technical analysis, market psychology, and risk management. This foundation allows me to mentor and guide hundreds of traders across the world, sharing my insights on price action and market sentiment analysis.

As the creator of the Bxtrender Indicator, I've developed a tool embraced by portfolio managers worldwide for its ability to pinpoint market trends and reversals. Today, my focus stays sharp on global equities, commodities, futures & options, where I strive for consistent and profitable trading outcomes.

When I'm not immersed in charts and market analysis, you might find me sharing my passion for trading through speaking engagements or online courses. My mission is simple: to empower traders with the knowledge and tools they need to navigate the financial markets with confidence and success.

Let's Connect:

Website: https://www.prorsi.com

YouTube: @jhunjhunwala_b

X (Formerly Twitter): @jhunjhunwala_b

Instagram: @jhunjhunwala_bh

Linkedin: https://www.linkedin.com/in/bharatmftacmtcftemsta

Introduction

My journey into the world of stock markets, particularly technical analysis, was a whirlwind of information. I devoured over 500 books by various authors and attended countless seminars and webinars. Yet, a nagging frustration persisted – a lack of simplicity. My early forays were plagued by jargon, an overwhelming array of tools, and complex methodologies. Half the battle was deciphering the language itself!

As I delved deeper, a revelation struck me: the market is ultimately driven by human psychology. It's about understanding the movements fueled by emotions. This led me to focus on price and trend analysis, free from jargon. Instead of naming the phenomenon, I prioritized comprehending what the price itself was telling me.

Similarly, risk management often felt like deciphering arcane math problems. Many resources convoluted the concepts, making them unnecessarily complex. Here, I've strived for clarity and practicality.

Finally, there's the often-touted "mindset training." In my experience, it's sometimes a buzzword more than a necessity. However, there are a few key principles that shape a trader's mindset, and I've included those essential pointers without requiring a course in brain anatomy!

This book is a culmination of my ongoing learning journey in the markets. It's a testament to the power of understanding over theoretical definitions. My aim is to provide a jargon-free, math-light experience, with a dose of mindfulness that doesn't require a deep dive into brain function.

Here, you'll find a strong emphasis on understanding price action with minimal reliance on indicators. The essential applications of moving averages and RSI are included, but the focus remains on price itself.

This book is designed to serve as a strong foundation for beginner traders and a valuable upskilling guide for experienced ones alike. Over 300 charts and illustrations make it a highly practical resource.

Welcome aboard! I hope this book earns a cherished spot in your trading library.

Contents

Money, Method & Mindset.

Unlocking the Practical World of Stock Trading using Technical Analysis, Beyond Theoretical Boundaries.

I have always believed that for a trader to embark on a successful journey in the financial markets, they need to follow the three M's in a specific order: Money, Method, and Mindset.

I'm sure many of you may have already begun to question what you've just read, especially if you've been on your trading journey for a while. It might seem contrary to what you've heard before. However, allow me to clarify my perspective, and I'm confident that by the end of this chapter, you'll understand my point of view.

The structure of this entire book follows the 3M approach. We will begin by emphasizing "Money" – determining the necessary capital to trade effectively and how much of your savings it should comprise to secure a comfortable living from the markets. Then, we'll delve into the "Method" section, where we'll concentrate on effective techniques like Technical Analysis and proven trading strategies. Finally, we'll explore valuable Mindset insights, which I've found crucial during my 15+ years in this world of "Mad Money."

I know that in-depth discussions about trading mindset can sometimes feel a bit heavy. To lighten things up, I'll sprinkle mindset tips throughout the book rather than dedicating entire section to the topic. Think of them as refreshing breaks during your learning journey, offering moments to reflect and recenter your approach.

Without further ado, let's dive straight into the first and most vital 'M' on the path to becoming a successful trader - MONEY

Drop I

The Basics of Trading: A Layman's Guide

Embarking on a trading journey transcends mere buying and selling; it demands rigorous analysis, strategic foresight, and unwavering commitment. Far from a simplistic path to wealth, trading parallels running a sophisticated business, integrating data analysis, market trend interpretation, risk management, and decisive action. It's a skillful endeavor, not reliant on luck but on persistent learning and strategy refinement. Aspiring traders must dedicate themselves to mastering the market's complexities, recognizing that success lies in perseverance and continuous improvement.

Chapter 1

The First M - Money

Let's talk about the most crucial trading tool when stepping into the market. This is perhaps the most fundamental thing you need for trading.

When I mentioned the most crucial tool for trading and making money, you might have immediately thought I'd discuss some advanced price action techniques or reveal a magical indicator from my extensive toolbox, honed through years of trading experience. However, you'll be surprised to learn that all these tools and strategies are rendered ineffective without the single most important element in trading. And no, I'm not referring to having a high-performance computer with a lightning-fast internet connection, nor am I talking about selecting a reputable brokerage service offering a variety of trading options. What I'm emphasizing here is the cornerstone of it all: MONEY! Yes, cash or funds are the primary prerequisites for entering the world of trading!

I've often heard trade pundits and gurus emphasizing the importance of having the right mindset and a solid strategy as essential elements for success in the trading world. However, there's a fundamental aspect that tends to be overlooked, and it's something without which both the method and mindset become futile for a trader. Before immersing oneself in the world of quotes and trading screens, aspiring traders must ensure they have a sufficient amount of "risk capital" available to begin trading.

Risk Capital

Risk capital refers to the funds you are prepared to invest in the financial markets, and you are willing to take the risk of potentially losing a portion of this capital, especially during the initial years of your learning journey. These losses, if incurred, should not cause significant financial distress or disrupt your peace of mind. The trading capital I'm referring to as risk capital should constitute the surplus amount left after you have covered all your contingencies, including education, medical expenses, and your daily bills. It's crucial to emphasize that this capital should not be borrowed; it should be entirely your own.

The immediate question that arises is, "How much capital will one require to start trading?"

So, let's break it down this way: Imagine you're a newcomer who has just entered the exciting world of trading for a living, and you're about to make your first trade soon! In this situation, I would suggest starting small, with the smallest amount you can comfortably invest. During these early stages, your primary goal shouldn't be making profits; instead, it should be focused on gaining an understanding of how the trading world operates. There's a significant likelihood that your first few trades may result in losses, and you might lose the capital you initially invested in those early trades.

Yeah, I understand that's not the answer you were looking for! You simply wanted to know how much capital you need to enter trading and generate a substantial return! However, before I can provide a direct answer, there are certain questions I'd like you to consider for yourself. So, if you've made the decision to trade "full time," have you taken the following factors into account?

The primary discussion I have with many aspiring "full-time" traders revolves around a fundamental question: If you have a stable career in another field, why rush into full-time trading? Generating an additional income as a trader can be a great opportunity.

Even if you've made the decision to pursue full-time trading, there are specific capital requirements that need to be addressed before determining the amount of trading capital for your trading account:

1. Your trading account should consist of profits earned from trading, not funds taken from other ventures.
2. It's advisable to have a minimum of two years' worth of living expenses saved in a separate bank account (in addition to your trading capital).
3. You should be prepared for a 50% likelihood of your first year being a losing one.

Now that we've taken the above factors into consideration, let's calculate the amount of trading capital needed to sustain a comfortable lifestyle as a full-time trader!

To calculate this, you'll need to determine two key factors:

1. Your average monthly gains over the past three years (let's call it AMG).
2. Your monthly expectations in terms of earnings (let's call it ME).

Once you have these figures, you can use a simple formula: divide ME by AMG.

For instance, let's say you have achieved an average monthly return of 3% over the past three years, and you aim to earn a monthly income of Rs 100,000 from your trading activities. In this scenario, the capital required for "full-time" trading would amount to approximately Rs 3,333,333.33 let's take it as Rs 34,00,000 (rounded off to account for additional expenses such as brokerage and trading-related taxes, excluding Income Tax).

Raised eyebrows, anyone? I'm sure many of you just received a reality check. Never underestimate the fact that money is the most critical element when it comes to making money in the world of trading!

Let's understand the above with proper numbers:

If a Trader has an expectation for making a post tax return of Rs 12 lacs per annum (Expectations)

Here are his/her monthly returns

December 2020	5.2
January 2021	6.1
February 2021	-3.2
March 2021	4.7
April 2021	-5.8
May 2021	5.8
June 2021	6.3
July 2021	-6.3
August 2021	4.9
September 2021	6.7
October 2021	-2.9
November 2021	5.4
December 2021	-7.2
January 2022	4.2
February 2022	6.5
March 2022	-3.5
April 2022	-4.9
May 2022	5.9

June 2022	-2.1
July 2022	7.2
August 2022	5.6
September 2022	6.9
October 2022	-6.1
November 2022	-7.5
December 2022	4.8
January 2023	7.5
February 2023	-3.7
March 2023	6.4
April 2023	-5.2
May 2023	-4.3
June 2023	5.3
July 2023	-2.8
August 2023	7.8
September 2023	-
October 2023	6.2
November 2023	4.5
Monthly Average	4.1

My monthly expectation is Rs 100,000, so the total trading capital required would be Rs 100,000 divided by 4.1%, which comes close to Rs 2,439,024 (rounded off to Rs 2,500,000).

The assumption of a 4.1% monthly return may be a bit optimistic. Let me clarify that even the best traders in the profession aim for a 3% monthly return. I would advise you to start with an estimate that is 40% lower than your historical returns and overestimate your monthly expectations by 50%.

In that case, my monthly requirement will be Rs 150,000, and the average monthly return will be 2.46%. So, the total trading capital required will be Rs 150,000 divided by 2.46%, which is approximately 61 lakhs (rounded).

My intentions are not to demoralize you, but what I'm trying to do here is provide you with the tough reality checks that other authors or coaches may not. You have to accept the truth to succeed in this game. Fancy numbers won't help.

Your trading capital plays a crucial role in determining your returns. So, before making any decisions, calculate your expectations and the capital required to achieve those expectations.

By now, I assume that the capital arrangements are sorted out. The next significant question is, how much time will it take for you to become a "Full-Time Trader"?

During my extensive 15+ years in the market and over half a decade of coaching, I've encountered numerous individuals with strong academic backgrounds such as doctors, CAs, engineers, lawyers, and more. What I've realized is that trading requires a distinct skill set. While these professions undoubtedly demand time and effort, assuming that success in fields like being a CA or doctor guarantees success in trading is far from the truth. I've witnessed undergraduate housewives achieve remarkable financial success, while MBA and engineering professionals have chosen to quit the trading journey.

Becoming a full-time trader requires knowledge, not just luck. Many aspiring traders mistakenly rely solely on luck when aiming to transition into full-time trading. To gain mastery over this knowledge, aspiring full-time traders must develop a comprehensive understanding of various aspects related to trading. The duration it takes truly varies from one trader to another. Some may feel mentally prepared in as little as six months, while others might require two years or even five years of dedicated study and practice.The key takeaway is that when you make the decision to become a full-time trader, your learning journey should focus on consistently generating profits. While losses may occur, the goal is to ensure that the potential for profit outweighs the losses.

How to Learn & Practice?

Anticipate dedicating 6 to 12 months of effort before achieving the level of consistency required to generate a monthly profit. Once you reach that stage, based on my observations, those monthly profits are likely to persist.

When you're in the process of learning a new market, it's crucial to invest several hours each day. If you're only dedicating an hour a day, it might take you a longer time to achieve profitability. It's important to note that this doesn't imply you have to be actively trading all day long. On the contrary, I now spend only about two hours (or even less) day trading, and my swing trading activities only require about 20 minutes each day. However, in the initial stages, it's essential to practice trading. Even when you're not executing actual trades, you should be analyzing charts, studying market trends, testing strategies, and enhancing your mental fortitude. Spending just two hours a day on trading is the ultimate goal. In the beginning, you'll need to invest more time than that if you aim to achieve consistent profitability within a few months.

Remember, it's not just practice that leads to perfection; it's perfect practice that fosters improvement. If you consistently practice the wrong techniques or repeat the same errors, you'll continue to face challenges, regardless of the number of hours you dedicate. Having traded for over 15 years, I can attest that I still make mistakes, but with experience, I've become adept at identifying and rectifying them promptly. Consequently, the frequency of my mistakes has diminished over time.

Successful traders need to possess self-reflection and self-reliance. They thoroughly evaluate their trading strategies, maintaining objectivity in identifying potential improvements. If a previously successful strategy no longer yields results, it's essential to probe into the reasons. Has the market environment shifted? Is there increased or decreased volatility compared to before? Are you frequently getting stopped out, or is your analysis fundamentally flawed? Asking these critical questions enables you to pinpoint the underlying issues and adapt accordingly.

Accomplished traders are committed to honing and optimizing their methodologies; it's their driving force. Once you've crafted a trading method, dedicate yourself to executing it with precision. Place your emphasis on the process rather than fixating on outcomes. Positive results naturally flow from the effective implementation of your plan. Stay flexible in adapting to market fluctuations, and proactively explore how your strategy can evolve in response to changing conditions—anticipate these changes before they occur. Consistently pose questions like, "If the market's volatility shifts, or if it transitions from trending to range-bound (or vice versa), how will my strategy be influenced? How should I adapt?"

Anyone can profit from trading during a trend, but it takes a genuine trader to thrive in any market scenario. This implies dedicating time to practice in diverse market conditions and acquiring the wisdom of when to abstain from trading—equally vital as recognizing the opportune moments to trade. Investing two focused hours daily to refine techniques, accommodate market shifts, and execute strategies with precision is far superior to spending five hours engaging in haphazard trades. Relying on impulsive "gut instinct" trades throughout the day undermines the cultivation of consistency and achieves the opposite effect. For consistent profitability, prioritize practicing consistency day in and day out!

Consistency is the ultimate key

Many traders experience a few months of profitability, but sustaining it is the real challenge.

Difficult times are inevitable. In my case, they arrived about five years into my trading career. After an initial profitable phase, I hit a slump. The market hadn't changed; it was my own distraction and wavering interest in day trading that caused the downturn.

Regardless of the reason, your trading profits may dwindle at some point. It's crucial to persevere if you want to continue trading. After some introspection, I rediscovered my passion for trading and recommitted to the process. It took a few months to regain my footing.

If you've traded successfully for several years, you likely possess the skills to do it again. Most traders I know who have over five years of experience continue to thrive. Even those who temporarily left trading but had previous success can typically return and become profitable again within six months. The tools are still there; it's a matter of reentering the mindset of consistency.

For more insights into the psychological challenges that impact traders and individuals, will be explored in the last section of this book "Mindset".

Wrapping up!

Whether you're devising your own trading strategies or adopting someone else's, it's important to understand that it will likely take you six months to a year to achieve the level of consistency needed for regular monthly profits. This assumes that you are dedicating several hours each day to deliberate and systematic practice. For some individuals, this journey may extend beyond a year; a year-long learning curve is not uncommon. It's crucial to be financially prepared for this endeavor and avoid relying solely on your trading income until it's sufficient to sustain your living expenses. Even then, it's advisable to maintain multiple streams of income for financial stability.

Your ability to generate income from trading isn't solely determined by your monthly returns; your capital plays a significant role. The positive aspect is that if you can maintain consistent profitability, even a modest trading account has the potential to grow into a source of income. However, it's important to note that the process may take more time when starting with a smaller account size.

The factors mentioned become significant only if you belong to the group of profitable traders. Remember, the vast majority of individuals who venture into short-term trading won't achieve consistent profits. What sets successful traders apart is the investment of time and dedicated practice. To genuinely claim the title of a consistent trader, you must accumulate several years of experience and effectively navigate through various market conditions and personal challenges.

Drop II

Navigating the Unpredictable World of Financial Markets

In trading, surprises are common. It's hard to guess what's next, like the weather. Markets can change fast, often in ways you don't expect.

What helps? A good trading plan. It's like a map that helps you through the market's ups and downs. Your plan includes your trading style, what risks you're okay with, and your goals. It also looks at market trends and possible risks.

Creating this plan needs effort. But with it, trading feels less stressful. You'll know what to do, even when the market is tough.

Having a solid plan is key for lasting success in trading. So, take your time to make a good one and stick to it. It's worth it.

Chapter 2

The Second M - Method

The second most crucial element for successful and profitable trading is having a well-established method, commonly referred to as a 'strategy.' Randomly entering trades at any given moment or price level is not a sustainable approach. Your trades must be underpinned by a sound rationale, which can be derived through various means, including:

1. Fundamental Analysis
2. Technical Analysis
3. News and Media Insights
4. Gut Feeling!

Trading without a solid strategy is akin to sailing without a compass. Having a method in place is your navigational tool in the complex world of financial markets.

Price movements in the market are typically instigated by catalysts, and these catalysts can encompass a wide range of factors that 'smart money' perceives as significant. As retail traders, we possess tools that allow us to decipher and follow these market moves. Various trading methods aim to achieve this goal, with some identifying opportunities in advance, others catching them in real-time, and some reacting after the event has already unfolded.

In this book, our primary focus lies on Technical Analysis, as it serves as a comprehensive study that integrates elements from all the aforementioned trading approaches. It provides us with a valuable backdoor perspective, allowing us to understand and navigate the intricacies of the market dynamics more effectively.

The Fundamental Analysis World

I frequently encounter a common question: why do I place such significant emphasis on Technical Analysis over Fundamental Analysis? The answer lies in the fact that the definition of Fundamental Analysis is not crystal clear to the vast majority of individuals who employ it. So, if I were to pose the question to you, 'What is Fundamental Analysis?' how would you go about defining it?

You might describe it as an analysis that delves into a company's financial records, specifically examining its Profit and Loss statement, Cash Flow statement, and Balance Sheet. Through this analysis, we calculate unique ratios that serve as indicators for assessing the true and just market value of a stock. If the stock is trading near or below this intrinsic value, it is considered an attractive buy, whereas the opposite holds true for stocks trading above their intrinsic value.

In reality, the description I provided earlier does not align with the true essence of "fundamental analysis"; rather, it falls more under the purview of "financial analysis." It's important to note that financial analysis inherently lags behind market developments since the data, such as quarterly financial reports, is typically released after most market pricing has already factored in these effects.

In reality, Fundamental Analysis encompasses a much broader spectrum, including:

1. Assessing the management's competence and leadership within the company.
2. Understanding the industry's product lineup, both current and future offerings.
3. Examining the overall economic climate and the company's operating environment.
4. Analyzing government policies and regulations affecting the company or its sector.
5. Monitoring geopolitical conditions that could impact the company's operations.
6. Evaluating the anticipated behavior of the U.S. dollar.
7. Anticipating trends in oil pricing and their implications.
8. Investigating the export policies of the countries where the company's products are sold.
9. Exploring potential internal connections within the company's hierarchy to gain insights into forthcoming significant announcements and developments.

This comprehensive approach to Fundamental Analysis provides a holistic view, allowing investors to make informed decisions based on a broader understanding of a company's operating context.

The reality is, my friend, that the truth can be quite daunting. It's a fact that it's virtually impossible for any single individual to diligently monitor all the aspects mentioned above. The constraints of time, knowledge, and resources make it a challenging endeavor. Even if we were to acquire these inputs, the sheer volume of companies to analyze using these criteria would be staggering.

Now, let's grasp a fundamental truth. What do all those factors mentioned earlier ultimately influence? The answer is clear: both the price and the trading volumes of a stock. When positive developments occur for a company in a favorable global environment, we can expect the stock price to rise, and conversely, it may fall when unfavorable circumstances arise.

So, what is Technical Analysis? At its core, it is the meticulous study of price movements and trading volumes.

In essence, Technical Analysis serves as a complementary perspective, providing insights that can be seen as a rear-view mirror to Fundamental Analysis.

Technical Analysis entails the examination of market trends by analyzing price movements, trading volumes, and a range of derivative indicators. Its primary purpose is to respond to price movements and make informed trading decisions based on this analysis.

When you search the internet for the definition of Technical Analysis, you'll often come across terms like "predict" and "forecast." However, it's essential to understand that predicting or forecasting prices is an impossible task unless you possess time-traveling abilities. So, don't be swayed by the notion that price movements can be accurately predicted. Technical Analysis is, in fact, a reactive study rather than a predictive one.

Technical Analysis proves most fruitful when your primary concern is understanding "what the price is doing" rather than fixating on "why the price is doing it."

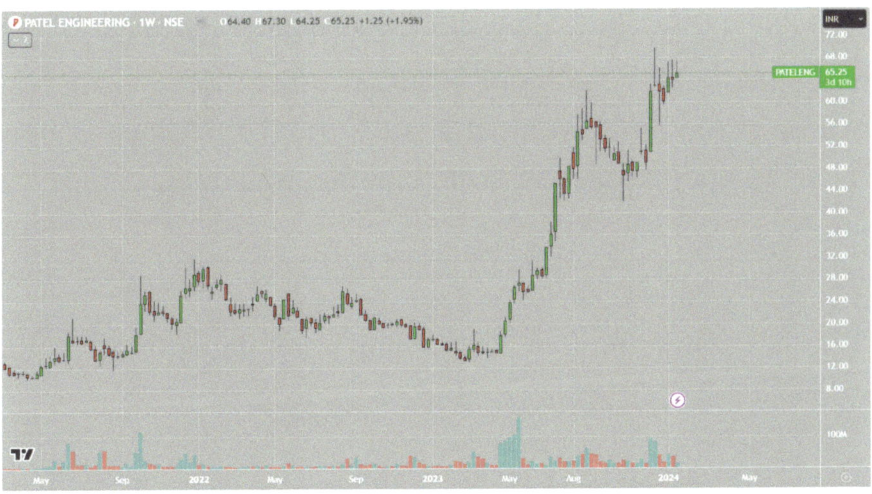

Take a glance at the chart, where the stock surged over 400% in just 50 trading sessions. As technical analysts, our focus isn't on dissecting the reasons behind the stock's rapid ascent (why); instead, we're keenly interested in devising strategies to capitalize on and ride this trend (what). Furthermore, we do not dwell on how far the price move will extend (forecast). Instead, we employ techniques that will promptly exit our position as soon as the stock begins to reverse its course (react).

TRP or Technicals?

Now, let's shift our focus to the third well-known method of trading: Following **News and Media**. We'll explore why this approach often proves to be an elusive pursuit.

The primary and most compelling reason to avoid relying on news and media analysts is that they are fundamentally "journalists" and not "analysts." In essence, their role involves reading scripts or stories, and they lack the professional skills necessary for effective trading. Often, they struggle to provide comprehensive explanations or insights into price movements. For instance, in the event of a sudden price decline, a "news reader" might struggle to discern whether it's merely a "technical blip" or a more substantial sell-off.

Take a look at the chart above, which illustrates the Nifty50. The red arrow signifies November 9, 2016, the day immediately following the announcement of demonetization, involving the withdrawal of 500 and 1000 rupee notes. This news came as a shockwave, leaving everyone in astonishment. Media outlets were abuzz with predictions of a cash shortage and a market collapse.

But here's what actually occurred: the opposite. Contrary to the media sentiment, the market responded differently. Were there any technical signals that contradicted the media narrative? Yes, indeed (we'll delve into those signals later). For now, consider the traders who may have sold their holdings or, worse yet, shorted the index based on the forecasts of media pundits!

This incident is just one of many instances where the media has presented a contrasting view. I don't have any intention to undermine their efforts, but if we have a strong grasp of technical analysis, we can at least cross-check the charts ourselves to gain deeper insights and form a more well-rounded perspective.

Furthermore, it's essential to recognize that media outlets are often motivated by ratings and the pursuit of higher TRPs (Television Rating Points). In their quest for viewership, other priorities can take a backseat, potentially leading to an overload of information that may not be particularly useful. Instead of offering clarity, this excess of information can introduce biases. Lastly, it's worth noting that media sources can be susceptible to manipulation by influential market players, often referred to as the "Big Boys" or "Smart Money."

The Gut's Feeling

Some individuals, particularly those with strong egos, may develop a profound belief in their luck. However, relying on luck has no place in a professional trading strategy.

For novice traders, one of the riskiest scenarios is when they trust their gut feeling, and by chance, the trade moves in their favor, turning a profit. This initial success can create a false sense of confidence, as they achieve profitability without adhering to a predefined strategy.

If these traders continue to rely on intuition rather than developing and following a well-defined, step-by-step, and repeatable strategy, their chances of consistent long-term success diminish significantly.

Trusting one's gut feelings may also lead traders to forgo using stop-loss orders because they believe in the eventual triumph of their approach. They may be willing to endure short-term losses in anticipation of long-term gains, leading them to hold onto losing positions far longer than experienced traders would.

Seasoned and advanced traders typically adhere to a well-defined and repeatable strategy. This approach eliminates the temptation to rely on gut instincts, reducing the influence of emotions in their daily market analysis and decision-making process.

Wrapping Up

It's clear that attempting to trade the markets with insufficient knowledge is a fruitless endeavor. To succeed, you must have a strong strategy supported by thorough and extensively tested results. Any method you choose to follow should be grounded in a well-documented history of backtesting.

It's essential not to place undue reliance solely on what you see, hear, or read in the markets. Price and trading volumes serve as gateways to uncovering the truth and are vital components of a successful trading approach.

Drop III

A Trader's Guide to Emotional Control

When it comes to trading, emotions can often cloud judgment and lead to poor decision-making. Many traders find themselves on an emotional rollercoaster, focusing more on the potential gains or losses rather than the market itself. But there's a better way: mindfulness.

Mindfulness in trading means staying present and focused on the market's movements, rather than being consumed by thoughts of profit and loss. Instead of letting emotions dictate your trades, you learn to observe and react to price action objectively.

One effective tool for practicing mindfulness in trading is keeping a trading journal. Think of it as your diary for your relationship with the financial markets. By recording your thoughts, feelings, and observations each day, you gain valuable insight into your trading habits and emotional patterns.

A trading journal helps you become more self-aware, allowing you to identify any biases or tendencies that may be affecting your trading decisions. It serves as a visual record of your progress and growth as a trader, helping you learn from both your successes and mistakes.

By practicing mindfulness and keeping a trading journal, you can develop greater emotional control and discipline in your trading. You'll be better equipped to handle the ups and downs of the market with composure and confidence, ultimately leading to more consistent and profitable trading results. So, start your mindfulness journey today and watch your trading skills soar.

Chapter 3

The Emergence of Technical Analysis

Now that we've chosen to incorporate Technical Analysis into our trading journey, it's crucial to gain some insight into its historical roots. While I won't delve into extensive details, understanding its origins is essential because it forms the foundation from which all our trading strategies will spring. So, let's explore the emergence of Technical Analysis briefly.

The Dow Theory

The origins of modern-day technical analysis can be traced back to the early 1900s, with Charles H. Dow playing a pivotal role in its development. Charles Dow was not only a writer but also the editor of a newsletter called The Wall Street Journal. In these newsletters, he introduced and applied various technical analysis techniques, many of which were then unfamiliar and not widely known.

Charles H Dow

Dow's groundbreaking work involved analyzing market behaviors using the Dow Jones Industrial Average (DJIA), and he was the visionary who conceived the idea of creating stock market indices. Unfortunately, he passed away in 1902 before officially formalizing what we now recognize as the Dow Theory—the cornerstone of modern technical analysis.

However, Dow's disciples and followers meticulously compiled his work, ultimately giving birth to "The Dow Theory" as it exists today. Unbeknownst to him at the time, Charles Dow had inadvertently crafted an advanced and time-tested theory. He is rightfully honored as the Father of Technical Analysis.

After Charles Dow's passing in 1902, the responsibility for advancing and refining his theory fell into the capable hands of his successor, William P. Hamilton. Hamilton's significant contribution came in the form of his book "The Stock Market Barometer," published in 1922. This work not only expanded upon Dow's original theories but also solidified the Dow Theory as a foundational component of technical analysis.

In 1932, Robert Rhea took the reins and published "The Dow Theory," further enhancing and honing Dow's initial concepts. In 1960, E. George Schaefer added to the legacy with his book "How I Helped More Than 10,000 Investors to Profit in Stocks," which included a dedicated section on the Dow Theory. Lastly, Richard Russell's 1961 publication, "The Dow Theory Today," offered a contemporary interpretation of Dow's ideas, which continues to be widely read and respected in the field of technical analysis.

In his timeless book "The Dow Theory" published in 1932, Robert Rhea remarked that "the value of the Dow Theory grows with time... those who apply it two decades hence will possess a more substantial advantage than we do today."

Now, well over 80 years later, we find ourselves in an even more advantageous position. Neglecting the Dow Theory in the 21st century could pose a significant risk to your portfolio.

As you progress through this book, you'll observe that each tool and concept we delve into harmoniously aligns with the Dow Theory. You will come to appreciate how mastering this theory is not just beneficial but indispensable. The Dow Theory serves as the bedrock upon which the entire science of Technical Analysis is built.

Understanding The Dow Theory

The Dow Theory rests upon six fundamental principles, and in my perspective, these very principles serve as the foundation for the entire realm of technical analysis. These six principles can be summarized as follows:

1. Market Averages Incorporate All Information
2. Market Movements Comprise Three Key Trends
3. Trends Progress Through Distinct Stages
4. Volume Should Validate Trend Direction
5. Mutual Confirmation of Averages is Essential
6. A Trend Persists Until Reversal Signals Emerge

Now, let's delve into these principles one by one.

1) Market Averages Incorporate All Information

The closing price of a stock serves as a collective decision made by market participants at the conclusion of each trading day. It reflects the consensus among all these participants regarding their current and future outlook on that particular stock. This phenomenon is commonly referred to as "discounting."

In essence, the price already incorporates and discounts all available information, including everything that is currently happening and any factors that may influence the price in the future. In simpler terms, whatever news you hear, read, or see has already been factored into the stock's price.

In the chart above, you can observe that discussions about the approval of a BTC ETF by the SEC were ongoing in mid-January 2024. However, it's important to note that the market had already discounted this development well in advance. So, what transpired during the actual event? Surprisingly, instead of a significant price surge that many had anticipated, there was a phenomenon of profit booking. The reason behind this might be that the information regarding the BTC ETF had been factored into the market for several months leading up to the announcement.

2) Market Movements Comprise Three Key Trends

Price movements in the market follow distinct trends, and Charles Dow identified three primary types of trends: the Primary Trend, the Secondary Trend, and the Minor Trend.

The Primary Trend holds the utmost significance in market analysis. Typically, when experts talk about a Bull Market or Bear Market, they are referring to this primary trend. This trend typically spans a duration of 12 to 18 months.

During a Primary Bull Market, prices advance as they establish higher peaks and higher troughs. Conversely, in a Primary Bear Market, prices decline as they create lower peaks and lower troughs.

You may observe that the price is trending upwards, and in the process, it is forming higher peaks and higher troughs - a characteristic of a Bull Market with the Primary Trend pointing upwards.

Similarly, in the chart above, you can observe that prices are in a downward trend, characterized by the formation of lower peaks and lower troughs - a clear indication of a Bear Market with the Primary Trend pointing downwards.

Secondary Movements, also known as reactions, are responsive movements that occur in response to the prevailing trend. They can be characterized as intermediate counter-trend reactions, which means they temporarily counteract the dominant trend. These reactions can manifest as declines in a bull market or advances in a bear market. The intensity of these secondary movements can vary in relation to the larger trend and where within that trend they occur.

If the primary trend is relatively young and has recently commenced, the secondary reaction that follows may typically be in the range of 10% to 15%. However, as the primary trend matures and evolves, the intensity of these secondary reactions tends to increase, occasionally reaching levels of 25% to 30%. Additionally, it's essential to consider that the duration of the recovery from these reactions is influenced by the depth of the correction. Shallow reactions might last for approximately 10 to 15 days, whereas deeper reactions can extend for a more extended period, ranging from 25 to 60 days.

In the chart displayed above, you can observe the white arrows representing secondary reactions within the broader primary trend. It's evident that when the primary trend initially began, the corrections were relatively shallow, and the subsequent recoveries were swift. However, as the primary trend continued to evolve, the corrections became more pronounced, leading to longer recovery periods.

The last category of trends is the **minor trend**, characterized by short-term movements lasting from 1 to 3 days in the market. These minor trends can occur within both the primary and secondary trends. They are often considered as market "noise" and can be influenced by factors like media manipulation and reactions from novice traders.

In the chart above, the minor reactions are indicated by the black arrows. These reactions are largely inconsequential and lack significant analytical value.

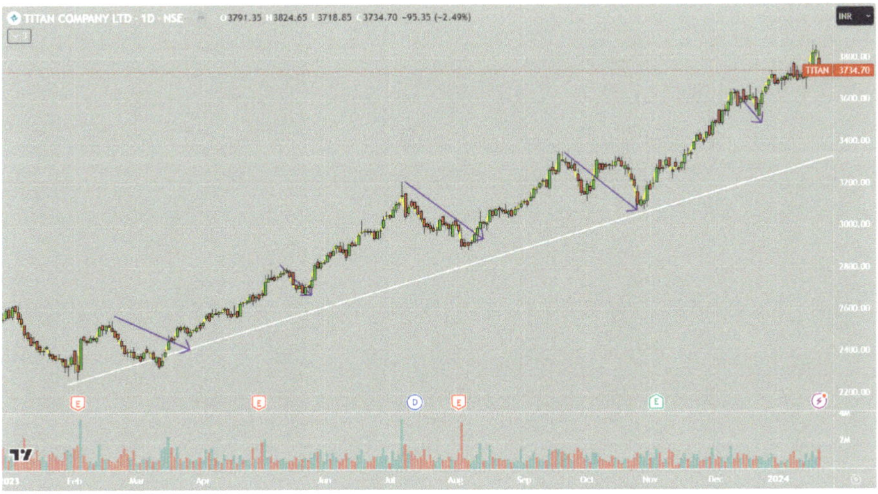

In the chart displayed above, I've highlighted all three trends concurrently. The white line represents the primary trend, the violet line signifies the secondary trend, and the barely noticeable yellow line, which holds minimal relevance, corresponds to the minor trend.

Now, let's eliminate the price and focus solely on the lines in isolation. This perspective will provide you with a broader understanding of what you should prioritize when embarking on a trading career.

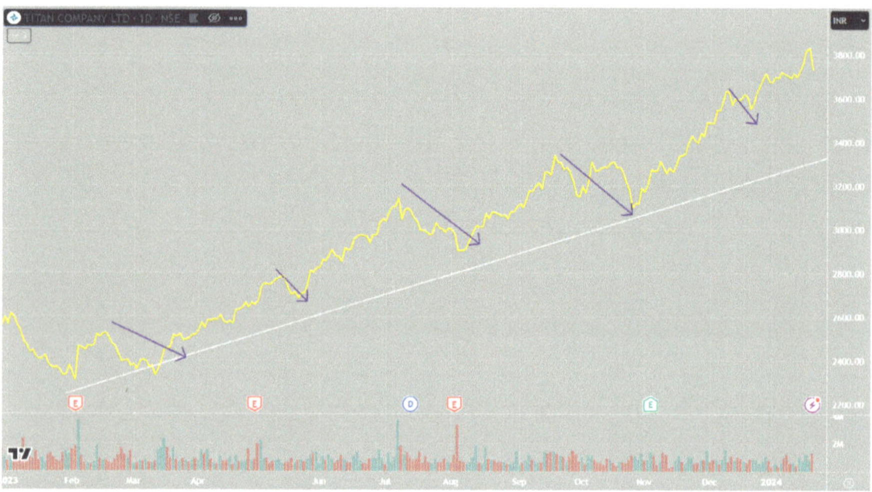

So, it's clear now that the primary trend and secondary trend are the ones worth trading, while the minor trend is essentially noise and not suitable for trading. However, it's ironic that many traders tend to fixate on the minor trend, often neglecting the bigger picture.

3) Trends Progress Through Distinct Stages

According to the Dow Theory, the primary trend consists of three distinct phases: accumulation, markup/markdown, and distribution.

Please take a look at the chart provided below.

The financial markets evolve through this cycle, indicating its continuous and cyclical nature.

Now, let's allocate some time to delve into each of these stages and gain a comprehensive understanding of them. We'll explore the importance of understanding these stages more deeply shortly.

The Accumulation Stage (Stage I): The accumulation stage, also referred to as Stage I, commences following the conclusion of a primary bear trend. During this phase, the prolonged decline experiences occasional significant rallies, injecting a glimmer of hope into the overall declining market sentiment. This stage initiates when the markets have effectively "discounted" all the most adverse news, and investor confidence begins to gradually rekindle. Prices cease their downward trajectory and start consolidating.

Take a moment to examine the chart below. In this instance, a year-long declining primary trend, which commenced in June 2014, came to a halt in July 2015. During this phase, prices ceased their downward movement, and the pattern of forming lower tops and lower bottoms transitioned into a phase characterized by nearly equal tops and bottoms, marking the **accumulation zone**. This is the first stage of the bull markets. The markets are setting up a base to start a new primary trend.

Take a moment to examine the chart below. In this instance, a year-long declining primary trend, which commenced in June 2014, came to a halt in July 2015. During this phase, prices ceased their downward movement, and the pattern of forming lower tops and lower bottoms transitioned into a phase characterized by nearly equal tops and bottoms, marking the accumulation zone.

The Markup Phase(Stage II): As the stock begins to break out from the accumulation zone, it captures the interest of other investors, including mutual funds and breakout traders who possess a good understanding of market dynamics. These investors start buying the stock, propelling its price higher. This marks the beginning of a primary uptrend, known as the markup phase. During this phase, the stock steadily climbs, forming higher tops and higher bottoms.

Take a moment to review the chart below. After a period of 10 months in the accumulation phase, the stock finally broke out in May 2016. Since then, the stock has been on an upward trajectory, forming higher tops and higher bottoms. This phase is where the stock tends to announce positive financial results, introduce new products, appoint renowned professionals to its board, secure numerous national and international approvals and orders, and witness overall favorable developments. It is during this phase that traders should be active, as we buy into the markup phase. For the same reason, this phase is also referred to as the participation phase.

This stage is alternatively known as Stage II.

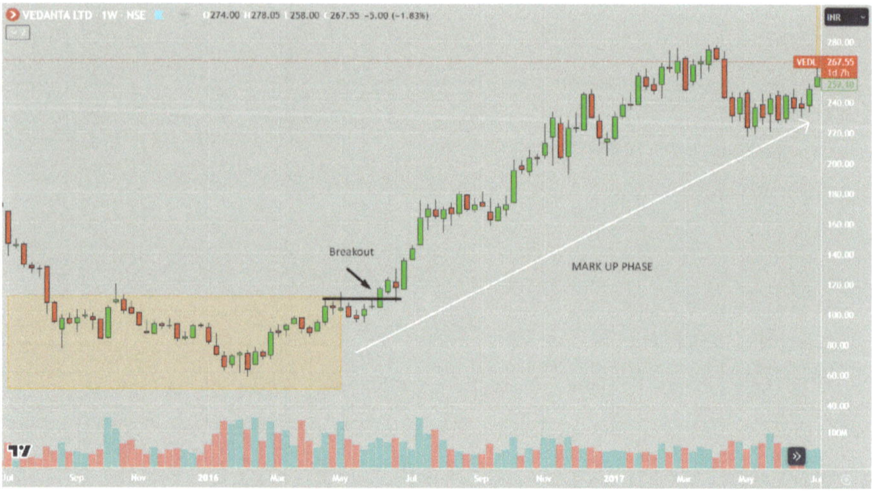

The Distribution Phase(Stage III): Eventually, the stock garners the attention of the media and other participants in the market. Media outlets start featuring the stock prominently, and discussions about it surge across various social media platforms. This marks the period when smart money, who had strategically accumulated the stock during the accumulation phase, begins offloading their holdings. Having reaped substantial profits during the participation phase, they now opt to secure their gains by selling their positions.

The distribution phase involves smart money investors commencing the sale of their shares to the public, capitalizing on their profits, and withdrawing their investments from the market. Meanwhile, the public remains active in buying, persisting even as the market embarks on a downward trajectory. Eventually, a tipping point is reached where the supply of shares surpasses the demand, leading to a decline in prices.

Typically, there's a noticeable surge in momentum or a sharp uptick in stock prices just before the distribution phase commences. This period is characterized by exuberance and euphoria, where even individuals who aren't usually involved in trading, like your grandmother, start discussing the company and its prospects extensively.

In the chart provided above, you can observe that the stock experienced a surge in momentum (fueled by media & FOMO buying), just before entering a sideways movement phase. When the stock begins the distribution phase, a change in its primary trend characteristics becomes evident. It will cease forming higher tops and higher bottoms, transitioning instead to a pattern of creating equal tops and bottoms.

It's not advisable to engage in short trading during the distribution phase because it's challenging to predict when a stock will eventually break down from the distribution zone.

Prices ultimately break down from the distribution phase and begin to move downward vigorously. This marks the commencement of the markdown phase.

Mark Down Phase (Stage IV): During the markdown phase, a significant descent in stock prices ensues, characterized by the creation of lower tops and lower bottoms. The sentiment surrounding the stock turns negative, earnings decline, geopolitical concerns arise, inflation may surge, and demand weakens. This phase is also referred to as Stage IV and represents a participation phase for traders seeking to take short positions.

In the chart below, following the breakdown from the distribution zone, the stock plummets swiftly. The decline appears relentless.

In the final stages of the decline, there is a heightened sense of concern within the market. Nearly everyone is selling, and the media is in full swing, amplifying the selling pressure by highlighting all the negativity and bad news associated with the specific stock. This is the moment when an uninformed participant sells out of sheer **exhaustion**, unable to endure any more losses. The last phase of selling is typically driven by media influence and fear, and the momentum is particularly strong during this period.

After this period, the stock enters another accumulation phase. Take a look at the chart below to see how the media fueled the last decline stage, followed by the onset of accumulation.

The cycle of accumulation, mark-up, distribution, and markdown continues in an ongoing fashion. This stock cycle typically precedes the business cycle due to the discounting mechanism inherent in the markets. Have a look at the Stage Cycle below.

4) Volume Should Validate Trend Direction

The typical relationship between price and volume should involve expanding volume during primary uptrends and contracting volume during declines. If the volume remains lackluster during price advances and starts expanding during declines, it could serve as an early warning sign that the prevailing trend might be on the verge of a reversal. An expansion of volume during rallies indicates strong buying pressure, suggesting that the stock remains a favored choice among large institutions.

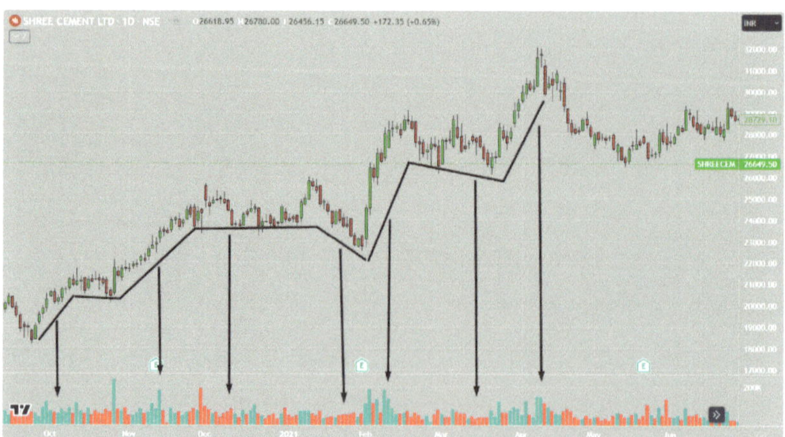

In the chart above, you can observe that the price was consistently rising with expanding volumes, and during secondary corrections, the volumes remained subdued. As long as this price and volume behavior remained consistent, the trend stayed intact. Throughout the upward move, you'll notice that the green bars, indicating buying interest, outnumbered the red ones.

Now, let's shift our attention to the chart below. After a significant advance with increasing volume, the stock began to decline with expanding volume. This signified that the primary uptrend might be experiencing a more substantial correction. Additionally, you'll observe that during the primary declining phase, the rallies were characterized by decreasing volumes, indicating a lack of buying interest from institutions.

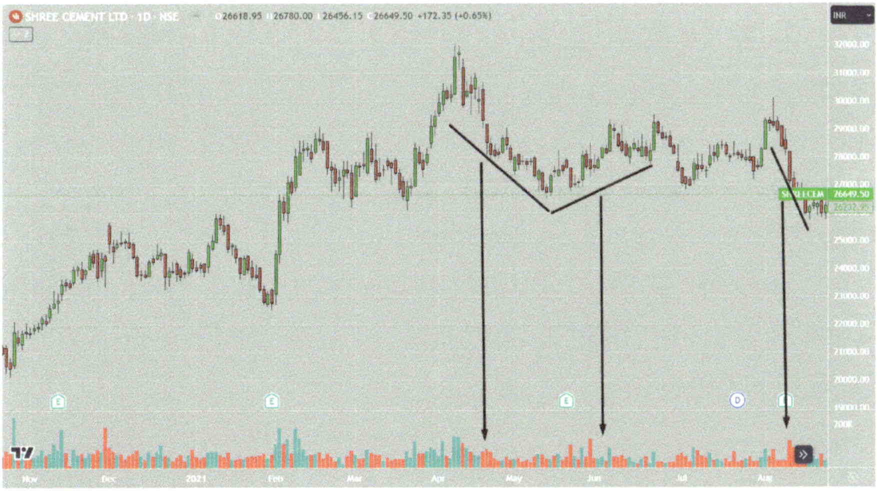

5) Mutual Confirmation of Averages is Essential

In accordance with the Dow theory, the validation of a trend hinges on the confirmation between different indices or market averages. This underscores the importance of confirming a trend in one index or average with the corresponding trend in another to bolster the reliability of the analysis.

Initially, Dow utilized the Dow Jones Industrial Average (DJIA) and the Dow Jones Transportation Average (DJTA) to validate the market's strength. The Industrial index monitored production, while the transportation index observed distribution. In an expanding economy, it's crucial for both production and distribution to progress harmoniously. Any divergence or anomaly between these two indicators can serve as a warning sign for economic growth.

This comparison was initially conducted in 1900, but as markets have evolved, we've expanded our analytical toolkit. Today, we can perform inter-market comparisons, intra-market assessments, sector-relative strength analyses, and much more using this fundamental principle. To illustrate, consider the need for strong overall market participation across various market segments, including Small Caps, Mid Caps, and Large Caps. If we observe a scenario where only Large Caps are advancing while there's sluggish movement in Small and Mid Caps, it might suggest that institutional investors are favoring safer investments, potentially signaling an impending correction in the overall market.

Take a look at the chart below. In March 2019, we observed that the Nifty Midcap 150 index was losing momentum, forming a lower top, while the Nifty 50 index continued to move higher, creating higher tops. This discrepancy between the two indices was quite evident. Notably, the Mid Cap 150 index started its correction ahead of the Nifty 50 index, exhibiting a leading behavior that indicated a potentially deeper impending correction in the overall market.

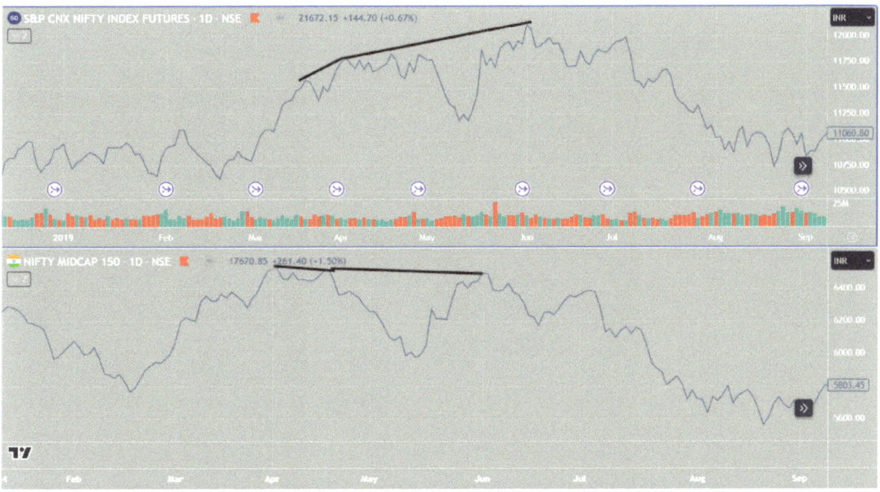

This principle of Dow Theory also aids traders in identifying outperforming sectors or stocks. When I refer to outperforming, I mean stocks or sectors that are advancing at a faster rate than the overall market or other sectors.

Have a look at the chart below. From November 2022 to March 2023, the Nifty was experiencing a secondary correction, but during the same period, the Nifty PSE index was forming higher tops and higher bottoms. It was evident that the Nifty PSE was "outperforming" the Nifty 50. As traders, our goal is to stay with the outperformer.

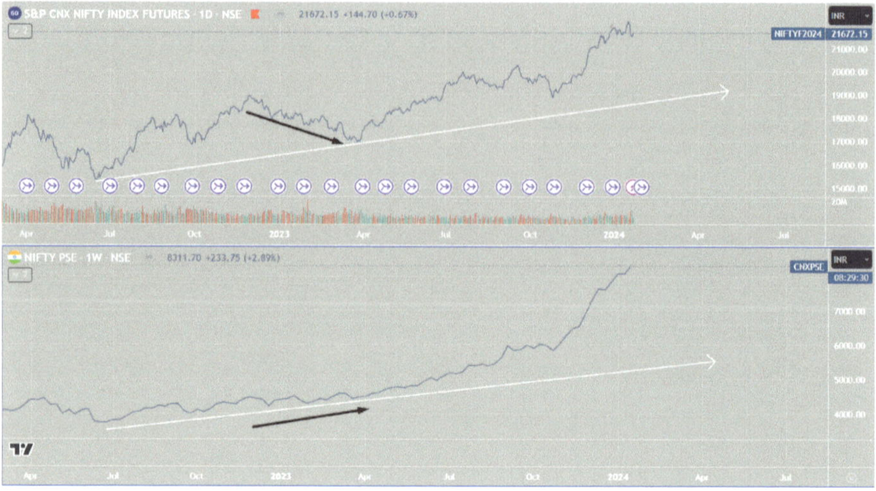

Now, imagine if you had invested in the pharmaceutical sector during this phase when it was undergoing a correction. It would have resulted in a significant missed opportunity!

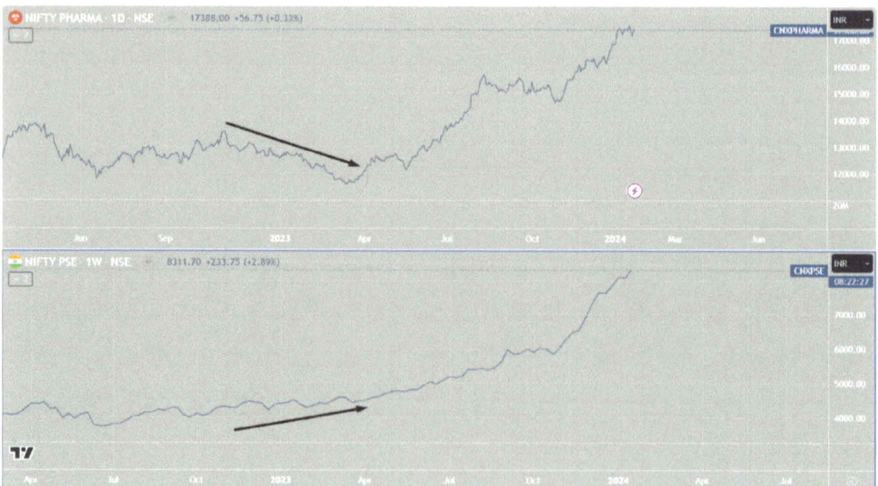

Take a look at the chart below. During the same phase, the pharmaceutical sector was undergoing a correction. Remember, money has a time value, and there's always an opportunity cost associated with it. Trading in the wrong sector or stock is akin to squandering both time and opportunities.

6) A Trend Persists Until Reversal Signals Emerge

The Dow theory maintains that a trend remains in force until a clear reversal signal is evident. In this context, a trend is characterized as a prolonged period of consistent movement in a stock price in a single direction. According to Dow theory, as long as this trend persists without any discernible reversal signal, it is considered to be ongoing and likely to continue. A reversal signal can be any event or development that indicates a previously established trend is on the verge of concluding and reversing its course. This could manifest as a sudden and substantial price shift, a breakdown in the price movement, or a noticeable increase in trading volume.

The Dow theory furnishes a structured framework for analyzing the stock market and detecting trends. It underscores the significance of comprehending the intricacies of the market, including the influence of weighted indices, the coexistence of multiple trends, and the various stages of primary trends.

To grasp this concept with our previous discussions in mind, when a trend is advancing, it typically forms higher highs and higher lows. As long as this pattern remains consistent, the trend is considered to be ongoing. However, once this pattern is disrupted, it becomes reasonable to assume that the trend is either on the verge of changing or has already shifted direction.

In the chart below, we can see that the price of Nifty 50 has been consistently rising, forming higher highs and higher lows. As long as this sequence remains unbroken, we consider the trend to be ongoing.

Sometime later, around mid-October 2021, we can observe (in the chart below) a shift in the market's character. The prices are no longer forming higher highs; instead, they have initiated a series of lower highs, though the prices are still generating higher bottoms. This change is the initial warning sign indicating a potential shift in the prevailing trend.

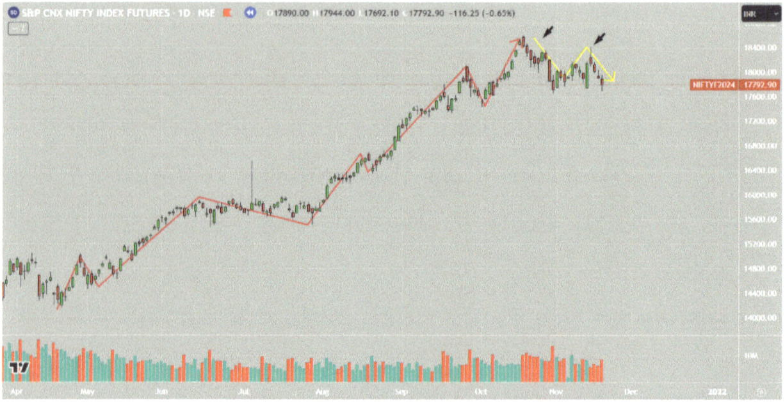

Finally, we can observe (in the chart below) that the last higher low has also been breached, confirming the change in trend as it begins to form distinct lower highs and lower lows.

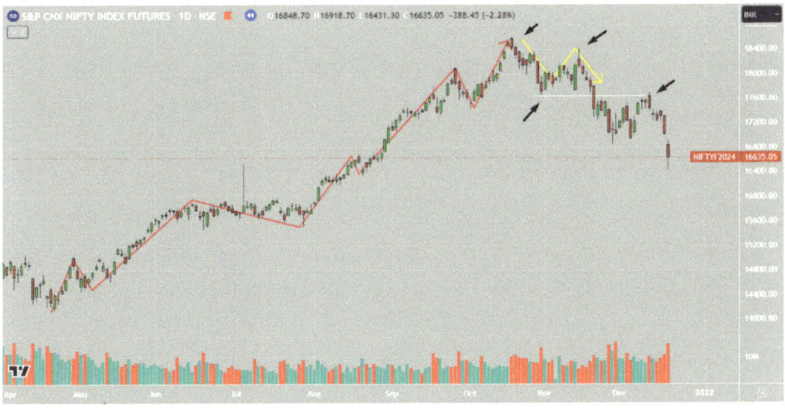

Crucial insights can be gleaned from volume analysis (the fourth principle we discussed earlier) and from other intra-market analyses (the fifth principle we discussed earlier).

Similarly, the primary downtrend changes to an uptrend. Take a look at the chart below and try to identify the transition. I have marked it for your convenience.

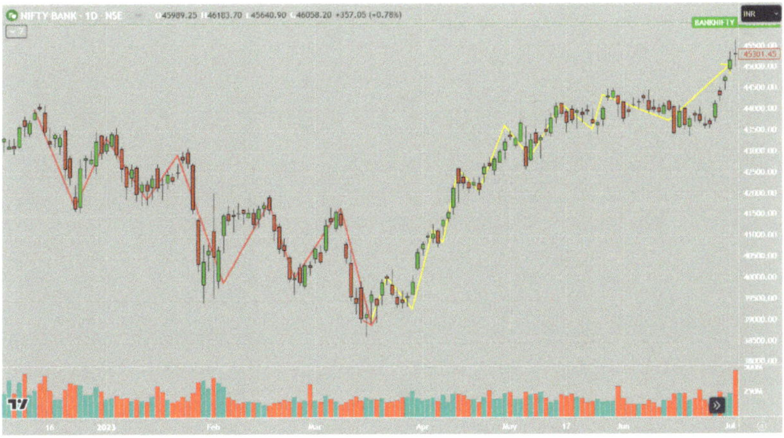

Wrapping Up

These are the six principles of Dow Theory, or rather, I would say these are the six principles you need to follow to trade in financial markets successfully.

These are the six principles of Dow Theory, or rather, I would say these are the six principles you need to follow to trade in financial markets successfully.

Drop IV

Embracing the Present

Trading thrives on the excitement of the moment, demanding traders stay present-focused. It's vital to concentrate on current market conditions, including entry setups, managing stop losses, and watching active trades, rather than getting lost in past regrets or future worries. Mindfulness, sharpening awareness of the immediate environment, enhances decision-making and adaptability to market shifts. Embrace the present to navigate trading's dynamics successfully, letting go of past and future to excel in real-time strategy execution. This approach, grounding oneself in the now, paves the way to clarity, confidence, and trading success.

Chapter 4

History Repeats Itself

Before we dive deeper into understanding support and resistance, let me introduce you to a fundamental principle of technical analysis: "History repeats itself."

A significant portion of technical analysis and the examination of market behavior revolves around the study of human psychology. Over the past century, analysts have identified and classified various chart patterns that manifest on price charts. These patterns provide insights into the bullish or bearish psychology prevalent in the market. Since these patterns have proven effective in the past, it is believed that they will remain effective in the future. They are rooted in the study of human psychology, which tends to exhibit consistent behavior over time. In essence, this principle suggests that comprehending the future lies in examining the past, and that the future often mirrors the past.

Understanding Support & Resistance

Mastering support and resistance is crucial as it forms the foundation of many essential price action trading concepts. Proficiency in understanding and utilizing support and resistance levels can significantly enhance your skills as a trader.

Price action trading heavily relies on the fundamental concept of support and resistance. Analyzing various levels of support and resistance, across different degrees, is a pivotal aspect of this trading approach. By effectively integrating these levels, traders can form their market opinions and make well-informed trade decisions.

Let's revisit the Dow Theory. As previously mentioned, trends in the market don't progress in a linear fashion. Instead, they advance, correct, and then continue in the main trend direction. This natural ebb and flow create peaks and troughs in the price movement. These peaks and troughs serve as significant zones for buying and selling activities. They act as crucial support and resistance levels in the price chart.

After prices have responded to a specific price level, they tend to exhibit a tendency to react at those same levels in the future.

In the chart below, you can observe that the previous bottom acted as a support level, where the price rebounded in the future. The June 2023 bottom served as support again in August 2023.

Similarly, in the chart below, we can observe that the peak created in February 2022 acted as resistance in April 2022, causing the price to decline.

We can describe a **support level** as a price floor that remains influential as long as it continues to hold. When the market approaches a support level, there is an expectation that the market's downward movement has a higher **probability** of being halted at that specific level.

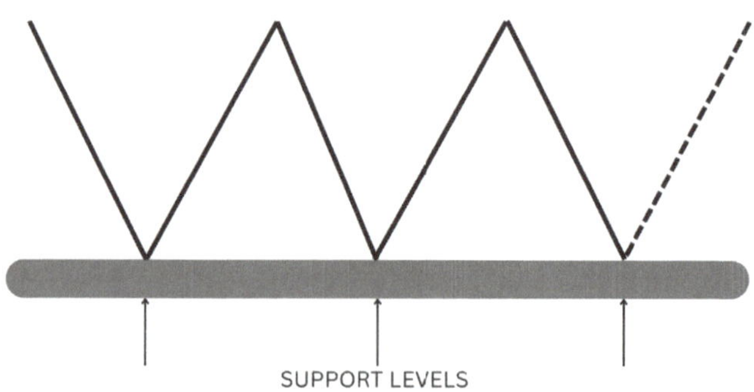

Similarly, we can define a **resistance level** as a price ceiling that remains relevant as long as it remains effective. When the market approaches a resistance level, there is an **anticipation** that the market's upward momentum has a higher probability of encountering a halt at that particular level.

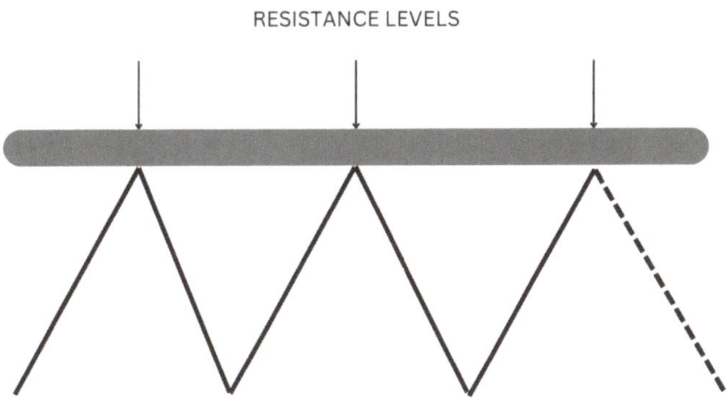

Why is Support & Resistance so important?

Now, you might be wondering, why are these support and resistance levels so important for a technical analyst? Our main objective is to trade the markets and generate profits, and these support and resistance levels play a crucial role in identifying potential "trading opportunities." Since prices have previously reacted at these levels, there is a significant likelihood that these levels will trigger price reactions once more. (Remember History Repeats Itself)

What Happens if a Support or Resistance Level Breaks?

In the definitions of support and resistance above, two key terms were highlighted: "probability" and "anticipation." When we engage in technical analysis, we are working with probabilities and seeking confirmation. Therefore, when a price approaches a support or resistance area, there is a probability that prices will respond to those levels. To achieve a higher level of accuracy as technical analysts, we must wait for confirmation of this probability materializing. So, when a price approaches a support or resistance area, it may take one of two actions: 1) react to those levels and move in the expected direction, or 2) break through those levels.

If prices respond as expected to our identified support or resistance levels, then that's excellent. We can execute our planned orders with confirmation (details on trading at these levels will be covered shortly). However, if prices break through the established support or resistance levels, it is anticipated that they will move toward the next support or resistance level.

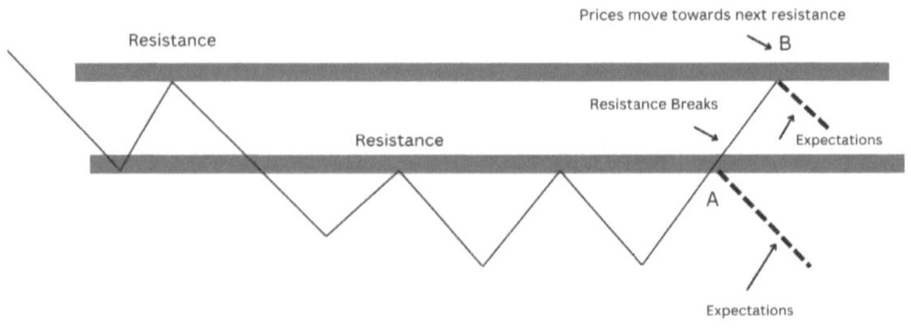

In the diagram above, you can observe that when the price reached point A, it had previously encountered resistance at those levels (based on historical data). Consequently, our expectation was that it might act as resistance once again. However, the price broke through point A and moved to the next point, point B, where it had reacted in a similar manner in the past. We hold the same expectation for point B. If it aligns with our expectations, that's great; if not, it may proceed toward the next resistance level.

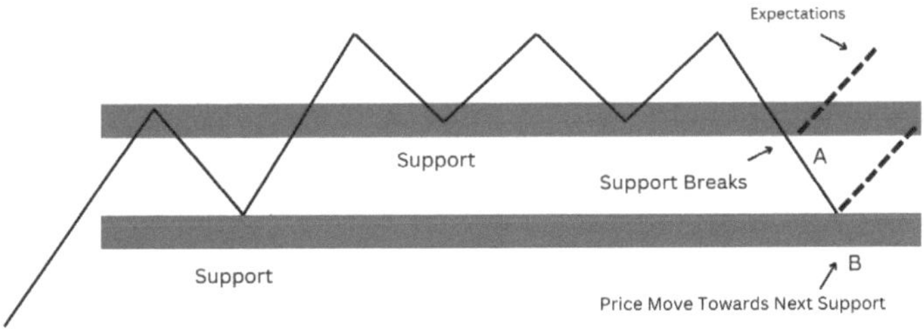

Likewise, the same principle applies to support levels. In the diagram above, you can observe that when the price reached point A, it had previously found support at those levels, as indicated by historical data. Therefore, our expectation was that it might act as support once again. However, the price broke through point A and moved to the next point, point B, where it had reacted similarly in the past. We maintain the same expectation for point B. If it aligns with our expectations, that's excellent; if not, it may continue toward the next support level.

Now, mentally superimpose the previously discussed support and resistance diagram onto the charts below. This exercise will help you identify potential price levels where historical support and resistance may come into play, aiding your trading decisions.

Resistance

Support

So, were there any magic spells cast at these support and resistance levels that caused prices to react when they reached those points? Certainly not! Instead, it's all about the **psychology that operates in the background**. Let's delve into this psychology to gain a deeper understanding.

Why Do Supports and Resistances Work?

Support and resistance levels are key components of technical analysis that traders rely on for making informed trading decisions. These levels are rooted in market psychology and reflect the collective actions of traders and investors. Let's delve into why supports and resistances work by examining what happens when the price approaches these critical levels.

1. **Short Sellers Consider Closing Positions:** When the price approaches a support level, traders who have previously taken short positions start to reevaluate their positions. They may anticipate that the price will pause or bounce back from the support level, prompting them to close their short positions by buying back the assets they previously sold short.

2. **Buyers Step In**: Simultaneously, buyers recognize the potential opportunity presented by the support area. They believe that the price has reached a level where it may find support and begin to rise. As a result, they step in to buy assets at or near the support level.

This dual action of short sellers closing their positions and buyers entering the market creates a confluence of trading activity at the support level. This collective behavior often leads to a reversal or at least a temporary halt in the price decline. The psychology at work here is based on the idea that support levels represent a point where supply (sellers) and demand (buyers) come into balance.

Similar dynamics occur at resistance levels, albeit in the opposite direction. Traders who have taken long positions may consider closing them near resistance levels, anticipating a potential price pullback. Meanwhile, potential sellers may recognize an opportunity to sell assets at or near resistance. This interplay of buying and selling forces can lead to a reversal or a pause in the price's upward momentum.

In essence, supports and resistances work because they capture the ebb and flow of market sentiment, as traders and investors react to key price levels. These levels serve as psychological markers where decisions are made, and this collective decision-making is what ultimately drives price action in the financial markets. Understanding and effectively using supports and resistances is a fundamental skill for traders and technical analysts alike.

Through the application of technical analysis, we endeavor to gain insights into the thought processes of fellow traders. By examining the behavior of major institutions, which wield significant financial resources capable of exerting influence over price fluctuations, we aim to decipher market actions.

So, it appears you're all set to engage in trading! You've likely identified where substantial capital is at play. But hold on, it might seem straightforward, but in reality, it's far from it. We can't simply leap into trades as soon as prices approach these levels. We must exercise patience and let the markets validate the actions of significant players at these support/resistance levels. We'll delve deeper into the concept of "confirmation" in a later section of this book.

Now that we've developed a theoretical understanding of Support and Resistance, it's time to apply this knowledge in a practical manner by marking them on charts. However, hold on a moment. The question arises: which specific levels on the charts should we consider as Support or Resistance? It's not a random selection; there's a method to identifying these critical zones on the chart.

The price chart will exhibit **significant support and resistance levels** based on the following criteria:

1. **Recent Swings**: Levels associated with recent price swings will have a notable impact on the chart.
2. **Strong and Drastic Moves:** Points where strong and abrupt price movements occurred will serve as important support and resistance levels.
3. **Dual Role Levels:** Levels that have historically acted as both support and resistance are of particular significance.
4. **Repeated Testing:** Levels that have been repeatedly tested by the market will carry substantial weight as potential support or resistance.
5. **Higher Time Frame Swings:** Keep an eye on important swing points identified on higher time frame charts, as they can also influence the chart's support and resistance dynamics.

Now, let's examine each of these criteria individually by analyzing them on the charts.

Recent Swings

In the chart provided, you'll observe rectangular markings indicating significant price swings. When we draw horizontal lines from these swing points, a noteworthy pattern emerges: these swing levels have historically provided support during secondary corrections within the primary trend.

As recent levels tend to leave a lasting imprint on traders' memories, if prices encountered resistance at these levels, traders would remember. Similarly, if prices rebounded from these levels, traders would still retain those levels in their memory banks. Consequently, when prices approach these remembered levels, traders are likely to react by entering trades, either supporting or resisting price movements.

Take a glance at the chart provided below.

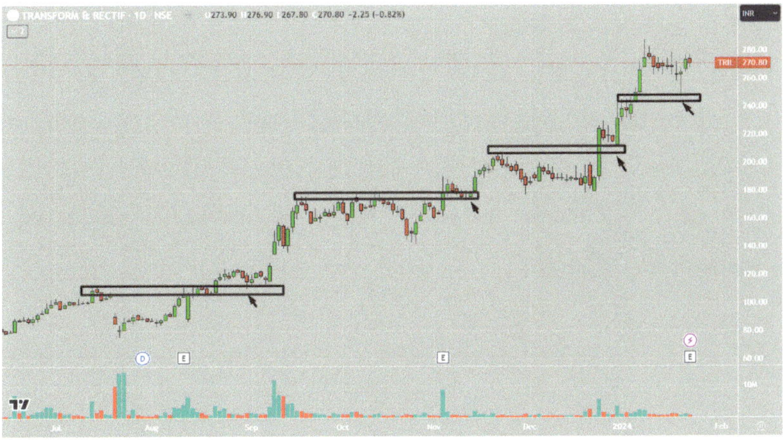

It can be stated that prices exhibit a form of memory.

Examine the chart below to see how these levels might also serve as resistance during the primary downtrend in the market. The recent swing levels repel prices downward after acting as resistance.

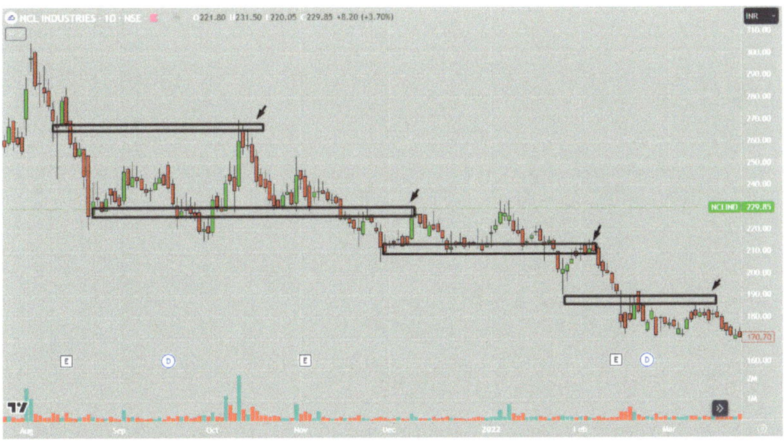

In both charts, have you observed a common occurrence? What happens to the support or resistance levels when they are breached? Take another look!

I hope you've grasped the concept! It's a role reversal at play here. This means that the levels which were functioning as support before now become resistance, and conversely, the levels that were acting as resistance now shift to support. This phenomenon is known as an **SR Flip (Support/Resistance Flip) or a Change in Polarity!**

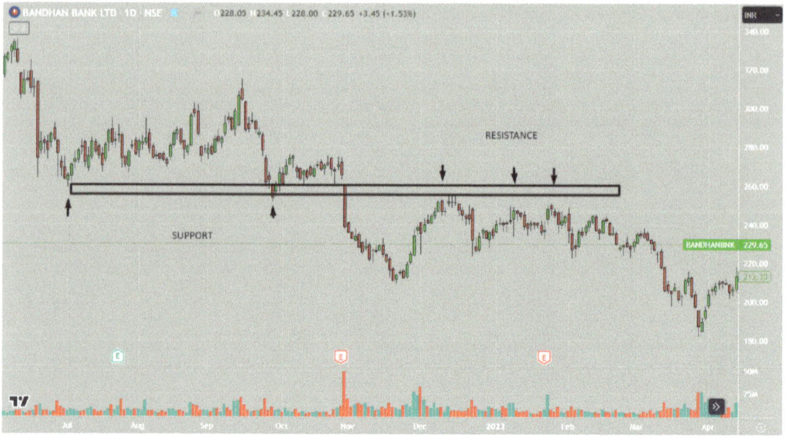

Strong and Drastic Moves

In the chart above, there was a notable and abrupt decline of over 30% towards the end of April 2022. The stock was initially trading within the range of Rs 660 to 640, but it swiftly underwent a correction, plummeting over 30% in a mere 11 trading sessions. Subsequently, prices gradually rebounded and returned to the same range of 660 to 640 by mid-September 2022. However, a repeat of the same sell-off occurred shortly afterward, with the stock experiencing a correction of more than 30% in just 12 trading sessions!

The significant sell-off in April 2022 served as a strong resistance level. What could possibly have transpired during that period? Consider delving into the underlying factors influencing the observed price action.

Let's delve into the psychology behind these levels that have acted as precise resistance points. What might have unfolded during mid-September? Several parties contribute to the price action in this scenario:

1. Buyers Trapped: Some buyers who got caught up in the drastic April 2022 decline likely found themselves trapped at these levels.

2. Fresh Sellers: New sellers, sensing an approaching sell-off zone, may have entered the market, adding to selling pressure.

3. Profit Bookers: Traders who had previously purchased at lower levels and witnessed a price rebound might have decided to book profits at September 2022 resistance levels.

4. Greedy Sellers: Traders who had succumbed to greed and bought at the September 2022 resistance levels may have panicked as prices fell, prompting them to sell to minimize losses.

This confluence of selling pressure at the September 2022 levels, driven by these various factors, significantly contributed to the price decline.

The same principle applies to buyers as well, especially when a sharp price movement serves as a support level. Please refer to the chart below for illustration.

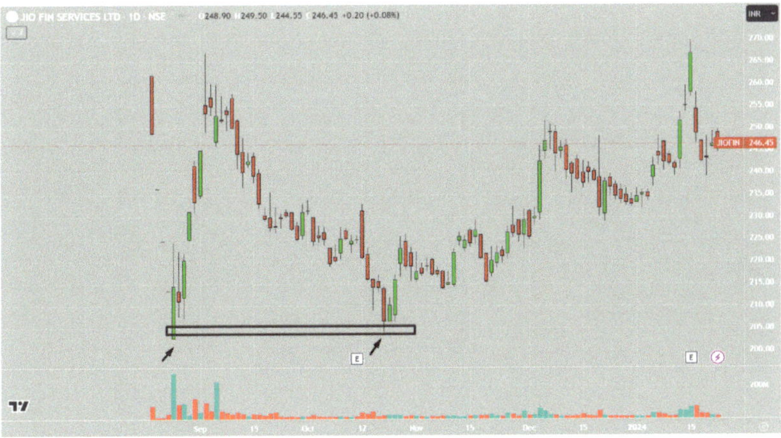

Dual Role Levels

Remember, we previously discussed the concept of an SR flip or change of polarity, and it's precisely the same phenomenon at play here. I encourage you to engage your analytical thinking and ponder why this level holds significance. The answer is straightforward: something significant must have occurred at this level to prompt the role reversal, transforming sellers into buyers or vice versa. Consequently, this level becomes a crucial reference point for the future and has the potential to act as a strong support or resistance level.

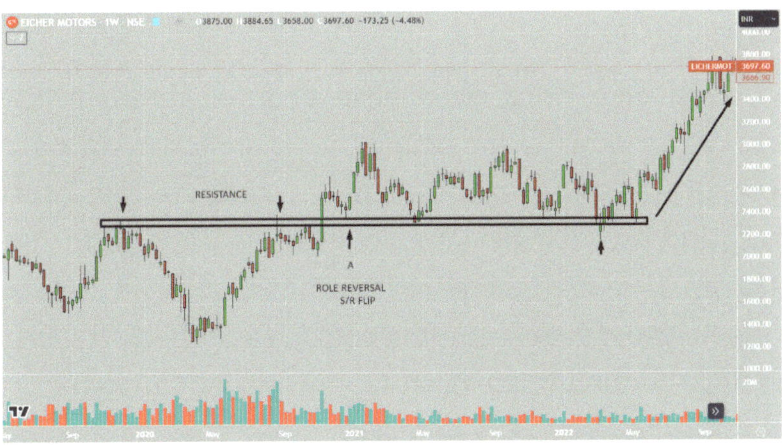

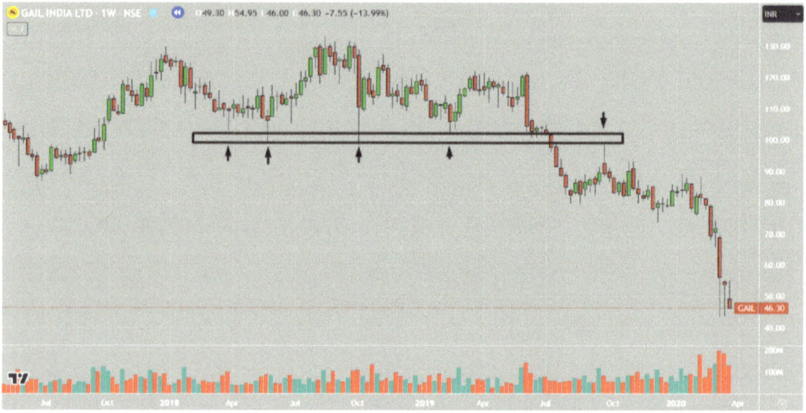

Repeated Testing

When levels on a price chart have endured multiple tests by the market, they acquire a heightened significance as potential support or resistance zones. This is due to the collective memory and psychological impact these levels hold for traders and investors. Repeated testing indicates that these price points have been pivotal decision-making areas where buyers and sellers have clashed in the past. As a result, traders often closely monitor these levels, expecting a recurrence of significant price reactions. The more times a level has been tested and validated, the greater its potential to act as a formidable barrier for price movement, making it a critical consideration in technical analysis and trading strategies.

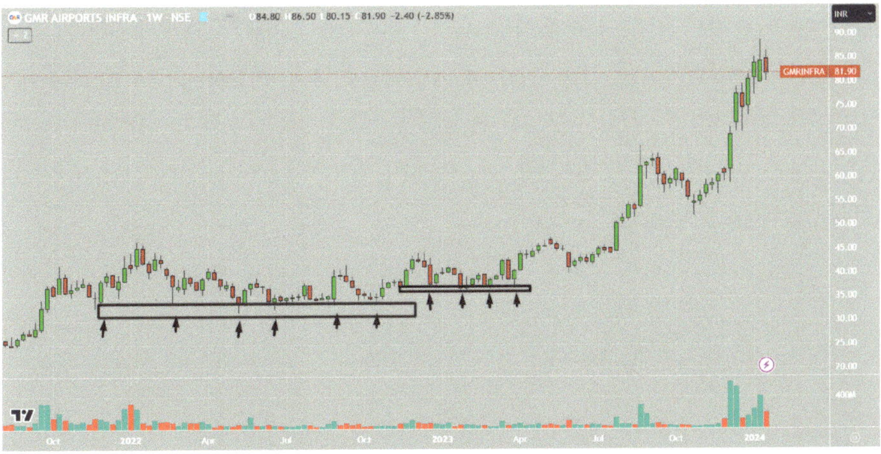

Higher Time Frame Swings

Monitoring crucial swing points on higher time frame charts is essential. These levels can exert a notable influence on a chart's support and resistance dynamics. Traders and analysts often consider these higher time frame swings as they provide valuable insights into broader market sentiment and potential areas of price reversals.

The support/resistance levels on a weekly chart carry greater significance than those on a daily chart. As we ascend to higher time frames, the importance of these swings intensifies. Wondering why? It's because with each step up in time frame, we filter out market noise, resulting in purer and more reliable price action analysis.

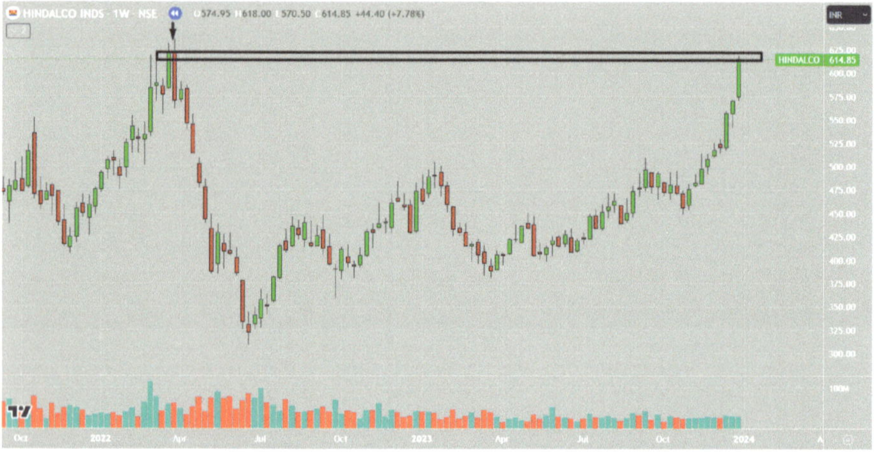

The chart displayed above represents Hindalco's weekly chart. In March 2022, the stock marked a significant swing high, followed by a sharp decline from those levels. As a result, the price range of 640 to 615 from that period may potentially serve as resistance in the future. Now, as we shift our attention to the right side of the chart, we observe that prices are approaching this same level in December 2023. At this juncture, it's advisable to transition to a daily chart to closely examine the price behavior in more detail.

You can observe how prices encountered resistance at those levels and initiated a correction. Had we solely relied on daily charts, we might have overlooked this crucial swing resistance zone. It's essential to remember the significant advantage offered by "Multi-Timeframe Analysis."

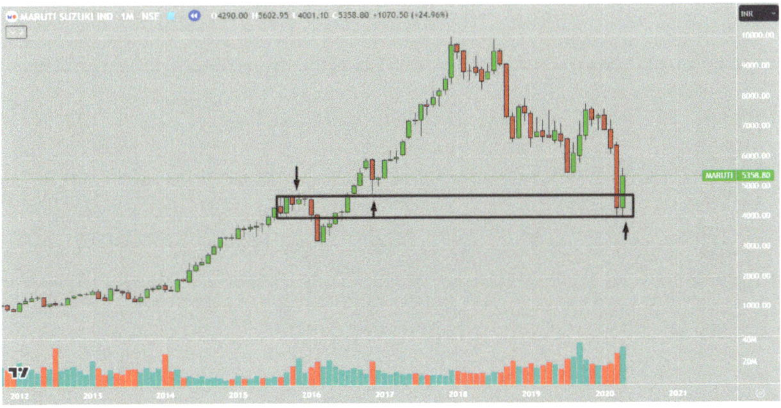

Likewise, in the chart above, observe the monthly chart of Maruti Suzuki India nearing monthly support levels within the range of 3500 to 3700 in March 2020, following the aftermath of the Covid Crash. We have identified the SR flip levels from October 2015 and November 2016 as significant support zones and extended them to the right side. Let's examine how the price action unfolded!

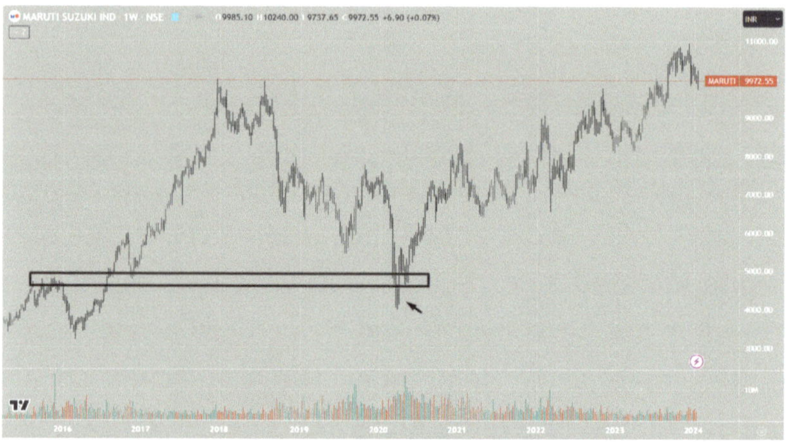

The stock witnessed a remarkable rally of over 120% in just three years! It's important to note that if we had solely focused on one timeframe, these crucial levels might have completely escaped our attention.

You may have observed that I've been using a zone to designate support and resistance levels rather than pinpointing an exact level. This approach is deliberate because we are dealing with emotions and various psychological factors when prices approach these levels. Emotions can't be precisely measured, so we employ a zone to account for the uncertainty. However, it's essential to strike a balance; the zone shouldn't be overly broad, resembling a highway. A range of around 1% is generally considered acceptable for this purpose.

Let's now practice marking support and resistance levels. I've provided some charts below for you to identify these key levels. Use your analytical skills and imagination to mark the levels, and then compare your markings with mine. Keep in mind all the factors we discussed earlier while identifying these support and resistance levels.

Challenge: I

Solution: I

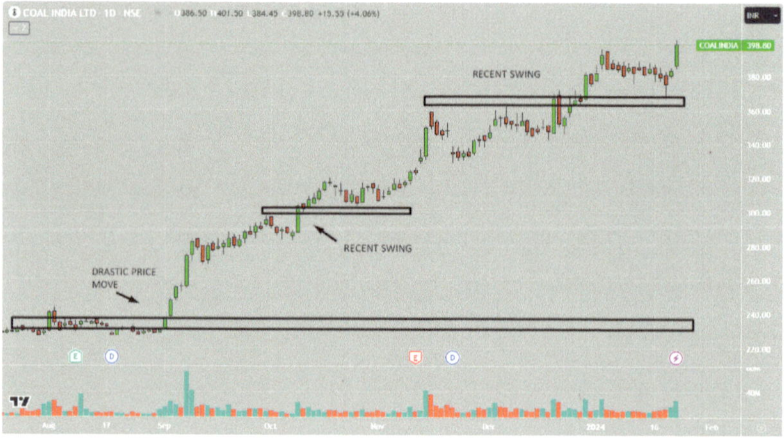

Challenge: II

Solution: II

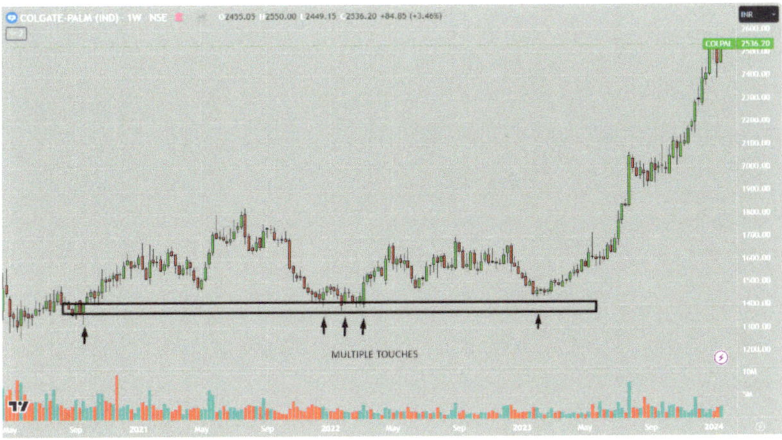

Challenge: III

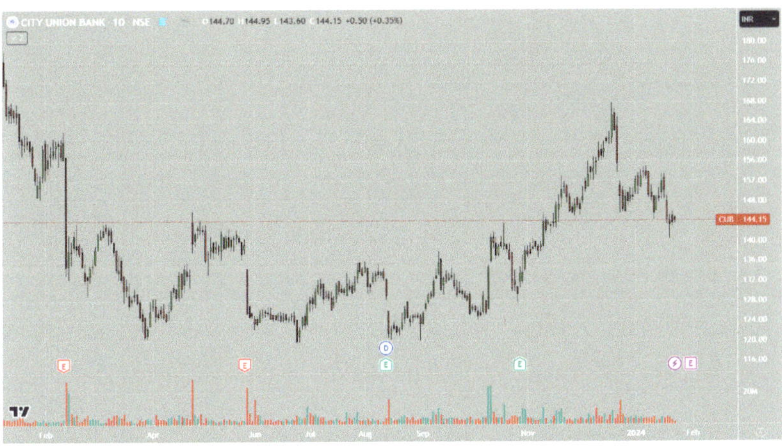

Solution: III

Challenge: IV

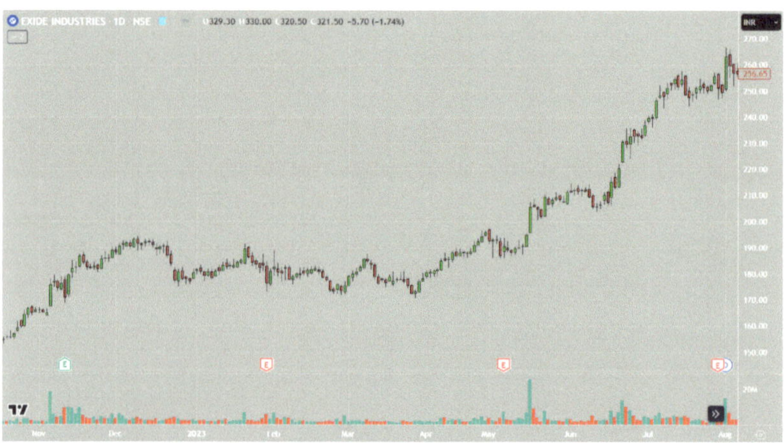

Solution: IV

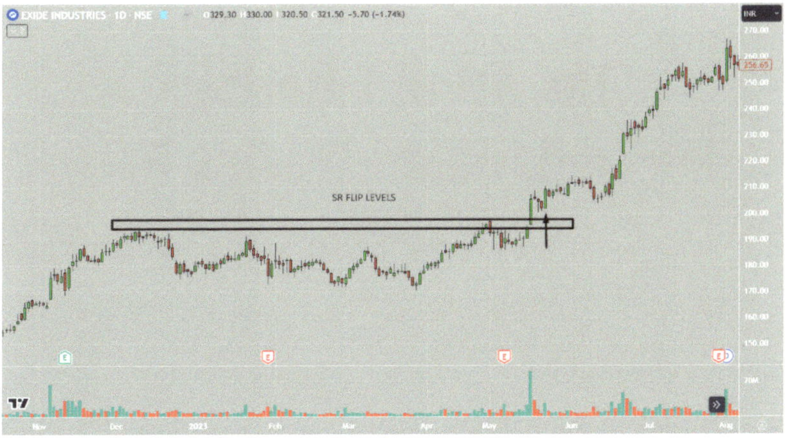

Wrapping Up

Comprehending and mastering support and resistance is paramount, as it forms the cornerstone of the entire foundation of Technical Analysis. Maintain simplicity and clarity in your approach; support and resistance represent zones rather than precise points. It's crucial to exercise patience and refrain from entering trades immediately when prices approach these zones; instead, we must wait for confirmation. Most importantly, initiate practice sessions to hone your skill in accurately marking these levels.

Drop V

The Art of Filtering: How to Navigate Trading Noise

In trading, distinguishing crucial signals from the distracting noise in market data is key. Signals, like technical indicators or market responses to news, offer valuable insights for entry or exit points. Noise, however, includes less helpful information such as minor price changes or speculative opinions, which can confuse and mislead. Success hinges on focusing on meaningful signals, thereby maintaining decision-making clarity amidst market fluctuations. Mastering this skill, though challenging, positions traders to make informed choices, steering clear of emotional biases. Remember, prioritize relevant signals over noise for strategic trading and resilience in the face of market volatility.

Chapter 5

Price Patterns

Now that we've explored the dynamics of support and resistance, let's delve further into this concept. Up to this point, we've primarily examined support and resistance levels using single data points derived from price action, such as swings. However, there are other crucial methods to consider, including trend lines, moving averages, Fibonacci retracements, and pivot points, some of which are covered in this book, while others are not. Our focus will be on what proves to be effective and, most importantly, what has yielded positive results in my personal experience.

Before we explore the various other methods to use Support & Resistance, let's address another crucial aspect of the second "M" - Price Patterns. As you may recall, in the previous chapter, I emphasized the importance of not hastily entering trades when prices approach support or resistance levels. Instead, we exercise patience and wait for confirmation. These price patterns will serve as our confirmation signals, guiding us when it's the right time to enter trades.

What is a Price Pattern?

Price Patterns are visual depictions of recurring price movements commonly observed in markets. These patterns serve as valuable tools , enabling us to recognize potential trade entry and exit points with the aim of identifying buying or selling opportunities.

Price patterns can be categorized into two types:

1. Shorter price patterns, typically spanning 1 to 5 days, reflecting shorter market activities. Like Candlestick Patterns, Bar Patterns etc
2. Lager price patterns, encompassing a broader range of market activities, usually extending over 15 to 45 days. These patterns form bases and include shapes like rectangles, head and shoulders, triangles, and more.

Price Patterns

Shorter Patterns

- Candlesticks
- Bar Patterns

Larger Patterns

- Head & Shoulders
- Triangles
- Wedges/Flags
- Rectangles

As traders, it's essential for us to grasp and utilize both types of patterns in our trading strategies.

Shorter Patterns

Shorter patterns, as the name implies, typically span 3 to 5 days and often serve as precursors to more extensive patterns. These shorter patterns can significantly influence the prevailing trend and help establish the foundation for the formation of larger and more significant patterns.

Shorter patterns also play a role as trade triggers, serving to confirm larger patterns and acting as catalysts for initiating trade entries, setting stop-loss levels, and on occasion, determining the opportune moments for booking profits as well.

These patterns can be effectively utilized for trading within the "minor trend," enabling traders to capitalize on short-term moves spanning 1 to 3 days.

Short patterns can be identified using either candlesticks or bar patterns, and there are additional variations of these tools available. However, we'll keep things straightforward and concentrate on the essentials. We'll utilize candlesticks for our analysis because they offer a more comprehensive perspective, and their simplicity makes them easy to understand and apply.

Candlestick Charting

Now, let's embark on our journey into the world of candlesticks. However, before we delve into it, here's a crucial point to consider. There are possibly hundreds of candlestick patterns, numerous books dedicated to them, and if we were to discuss them all, this book might need to be divided into multiple parts! Through my 15+ years of trading experience, I've come to realize one fundamental truth: understanding the psychology behind price pattern formation is the key. Regardless of the number of patterns, what truly matters is deciphering the message the markets convey through them. Names may vary, but it's the message that holds significance.

At the end of a trading session, we have access to four critical data points: the day's high, low, open, and close. As traders, it's essential to attribute significance to each of these points, as they collectively convey valuable information. Now, imagine this data being visually depicted and presented to you - how impactful would that be? Just as the saying goes, "a picture is worth a thousand words," candlestick charting embodies this idea. Candlestick charts effectively paint the day's price information, presenting it visually for enhanced understanding and analysis.

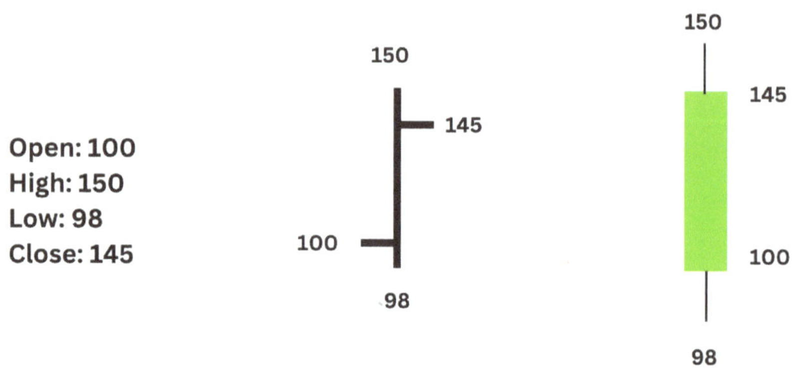

Examine the illustration above – which figure is more engaging to you? The answer is the green box, right? That's the candlestick chart! Now, let's delve into the anatomy of these candles, and then we'll revisit the same image for a deeper understanding.

Candlestick charts have a rich history dating back to the 17th century when the Japanese used them to analyze rice prices. However, it was in modern technical analysis that candlestick patterns gained prominence, thanks to Steve Nison, who introduced them in his book "Japanese Candlestick Charting Techniques."

Candlestick charts effectively convey various price details, including the open price, close price, highest price, and lowest price, utilizing candlestick-shaped symbols. Each of these symbols represents the condensed trading activity that occurred within a single time period.

The primary rectangular portion within the symbol is referred to as the "real body." It serves the purpose of illustrating the price range between the open and close prices for that specific time period. Meanwhile, the lines extending from the top and bottom of the real body are known as the "upper shadow" and "lower shadow" (or "wick"). Each shadow represents the highest or lowest price traded during the time period being represented. In a Bullish market scenario (where the closing price is higher than the opening price), the body is typically depicted as white or green. Conversely, in a Bearish market (where the closing price is lower than the opening price), the body is typically rendered in black or red.

Candlestick charts serve as a tool to unveil market psychology, offering insights into the emotions of both sellers and buyers, characterized by fear and greed. This understanding is derived not only from the shapes and colors of the candlestick patterns but also from the multitude of recognizable patterns that manifest within candlestick charts.

Think of it this way: when you encounter a red candle, it signifies that the market closed lower than where it opened, indicating selling activity. Conversely, when you spot a green candle, it's a clear indicator that buying prevailed, with the market closing higher than its opening price.

When you come across a large green candle, it signifies strong buying pressure, as the price concluded significantly higher than its opening level. Conversely, the opposite holds true for a large red candle, indicating strong selling pressure, with the price closing notably lower than its opening price. It indicates that strong buying/selling activity has taken place with strong momentum support!

Take a moment to ponder and generate your own conclusion: If the day's opening and closing prices are extremely close to each other, resulting in a very narrow range candle, what does it suggest about the market's activity on that particular day?

Visualize this scenario in your mind: imagine a day where the opening and closing prices are extremely close, forming a candle with a very narrow range. What has happened on this day? Nothing! Yes you are getting it now. This was a low momentum neutral (indecisive) day! Just look at the chart below:

Now that we've comprehended how the candle's body is constructed and the insights it provides, let's shift our focus to the shadows – both the lower and upper shadows. As we've learned, these shadows delineate the day's highs and lows.

Let's rev up our imaginative engines once more and envision the significance of shadows. Picture this: on a given day, you observe a candle with a substantial shadow, be it a tail or a wick. What does this isolated shadow convey? It signals that a multitude of market participants has exerted significant pressure on prices, moving them considerably away from a specific level.

Take a look at the illustration below. In Figure A, notice that there's an upper shadow, and the body of the candle is positioned below the shadow. What does this configuration indicate? Let's begin adopting this analytical approach: It implies that prices initially surged higher from the open during the day, but as the session progressed, selling pressure emerged, pushing the price back down near the opening level. Even though the candle is green, it suggests that the day was primarily influenced by sellers. Now, let's apply the same analytical method to candle B.

Now, let's dissect Figure B to comprehend the dynamics at play. The market commenced with an opening followed by a sell-off. However, as the day progressed, buying activity intensified, driving the market back up to the opening level. Despite the day ultimately closing in the negative, the price action exhibited a bullish undertone, as evidenced by the recovery from the early selling pressure.

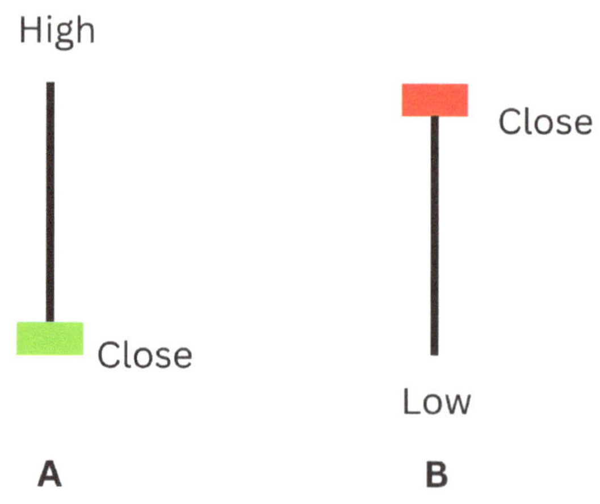

Take a moment to reflect on this: as you practice and refine your ability to analyze price action in its unadulterated state, gaining an understanding of the underlying psychology driving price movements, the specific name assigned to a candle becomes inconsequential. What truly matters is the pattern itself, as that's where our focus lies.

In simpler terms, if we can get good at understanding how prices move naturally, we won't need to memorize the names of candle patterns. Many traders spend a lot of time just trying to remember the names of candles. But really, does the name matter that much?

Now that we have a good understanding of what goes into the formation of a candlestick pattern, let's take a unique and different approach to studying candles. While we will certainly discuss some of the most famous candle patterns, our approach will be unlike anything you may have encountered before.

Before we delve into the various types of candlestick patterns, it's crucial to grasp that you cannot rely solely on candle signals for trading. You must harmonize these signals with the support and resistance levels we discussed earlier. The right candle should be employed at the appropriate levels to derive meaningful signals from the market.

Now, let's begin our exploration of candles, one at a time.

The Long Tail & Wick Candles

A candle with a small body and a long tail signifies strength within the session. It suggests that there was an initial sell-off when the price opened, but as the session progressed, buyers regained control and pushed the prices higher, often closing near or above the opening level. When this type of candle appears near a support area, it serves as confirmation for that support level. It's expected that prices will likely begin advancing after this pattern forms on support. Additionally, the low point of this candle may serve as a strong support level.

A strong long-tail candle is characterized by a tail that's at least twice the length of its body.

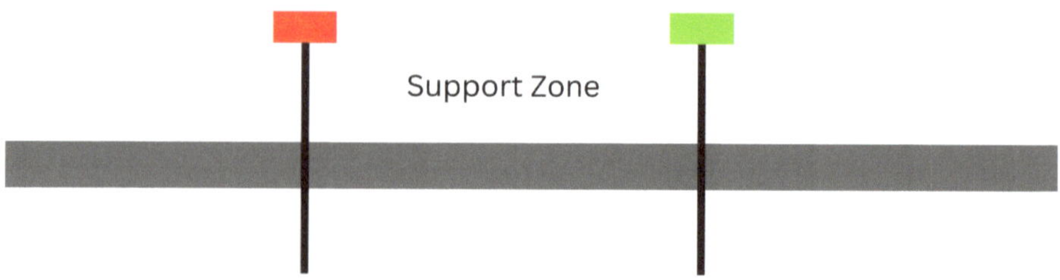

Long Tail Candle

In the chart above, pay attention to the initial long-tail candle on May 3rd, 23. It provides confirmation of the Support and Resistance (SR) flip levels as it penetrates through these levels and then rebounds. This rebound suggests the presence of buyers at the support zone. Subsequently, on May 15th, another long-wick candle emerges, reaffirming that demand for buying is still strong, and prices take off. It's also worth noting that the low point of the May 3rd candle, at 186, remained unbreached, indicating its significance as a strong support level.

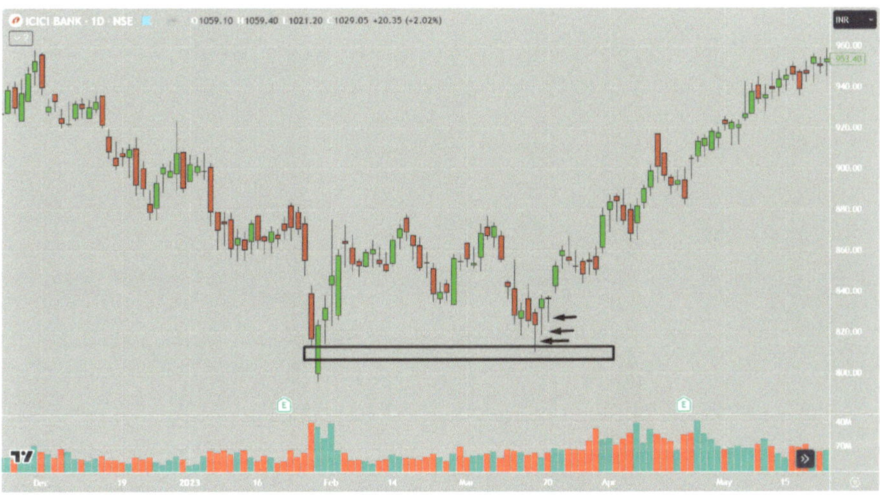

In the chart above, observe that on January 30, 2023, a swing was established, signaling buying interest. This particular area later served as a support zone on March 16, 2023. What's noteworthy is the presence of a series of long-tail candles, indicating a substantial buying interest. Whenever sellers attempted to drive the price below the support level, buyers intervened and prevented it, resulting in the formation of multiple long-tail candles.

Likewise, long-wick candles convey weakness in the market. They begin with an open and upward movement, only to be followed by selling pressure that drives the price back down, often near or below the opening level. The length of the wick correlates with the intensity of the selling pressure. When such a pattern emerges at a resistance level, it reinforces the signal, indicating the presence of genuine sellers at the resistance zone who are determined to push the price lower.

Take a look at the illustration below. The rejection at the resistance zone serves as a reaffirmation of the market's weakness and the prevailing selling interest at these levels.

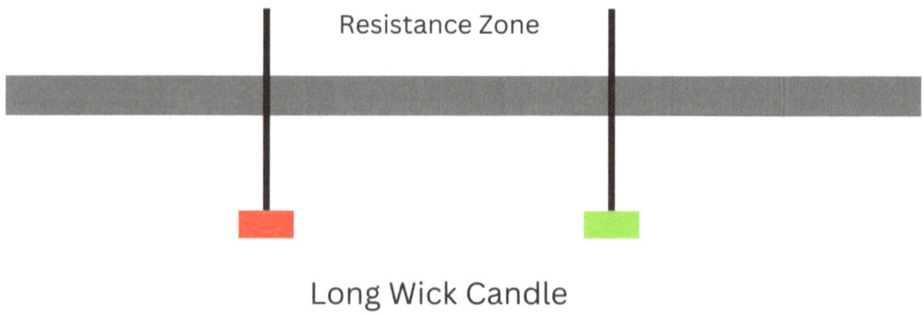

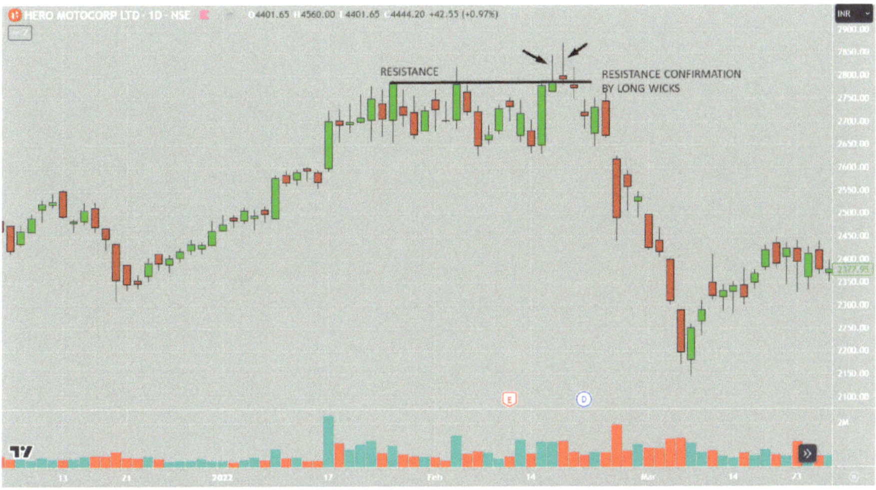

In the chart above, you can observe that the prices struggled to establish new higher highs starting from January 2022. Instead, they consistently held within the 2800 - 2700 zone. Take note of the numerous attempts made to breach this resistance level (as we discussed in the support/resistance chapter). Ultimately, there were two final attempts on February 16th and 17th to break through this resistance. However, these attempts failed, resulting in the formation of long-wick candles, and subsequently, the prices experienced a breakdown.

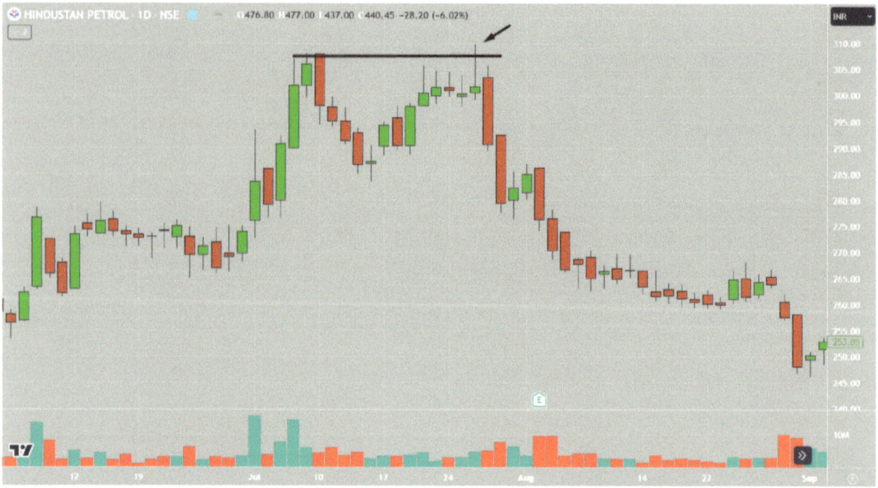

In the chart above, you can spot a swing level that formed on July 10, 2023. Subsequently, prices encountered resistance at this swing level on July 26th, leading to the creation of a significant rejection candle in the form of a long-wick candle. This candle clearly signified that sellers were gaining the upper hand, preventing prices from advancing beyond this level. Ultimately, the upward momentum succumbed to selling pressure, resulting in a correction.

When we examine the two candles from a momentum perspective, it becomes clear that the long-tail candle signifies strong bullish momentum at a support level, while the long-wick candle indicates the presence of strong sellers or bearish momentum at a resistance level.

The long-wick candle is commonly referred to as the "shooting star," and the long-tail candle is known as the "hammer." So, what truly mattered here – the name or the action it represented?

Large Body Candles

A candle with a large body signifies strength and momentum, indicating dominance by the market participants.

Bullish large body candles take shape when the market opens at a support level and is then driven upward by enthusiastic buyers. These candles typically have a minimal or non-existent lower tail, reflecting sustained buying throughout the day. The closing price is close to the day's highs, creating a wide range between the open and close. This wide range indicates strong momentum and a strong sense of determination from the buyers. The low of such candles often serves as a strong support level and is frequently employed as stop-loss points by many traders.

Conversely, a bearish large body candle exhibits the opposite behavior. Prices open at a resistance zone and are then driven downward by sellers, resulting in a candle with a minimal or non-existent upper wick. The selling pressure is so intense that the range between the open and close is wide, and the session concludes near the day's lows. This configuration signifies significant selling momentum and a strong bearish sentiment. The high of these candles functions as a formidable resistance level and is commonly used as stop-loss points by traders who opt to short at the resistance.

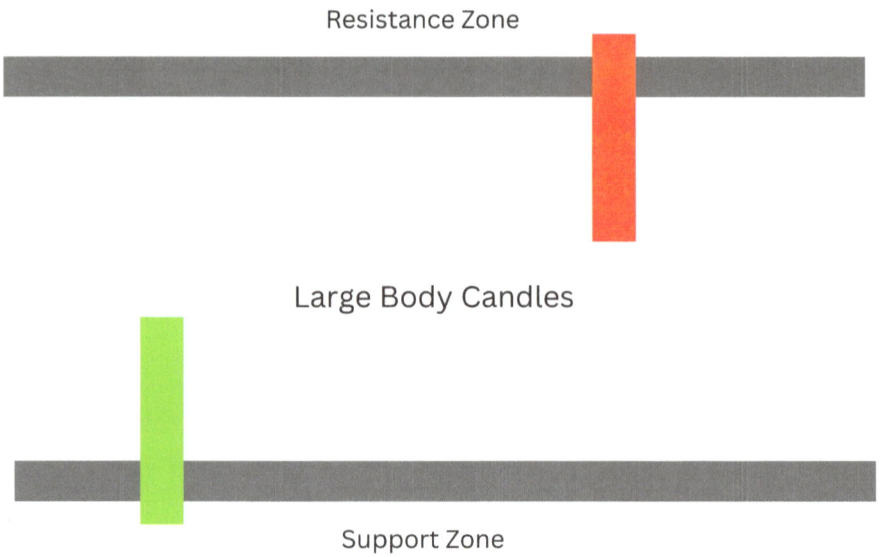

Examine the chart below where a low was established in February 2023, and afterward, prices consistently resisted falling below the 1800 levels. These levels are likely to serve as support since selling pressure was halted here. Towards the end of March 2023, prices retested these levels, forming a strong bullish candle. This confirmation indicates a substantial demand for the stock at this level. Following the formation of the large candle, we observe an uptrend taking shape.

On that candle, the price opened at 1834 levels and didn't hesitate, continuing to rise until it reached 1916 before eventually closing at 1910, very close to its highs. The low of the candle also remained unbroken for an extended period. This demonstrates strong momentum from the buyers.

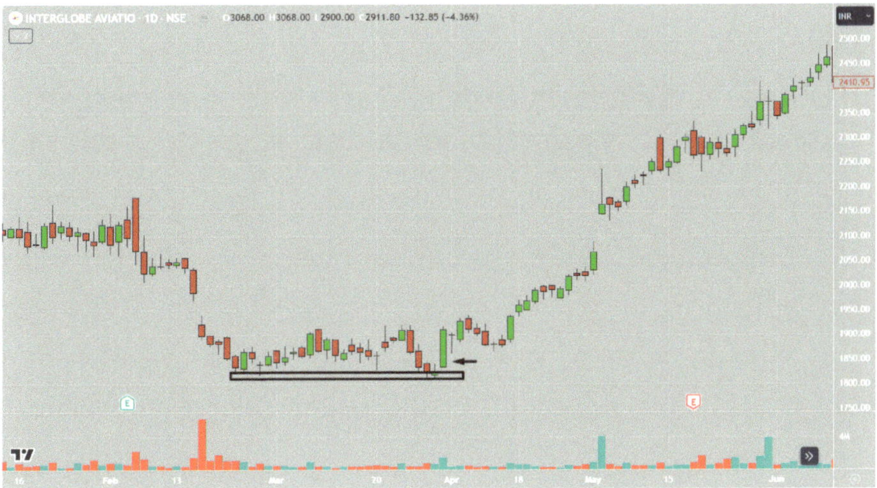

Now, let's delve into the bearish scenario.

In the chart above, it's evident that the price established a swing high in October 2022 at the 348 - 350 levels, and since then, this swing high has not been surpassed, establishing it as a strong resistance zone. In November 2022, a significant red candle appeared precisely at this resistance zone, and prices experienced a substantial sell-off. The day opened at 349 and closed at 315, resulting in an almost 10% decline in a single day. This event marked a pivotal moment that altered the course of the entire trend.

You might have a valid question at this point: were there any other indications on the charts before this significant 10% single-day decline that such a move could occur? The answer is evident in the chart below: all attempts to break the resistance failed.

These candles are known as "marubozu" and "belt holds." The bullish candles can be referred to as "bullish marubozu" or "bullish belt hold," and vice versa (I mentioned this just in case some of you are particular about the names).

At times, as the price nears a support or resistance level, it may form a series of small candles before a substantial, wide candle appears to validate those levels and initiate significant price movements. This occurrence is known as an "engulfing pattern." When a large green candle engulfs a smaller one at a support level, it's called a "Bullish Engulfing" pattern, and conversely, when it's a large red candle at resistance, it's referred to as a "Bearish Engulfing" pattern.

Bullish Engulfing at Support

Bearish Engulfing at Resistance

Small Body Candles

As we've discussed earlier, a large tail/wick candle signifies significant momentum and action, while a large body candle indicates strong market activity. However, what happens when the candle's body is small, with either no tail/wick or a very short one? In such cases, it reflects market inactivity or, in other words, a lack of decisive action by market participants.

The color of the candle, whether red or green, becomes less significant when the open and close are very close to each other. In such cases, it's the wicks or tails that truly matter. We can categorize these candles into two types: 1) Small body candles with shorter wicks and tails, and 2) Small body candles with longer wicks and tails.

1) Small body candles with shorter wicks and tails

Candles with Small Bodies & Small Shadows

Candles with small bodies and almost no wick or tail suggest a lack of momentum. and indecision among market participants regarding the direction of price movement. If these candles appear after a significant price move, they may indicate a potential slowdown or pause in that move.The subsequent candle following these indecisive ones will play a crucial role in determining the market's next move. It's important to note that these candles hold significance primarily at support and resistance levels, rather than appearing randomly on the charts.

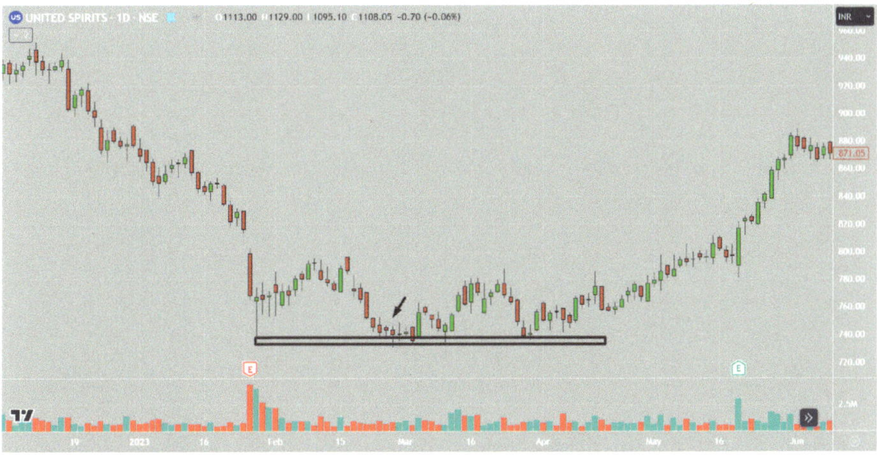

In the chart above, you can see that during the primary downtrend, there were significant red candles forming in the direction of the downward trend. However, after a pullback and a swing formation in the last week of January 2023, the downtrend resumed. Now, something interesting happened as the price approached the support level – the size of the bearish candles began to shrink (marked with an arrow). What does this tell us? It sends a signal that the downward trend might be losing momentum, and sellers are becoming indecisive.

Likewise, in the chart below, you can observe that prices initially advanced, creating the first swing in early August 2023. However, when they advanced towards the same swing again, the size of the candle began to shrink. This indicated indecision among buyers or a drying up of bullish momentum. Eventually in September 2023 end, a series of long-wick candles appeared, and the uptrend broke down with a wide-range bearish candle.

It's important to note that not every time a small body candle reaches a resistance or support level, it will necessarily change the course of the trend. As mentioned earlier, small body candles are indecisive, and it's the subsequent candles that will determine the trend's direction. When we have continuation candles aligning with the existing trend, these small body candles with little to no shadows can indicate a brief pause in the ongoing trend before it resumes.

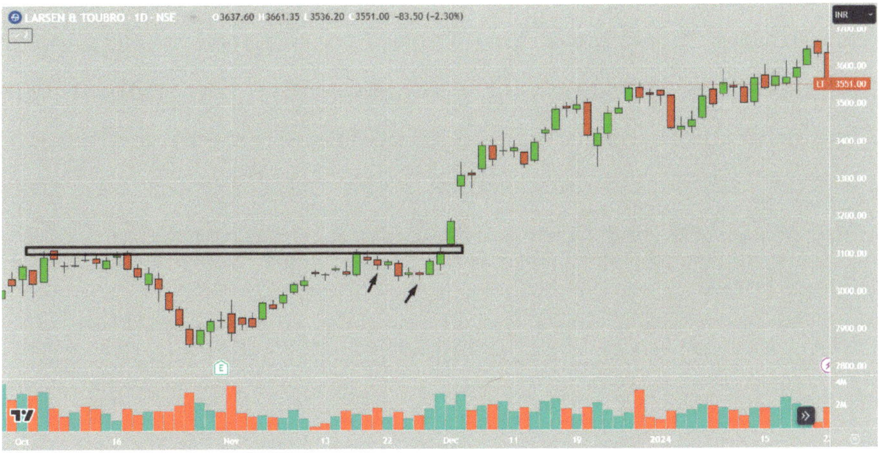

In the chart above, you can observe that an uptrend was dominant in the stock. However, during late November, there was a period of consolidation characterized by small candles. At this point, prices were near a resistance level. Eventually, the price broke out, forming significant green candles from the resistance zone. This indicates that the small range candles during the consolidation phase were actually a constructive consolidation, preparing the way for the breakout.

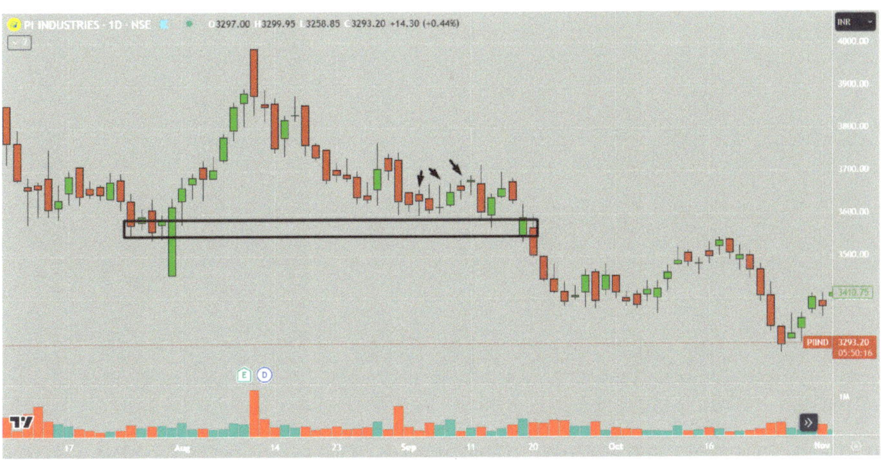

Similarly, you may notice in the chart above that the price was moving downward and then consolidated at a support level during September 2023. Subsequently, the support level broke, and the price continued its downward trend. In this case, the small range candles, which have small bodies and small shadows, acted as a brief pause before the continuation of the existing trend.

So, in conclusion, small-bodied candles with small shadows are not necessarily indecisive candles. The trend before their appearance and the price action that follows will ultimately determine the further course of the market.

These candles with small bodies and small shadows are commonly referred to as "doji" in the world of candlestick literature.

2) Small body candles with longer wicks and tails

Candles with Small Bodies & Large Shadows

We've already established that a small-bodied candle signifies indecision, and a small wick or tail doesn't make much of a difference. However, imagine a scenario where the candle has a small body but boasts large lower and upper shadows. What does this indicate? It suggests that significant buying and selling activities occurred throughout the day before the prices eventually closed near their open. Despite the session resulting in a small body, the intraday movements were anything but not calm, creating substantial price fluctuations. In simpler terms, this session was marked by nervousness and volatility, with market participants engaging in extensive buying and selling.

A small body with small shadows signifies indecision, whereas a small body with large shadows indicates a combination of indecision and volatility.

In the chart below, as the price approached the resistance levels, you can observe the appearance of small body candles with large shadows. These candles signaled a significant amount of buying and selling activity at the resistance zone, reflecting a lot of "change of hands" among market participants. Ultimately, this price action led to a correction.

I'm sure you've noticed the mention of "change of hands" in the paragraph above. When I refer to lots of action occurring on a long shadow candle, it indicates that someone is buying and someone is selling, especially at resistance. So, who will be the buyer, and who will be the seller? Take a moment to think about it.

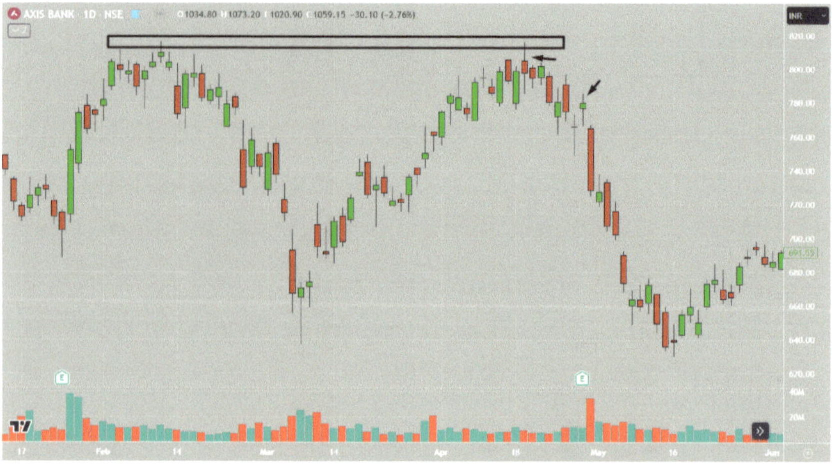

In a similar fashion, when observing the chart above, it becomes evident that in February 2023, the appearance of long-shadowed candles signaled the onset of increased volatility within the system. This heightened volatility ultimately resulted in a correction in the stock.

In the chart displayed below, you'll observe a significant drop during February and March 2020. This decline was interrupted by a notably large candle characterized by a small body and long shadows. This candle reflected a multitude of emotions and heightened volatility, signifying a substantial shift in ownership with "smart money" buying in. Consequently, the trend reversed and moved upward. Similarly, in January 2023, a correction was halted by a candle featuring a small body and a prominent shadow.

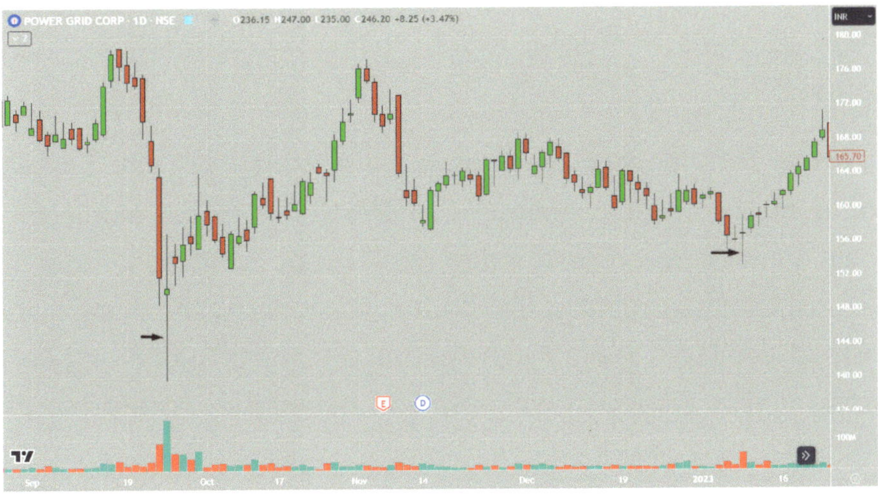

There are two nuances associated with this pattern:

1. Unlike the "doji" candle we discussed earlier, which may occasionally act as a continuation pause, this pattern has a low probability of serving as a continuation pattern; it typically signals a reversal in the trend.

2. This pattern tends to be more effective following a strong rally when prices have approached a resistance level. This implies that it is more indicative of a topping pattern than a bottoming one.

In the world of candlestick literature, these candle patterns are referred to by various names such as "high wave candles," "spinning tops," "long leg doji," and so on.

With this, I want to convey that you've encompassed all conceivable candlestick patterns that have been both discovered and perhaps even those yet to be uncovered. As I've previously emphasized, comprehending the underlying principles behind these patterns is crucial, rather than fixating solely on their names.

Now, let's engage in a fascinating exercise. I will present some of the most renowned candlestick patterns along with their names and corresponding visual representations. I kindly request that you avoid being influenced solely by the names, and instead, focus on grasping the actual dynamics underlying each pattern. This approach will help you develop a more profound understanding of price movements.

Begin adopting this thought process:

1. What insights does this price action offer?
2. Is this price action occurring in the appropriate context?
3. What course of action should I take once this action has concluded?

MARUBOZU

Take a glance at the chart below and pose these three questions to yourself:

1. 1) What insights can be gleaned from this price action?
2. 2) Is this price action unfolding in the relevant context?
3. 3) What steps should be considered once this action comes to an end?

I'm assisting you with this particular exercise, but I encourage you to undertake the remaining exercises independently. I aim to strike a balance and avoid delving excessively into academic content, as there is a wealth of material available for academic purposes.

Answers

1) What insights can be gleaned from this price action?

The trend was strong and upward, culminating in a swing high during August 2023. Following this high, a correction began in September 2023. However, after the correction, the subsequent upward movement lacked strength, evident from the presence of small candles suggesting weakened momentum. Eventually, as prices neared a resistance level, a powerful bearish candle emerged, characterized by intense selling activity and closing prices at the day's low. This occurrence strongly suggests a potential shift in favor of the sellers at this point.

2) Is this price action unfolding in the relevant context?

Indeed, the price action holds significance as it follows a substantial rally and occurs precisely at a resistance level. Consequently, this action appears to align seamlessly with the prevailing trend.

3) What steps should be considered once this action comes to an end?

If I am currently in a long position, it seems prudent to take profits at this point. To consider establishing a new position, I would prefer to wait for further confirmation from both the trend and price action to take a short or reenter long. This situation serves as a clear exit signal for long positions.

You're catching on! It's quite enjoyable, isn't it? By focusing on understanding the patterns without relying on their names, you're developing valuable analytical skills!

Going forward, make it a habit to pose each question to yourself when examining individual charts.

BULLISH MARUBOZU

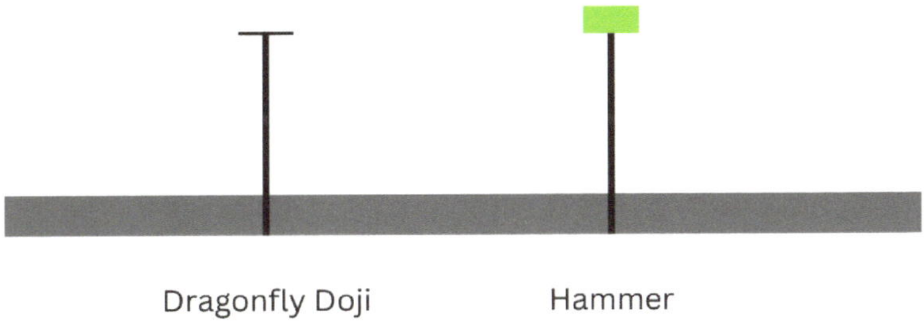

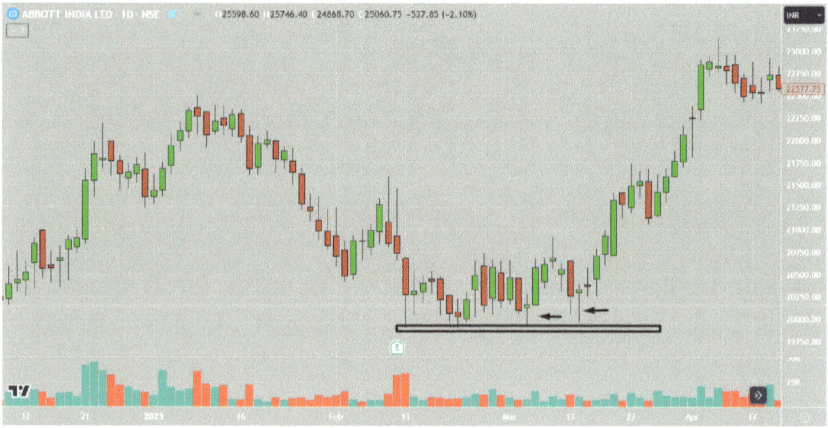

HAMMER

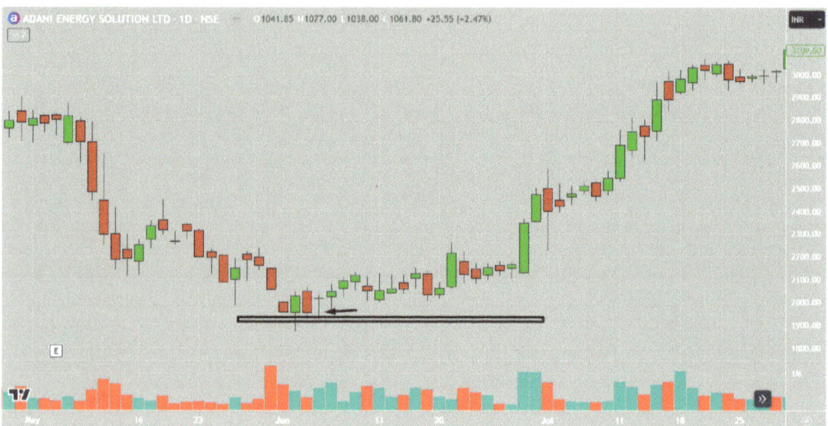

DRAGONFLY DOJI

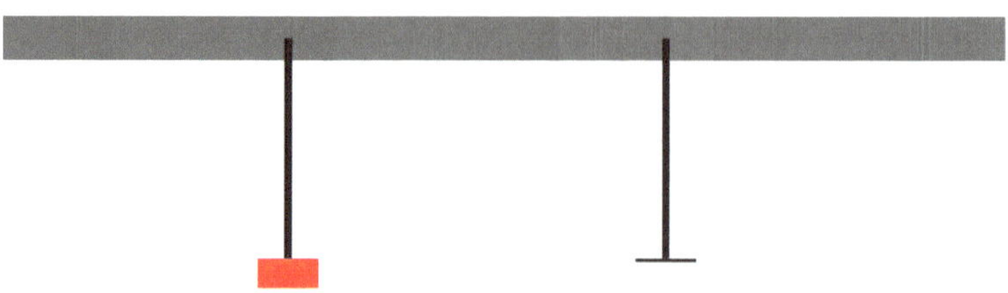

Shooting Star Gravetone Doji

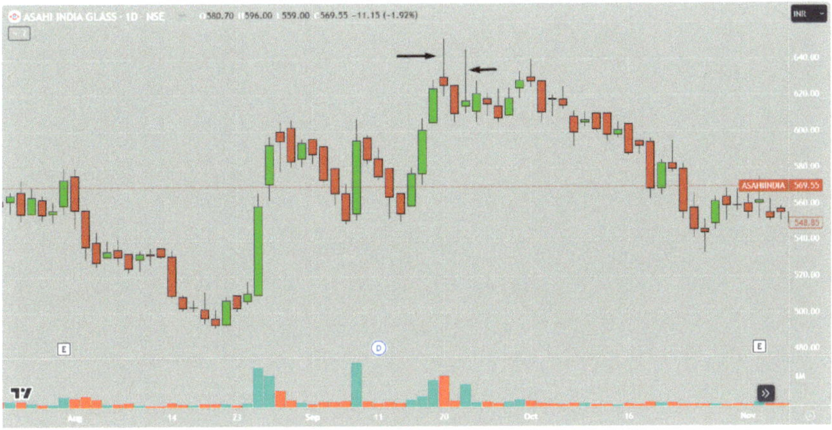

SHOOTING STAR

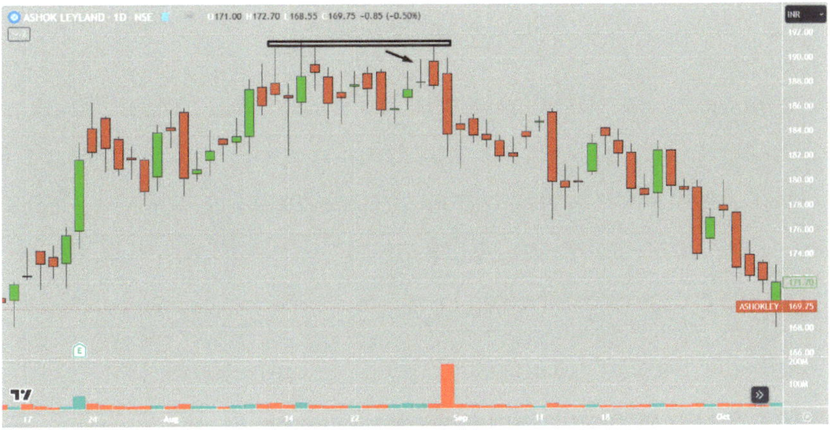

GRAVESTONE DOJI

Bear Engulfing (at Resistance)

Bull Engulfing (at Support)

BEAR ENGULFING

Let's analyze this chart together. In early November 2023, the stock reached its low point and then began a rally towards the previous resistance level of 800. However, as it approached this level, some increased volatility became evident, and the stock struggled to break through.

Then, in early January 2024, a significant Red Candle appeared, completely engulfing the previous small-bodied candles. Consider it this way: as the resistance level drew near, the body of the candle started shrinking, indicating a potential loss of momentum. This loss of momentum was subsequently confirmed by the appearance of a Big Red Candle, signaling the need to close any long positions. Ultimately, the trend reversed, forming lower highs and lower lows.

The fact that the Big Red Candle completely engulfed the prior small candles has led to the naming of this pattern as the "Engulfing Pattern."

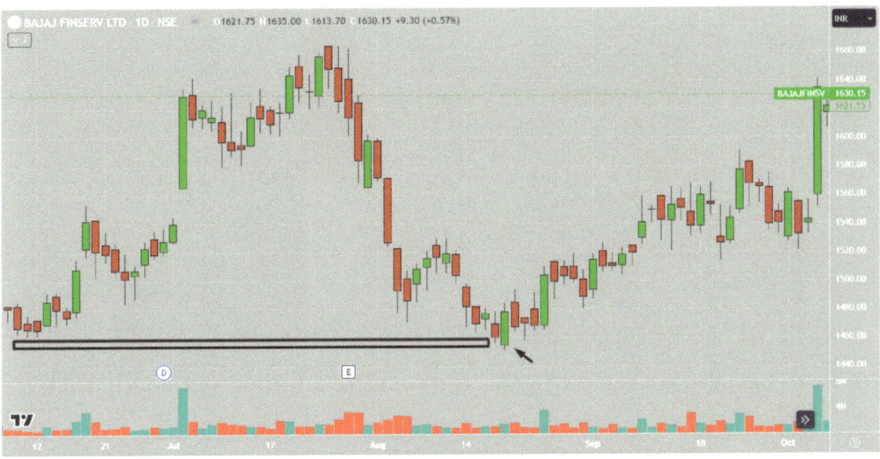

BULL ENGULFING

The same underlying factors also influence the Bullish Engulfing Pattern. In the chart above, we observed a substantial correction in prices from the end of July 2023 until mid-August 2023. However, take note that as prices approached the support range of 1460 - 1440 in August 2023, the significant Red Candle began to shrink, signaling a weakening of selling momentum.

Finally, at this support level, a prominent Green Candle emerged, completely "engulfing" the preceding red candle. This formation of a "Bullish Engulfing" candle at a crucial support zone indicated that the downtrend might pause or take a temporary break. Therefore, it was advisable to close short positions until further confirmation of the trend direction.

Whether it's a single-candle pattern or a multi-candle pattern, the analytical approach should remain consistent. Simply strive to understand what lies behind the price action.

Bear Harami & Resistance   Bull Harami at Support

Harami formations are indicative of indecision in the market. Harami candlesticks suggest a waning of momentum and the possibility of a reversal following a strong trend. The term "Harami" itself, meaning 'pregnant,' is quite illustrative. In this pattern, the second candlestick must be nestled within the body of the first, though their shadows may extend slightly.

This is undeniably one of the most significant and strong patterns in trading. In fact, it has the potential to serve as a comprehensive trading system all on its own. A detailed discussion of this pattern could easily occupy a substantial portion—perhaps around 25%—of this book. However, for brevity's sake, we'll keep the description concise for now, as the above explanation already provides a comprehensive understanding of the pattern.

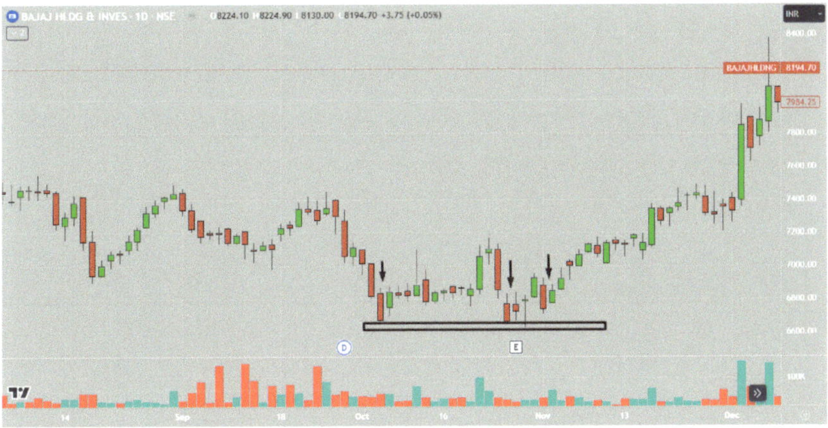

BULLISH HARAMI

Let's focus on a straightforward observation: in the midst of an ongoing downtrend, there comes a point where the prices cease to create lower highs and lower lows. Instead, the trend shifts into a sideways movement, characterized by the emergence of several small candles. These small candles then become enclosed within a larger red candle, signaling that the sellers are struggling to sustain downward momentum in the trend.

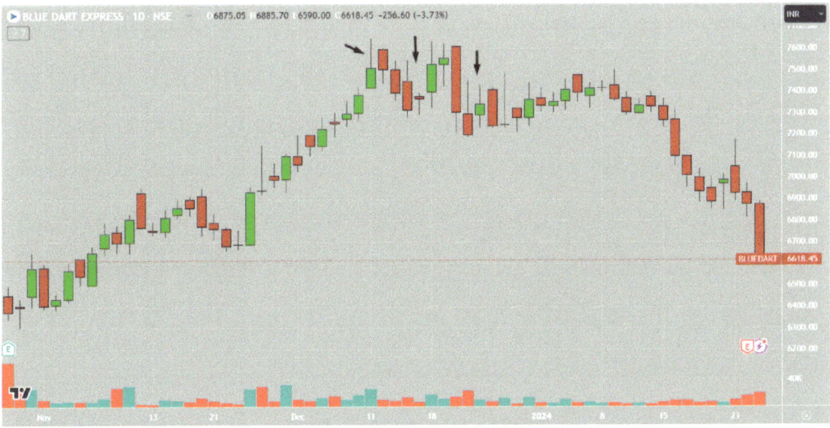

BEARISH HARAMI

Keep in mind that the color of the small candles contained within the larger candle holds no significance. It merely signifies indecision or a loss of momentum. What truly matters is the size of the candle's body, not its color.

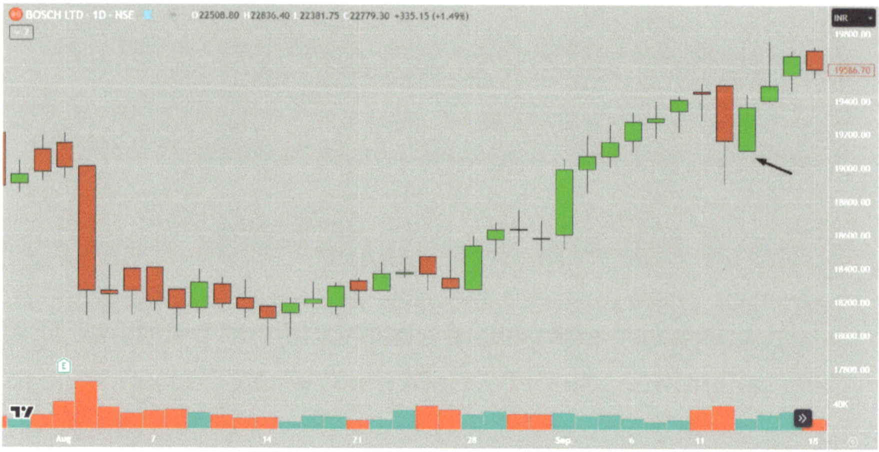

Now, take a look at the candle above, and let's determine whether it qualifies as a harami pattern. I've noticed that many social media enthusiasts label it as one, but it actually isn't. The primary role of a harami candle is to disrupt the existing momentum, which occurs when bullish or bearish activity suddenly halts in an ongoing trend. This pause in action often manifests as a small, indecisive candle body, not a large one. Although the green candle is contained within the body of the red candle, it doesn't constitute a harami pattern. Most computer programs would filter it out as such. Remember, stock markets are driven by emotions, and understanding these emotions is essential for comprehending the patterns!

Dark Cloudcover (at resistance)   Piercing Bull (at support)

The Dark Cloud Cover pattern, when observed following an uptrend, serves as a reversal signal, suggesting the possibility of challenging times ahead—a warning of potential "rainy days." Conversely, the Piercing Line, which is the opposite of the Dark Cloud pattern, acts as a reversal signal when it appears following a downtrend.

Whenever you sit down to interpret a pattern, remember to ask yourself these three key questions:

1. What insights can be gleaned from this price action?
2. Is this price action unfolding in the relevant context?
3. What steps should be considered once this action comes to an end?

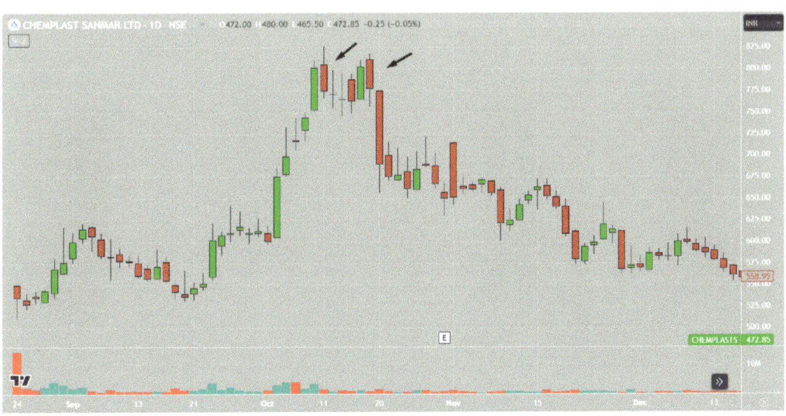

DARK CLOUD COVER

PIERCING CANDLE

We've covered single and double candle patterns, but there are also three-candle patterns to explore. Whether it's a single, double, or triple candle pattern, what truly matters in understanding these patterns is grasping the psychology of the traders responsible for their formation.

Morning Star at Support

Evening Star at Resisatnce

There's no need to be overwhelmed by the name or the pattern itself. If you deconstruct the pattern, you'll realize that it's essentially a naming convention. What's crucial is comprehending the factors influencing the price movement that resulted in the formation of this Morning and Evening Star pattern.

MORNING STAR

First, let's examine how a Morning Star pattern takes shape. It begins with a bearish candle, aligning with the prevailing downtrend. Next, a neutral candle appears (in the illustration, it's colored grey because the color isn't critical). Finally, a strong and wide bullish candle follows, effectively altering the trend's direction.

The neutral candle appearing at a support level indicates that the ongoing trend might be losing momentum, as evidenced by its shrinking size. Then, the substantial bullish candle signals a potent bullish move occurring at the support level, implying the presence of genuine buyers and a shift in the trend's course.

In essence, what transpires is a transition in the trend occurring within three candles. The intriguing part is that we've already discussed this concept earlier when exploring large-bodied candles, small-bodied candles, and candles with small shadows. The names associated with these patterns often serve to create a sense of excitement but don't fundamentally change the underlying principles.

EVENING STAR

Now, try to employ the same analytical approach (by yourself) as we discussed earlier, to the chart above in order to comprehend the Evening Star pattern.

By now, it should be evident that the name is merely an elaborate label that often overdresses the underlying price pattern. Our key focus should remain on unraveling the dynamics behind the pattern's formation and comprehending it within the context of the prevailing trend. This approach allows us to decipher numerous candlestick patterns without necessarily knowing their names.

The Most Vital Candlestick 'Insights' You Must Be Aware Of!

Now that you've grasped the essence of reading price action, let's delve into some of the most crucial concepts related to understanding candlesticks. These valuable insights may not be readily available in many other sources, making them invaluable nuggets of knowledge.

1) Candlestick patterns should not be relied upon in isolation

It's crucial to validate the candle's signals by incorporating other technical analyses such as trendlines, moving averages, and more.

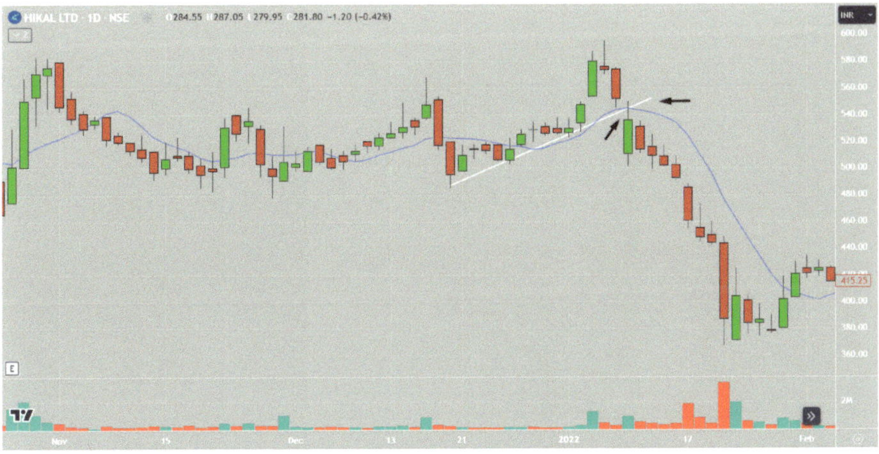

In the chart above, the confirmation of an Evening Star pattern occurred when prices broke down from the trendline and closed below the moving average. We will delve deeper into trendlines and moving averages in subsequent sections of this book. Employing multiple confirmations enhances the likelihood of success in our favor.

2) Trend is your Friend

Never underestimate the significance of support and resistance levels. Always bear in mind that a bullish candle pattern tends to be most potent within an upward-trending market. The ideal scenario to seek out a bullish candle is during a pullback phase, especially when the overall trend is approaching a support zone within a larger uptrend.

In the chart below, you'll notice that the trend was upward. During pullbacks, corrections consistently halted at the swing support zone. Whenever a bullish candle materialized at these levels, it propelled the price upward, allowing the trend to persist.

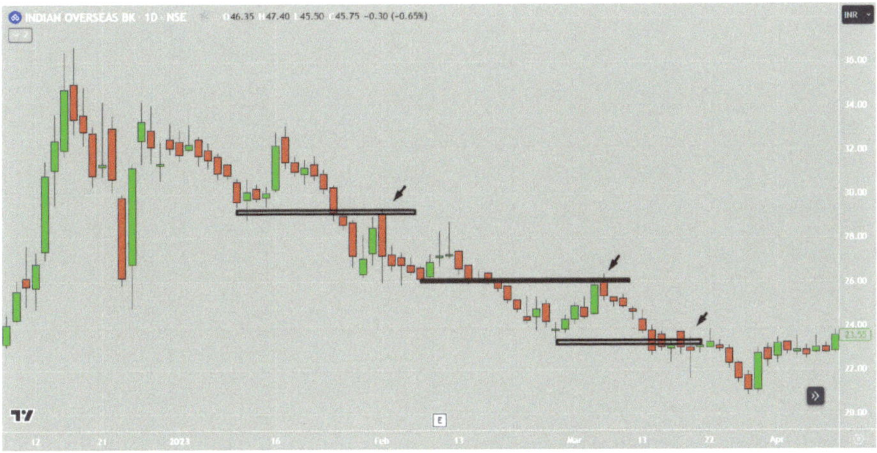

Similarly, when observing the chart above, you'll notice that as the trend moved downward, each rally came to a halt at the previous resistance level, often initiated by the formation of a bearish candle. Once the bearish candle materializes, the trend extends further downward, following the overall trend direction.

3) Right Pattern at the right place

It's crucial to grasp a fundamental concept: we must seek the appropriate pattern in the appropriate context. A trend that has been ascending for a while cannot be propelled further upward solely by the appearance of a strong candle. A strong, large candle at the beginning of a trend conveys a different message compared to a similar candle appearing at the maturity stage of the trend, where it sends a conflicting signal.

In the chart above, you can observe that when the trend initially began, the presence of significant green candles indicated strong and knowledgeable investors entering the stock. Notably, the trading volumes expanded during this phase. However, as the trend progressed and experienced a rapid 100% surge within a short timeframe, large green candles emerged in December 2022.

Now, consider what these candles were capable of pushing upward. The trend had already made substantial gains. Additionally, you may notice that the trading volumes declined during the latter part of the price advance. The appearance of a large green candle at the peak represented a "liquidity run," typically initiated by uninformed participants. This liquidity run allowed smart money, who had entered the trend during the formation of the earlier significant candles at the trend's initiation, to book profits.

Examine the chart provided below. Consider what you anticipate the hammers will achieve once prices have surged by over 100% from their initial lows!

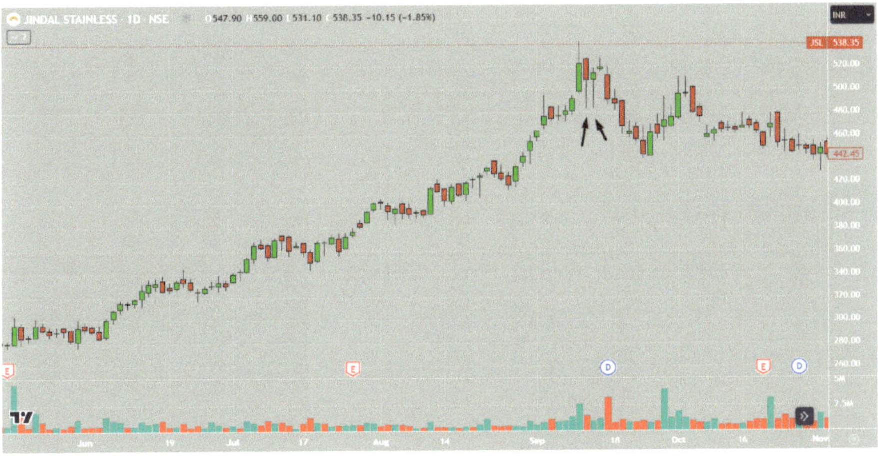

These hammers found at the upper end of the chart are also referred to as “hanging man” patterns within the academic realm of candlestick analysis.

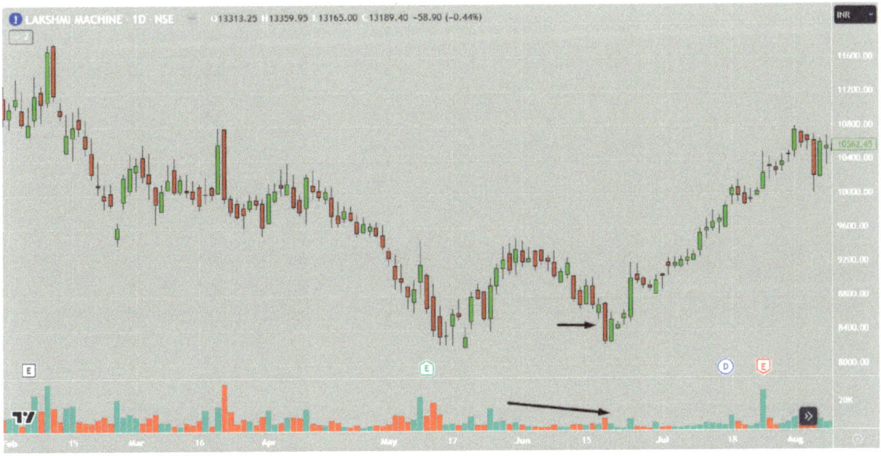

Take a look at the chart above. On June 20, 2022, there's a notably strong red bar following a substantial decline in price. Moreover, this bar appears at a swing point characterized by lower trading volumes during the descent. What can we infer from this? It suggests that this bar primarily represents the actions of the final sellers who may have been swayed by media influence and decided to liquidate their holdings.

4) Leading Indicator

As I've emphasized numerous times, candlestick charts are among the most effective tools for securing profits, making them a leading indicator. Candlesticks often offer early signals that hint at potential market movements. For instance, when multiple candles within a specific zone indicate a consistent outcome, they serve as a leading indicator.

Examine the chart above, and you'll notice that prices began consolidating during the first week of February 2023 before eventually breaking down in late February 2023. If you closely observe the sideways movement and the candle formations during this period, you'll find that the price action offered numerous clues about significant selling activities carried out by prominent players.Big red candles, long-tailed bearish candles, and small-bodied candles—all sorts of counter-trend indications were present.

Charts communicate with us, and it's our responsibility to hone the skills needed to listen and interpret their messages effectively.

Wrapping Up

This is all about candlesticks, which provide one of the most effective means of analyzing price action, often muddled and made ineffective by modern-day technical analysis. Approach this study with simplicity, and you'll discover its inherent beauty.

In recent times, technical analysts have made various modifications, such as creating Heiken-Ashi candles, volume-weighted candles, and more. However, in my view, these modifications often introduce lag to the inherent beauty of the subject. Instead of aiding us, these "modifications" can often confuse us since they tend to lag behind. My advice: Keep it simple!

Drop VI

Navigating Uncertainty: A Trader's Guide to Managing Stress

Trading in financial markets demands courage, as it's rife with unpredictability and inevitable losses are part of the journey to success. For novices, the volatility can seem overwhelming, yet maintaining a long-term outlook is crucial. Embracing uncertainty and building resilience are key. Visualization exercises can help manage fears, imagining worst-case scenarios while remaining poised, underscoring the importance of a solid trading strategy. This approach helps control emotions and stress, allowing traders to face market challenges with confidence and a disciplined mindset. Remember, resilience and a strategic approach turn volatility into an ally on the path to trading success.

Chapter 6

Gaps: Advanced Short Patterns

A gap in a chart signifies a region where no trading activity occurred. It materializes when an stock's price makes a significant upward or downward leap, leaving no transactions in the middle. In essence, it indicates that the market opened at a different price compared to its previous close.

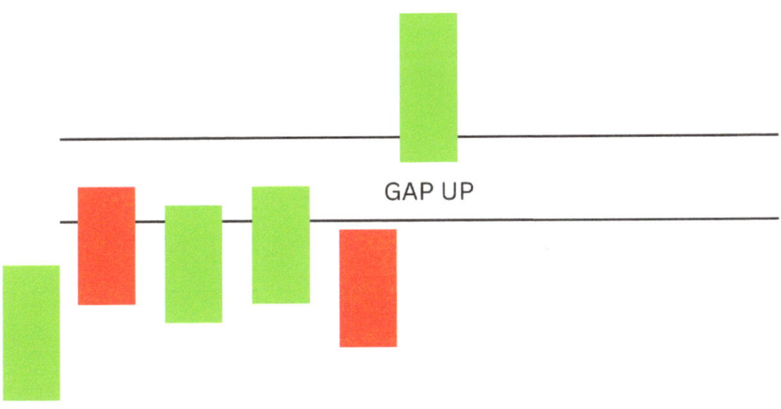

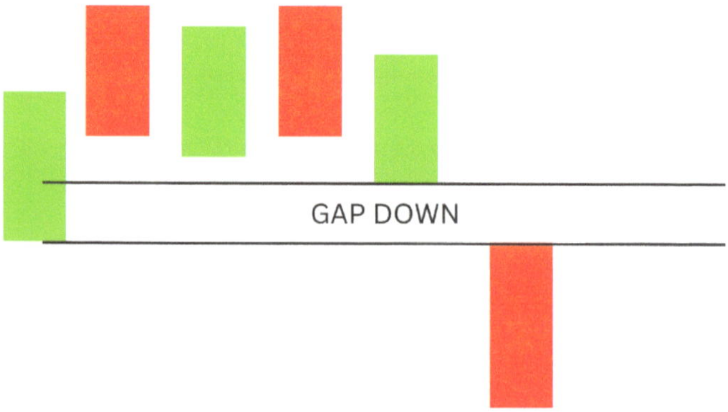

What leads to the occurrence of a gap? The primary reason is often rooted in fundamental factors. Events like earnings reports, product announcements, analyst upgrades or downgrades, and the appointment of new senior executives can trigger gaps. These occurrences have the potential to drive substantial market movements in either direction between trading sessions.

From a technical perspective, however, their significance lies in their context within the overall trend. For a technical trader, it's crucial to vigilantly monitor gaps as they materialize. Their occurrence concerning the prevailing trend will determine whether they contribute constructively to the existing trend or not.

Distinguishing Gap Down Stocks from Gap Up Stocks

Gap down stocks and gap up stocks are terms used to describe the direction of price movement on either side of a gap. A full gap down occurs when the opening price is lower than the previous low price, whereas a full gap up (as illustrated above) happens when the opening price exceeds the prior high price. Refer to the illustration above.

Gaps serve as highly charged emotional zones in trading, where numerous transactions occur, involving significant buying and selling activities. This heightened emotional atmosphere adds a layer of technical significance to gaps. Consequently, gaps often function as crucial support and resistance levels on price charts, owing to the intense emotions associated with them.

Gaps can be categorized into three distinct types: breakaway gaps, runaway gaps, and exhaustion gaps.

Breakaway Gaps

Breakaway gaps come into play at the onset of a fresh trend. Typically, this occurs when the financial instrument has been trading in a sideways consolidation pattern, and a noteworthy news event unfolds.

Breakaway gaps are often viewed as gaps that confirm the continuation of the emerging trend, thanks to the strength of the newly established market direction.

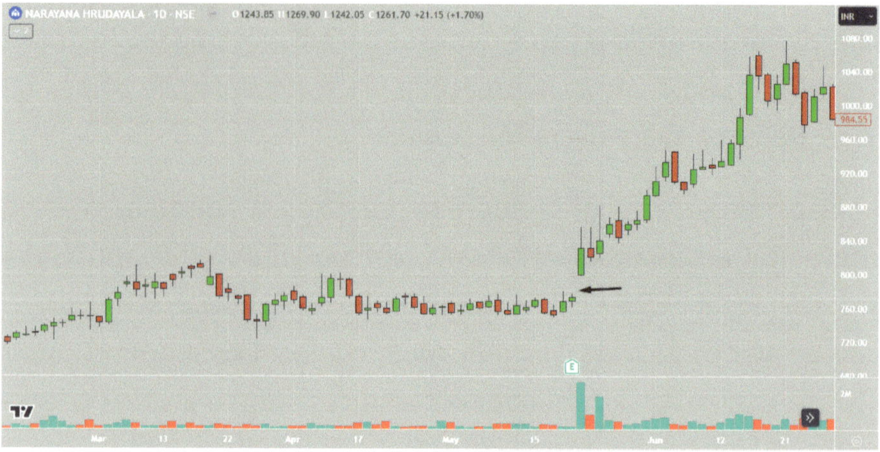

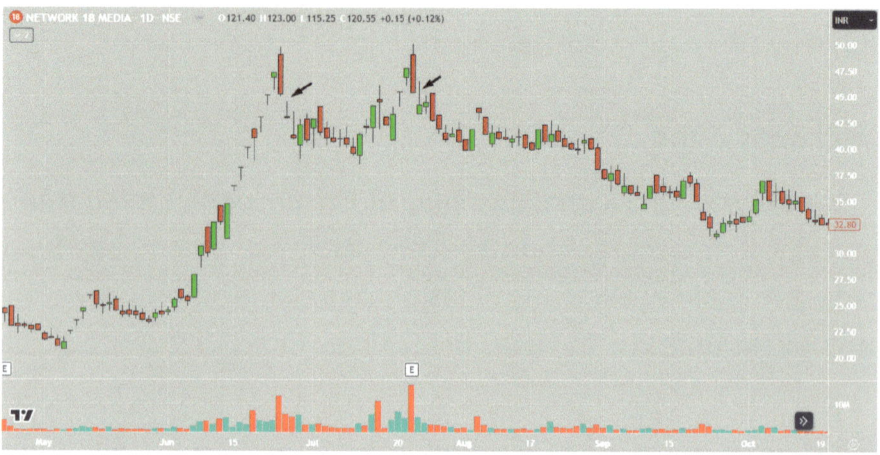

Runaway Gaps

Runaway gaps serve as a clear indication of trend continuation.

When it comes to trading runaway gaps to support the ongoing trend, it's regarded as one of the most secure trading strategies. To further bolster this safety, traders often opt to confirm their runaway gap analysis with additional signals.

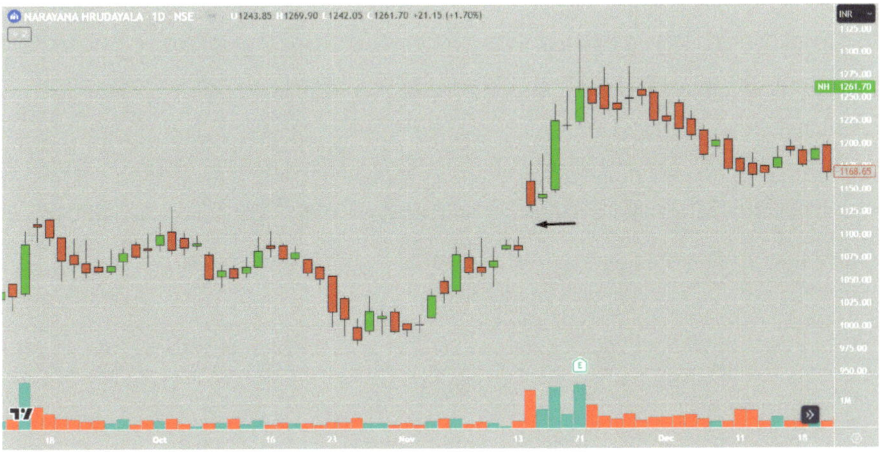

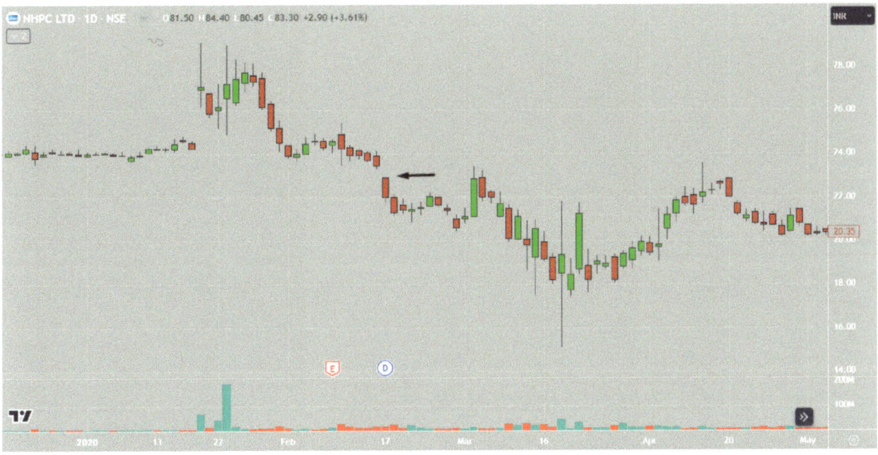

Exhaustion Gaps

Exhaustion gaps materialize towards the conclusion of a trend, serving as an indicator that the prevailing trend is nearing its termination or possibly even a reversal.

This particular pattern can be employed as a reliable indicator that a trend is reaching its conclusion.

For those engaged in trend-following trading strategies, it's imperative to assess their positions considering other concurrent signals that may hint at a potential trend reversal.

Exhaustion gap-ups are formed by the final group of buyers, while exhaustion gap-downs are generated by the last group of sellers.

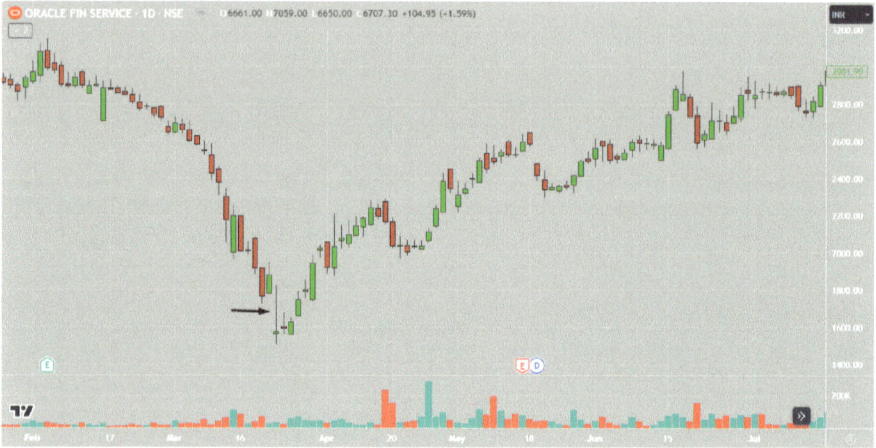

While gaps appear as strong trading zones with ample opportunities, it's crucial to remember that blindly chasing a gap for entry is not advisable. As we've previously established, gaps represent significant support and resistance levels, increasing the likelihood that prices will retest them. This retest can present an opportunity for strategic trading. Alternatively, traders can patiently await the formation of consolidation patterns after the gap to make well-informed trading decisions.

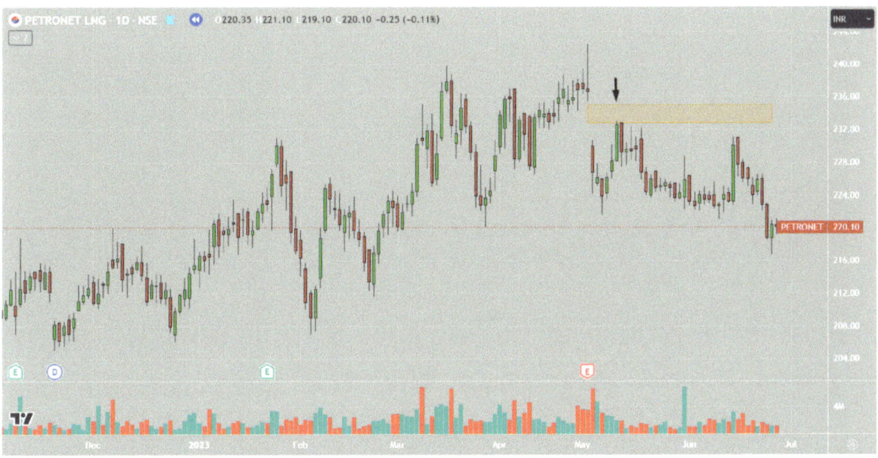

The stock exhibited a 4% gap-down opening on May 4, 2023. Would you consider entering at this point? Certainly not! However, on May 11, 2023, prices retraced back to the gap area, offering a more favorable risk-reward ratio. This area can be identified as an SR Flip zone, as discussed in our Support/ Resistance lesson.

Similarly, in the chart below, the stock experienced a 6% gap-up on April 28, 2023, compared to the previous day's closing price. Pursuing an entry immediately after such a gap doesn't appear prudent. Instead, it is advisable to exercise patience and await a retest. On May 19, 2023, prices retraced to the gap area, creating an ideal opportunity to initiate a trade with well-controlled risk.

Another approach to trading gaps is to be patient and wait for trading signals that occur after the gap forms. In many cases, the gap area will eventually be retested. However, if the gap is not retested, or if you happened to miss the initial entry opportunity, you can opt to wait for consolidation to occur after the gap before planning your trades.

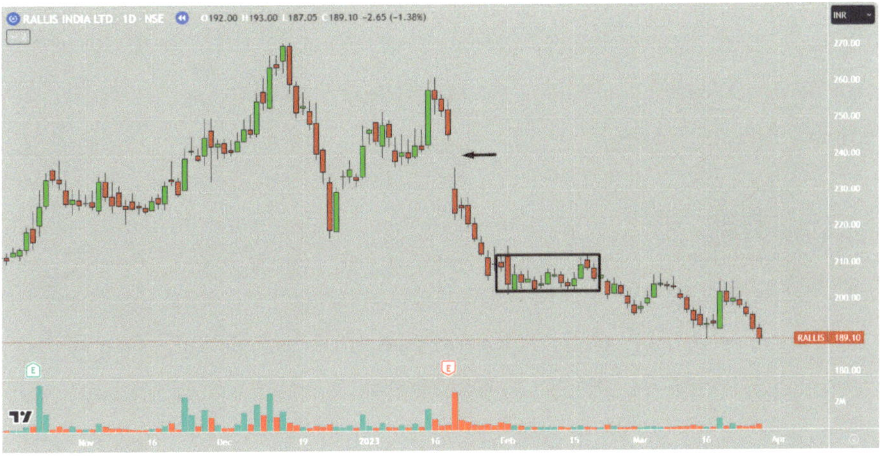

It's evident that on January 19, 2023, there was a gap-down, and interestingly, the price did not attempt to retest the gap area, making a trade entry unfeasible. However, subsequent to that gap, a consolidation phase emerged (highlighted within a box), signifying that the trend was pausing before continuing. This consolidation zone serves as a potential entry point. Once prices exit this zone, it can be an opportune moment to initiate a trade.

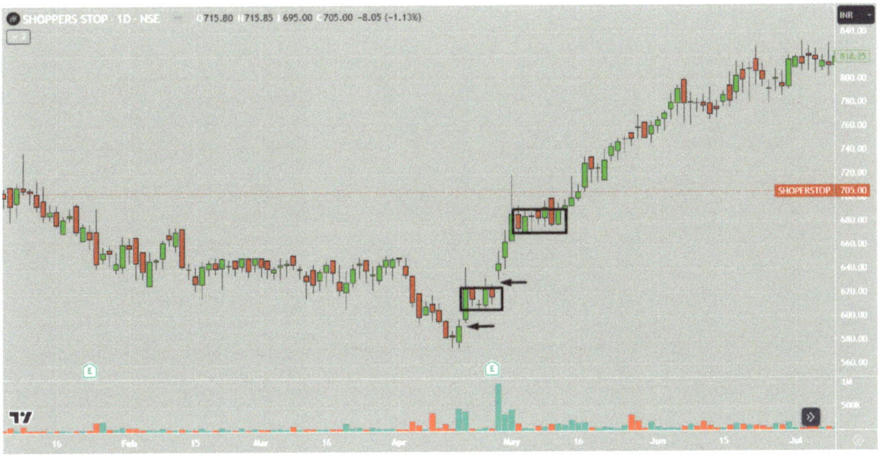

Using the same rationale, let's analyze the chart above. The initial trade opportunity was overlooked, but subsequently, potential trades could have been executed within the consolidation zones.

The Gap Trap

"Fading the gap" is a strategy that involves closing gaps within the same trading day they occur. For instance, consider a scenario where a stock experiences a gap-up opening, with the opening price higher than the previous day's closing price, likely driven by positive earnings news. Now, as the trading day unfolds, traders delve deeper into the company's information, discovering unfavorable aspects, leading to increased selling activity. Eventually, the stock's price retraces to the previous day's closing level, effectively filling the gap.

This strategy can be particularly advantageous for experienced market participants, capitalizing on the irrational exuberance often exhibited by less experienced traders. The volume that initially causes the gap is frequently a result of FOMO (Fear of Missing Out) in trading, making it a potential opportunity for seasoned traders to "fade the gap" and profit from the price reversion.

Observing the chart above, let's examine a specific scenario. On July 31, 2023, the company released its earnings report, resulting in a gap-up opening driven by positive earnings news. Traders, influenced by this news, eagerly rushed to acquire the stock in anticipation of a continued upward move. However, on the very same day, the stock reversed course, descending and effectively filling (or fading) the initial gap. This reversal caught traders who chased the gap by surprise, and subsequently, the stock continued its corrective downward trajectory.

This occurrence serves as a noteworthy example of the stock market's capacity for rapid price adjustments, as in line with Dow Theory, and highlights how traders' reactions to news events can sometimes lead to unexpected outcomes.

Wrapping Up

Price movements in the financial markets serve as valuable signals to traders, guiding them on whether it's an opportune moment to buy, sell, or remain on the sidelines. Among these price movements, there are gaps, such as stock gaps, which represent significant leaps in a security's price, typically occurring outside of regular trading hours due to external influences, often news-related. When analyzing these gaps, it's imperative for traders and investors to ascertain the underlying cause before making any trading decisions.

Drop VII

Letting Go of Trading Regret: Embracing the Present for Future Success

Trading is a journey marked by highs and lows. It's tempting to fixate on past errors, but this can lead to regret and shake our present confidence. The key is to stay present-focused, adhering to your trading plan with discipline. Forgive past mistakes and approach the future with determination. Reflecting on past errors through a list and aligning them with your plan can foster self-compassion and a forward-looking mindset. Embrace continuous improvement over perfection, letting lessons inform but not overshadow your present path to success.

Chapter 7

Trendlines

Trendlines are a fundamental tool in the world of trading, widely utilized by traders of all experience levels, from novices to seasoned professionals. Their popularity stems from their straightforwardness and efficiency. Trendlines serve as graphical representations of a financial market's path, aiding in the visualization of the general trend in price movement, whether it's upward, downward, or sideways.

Trendlines are like maps that show us where the buyers and sellers are in the market. They help us see if prices are going up, down, or staying the same. Knowing how to use trendlines can help us make smart trading decisions, especially in markets that can be a bit crazy, like the stock market or when trading things like gold and oil.

But, like any tool, trendlines have their good and not-so-good sides. It's important to know both to use them well. Also, when trendlines break, it can tell us even more about what might happen next in the market. So, in the next parts, we'll dive deeper into this stuff and look at some real chart examples to help you understand it better.

At its simplest, an uptrend line is drawn beneath clearly recognizable support zones (valleys), referred to as an ascending trend line. Conversely, in a downtrend, the trend line is plotted above easily identifiable resistance zones (peaks), termed a descending trend line.

How does a trendline work?

A trendline is like a helpful guide for understanding where prices might go. To draw one, you connect a line between the highest points (swings) or the lowest points (swings) in a series. If you connect the lows, you get an upward trendline, and if you connect the highs, you get a downward trendline. Think of these lines like barriers: in an uptrend, the line helps support prices from going too low, and in a downtrend, it acts as a barrier to stop prices from going too high. These lines are often called "dynamic support and resistance" because they move along with the price trend.

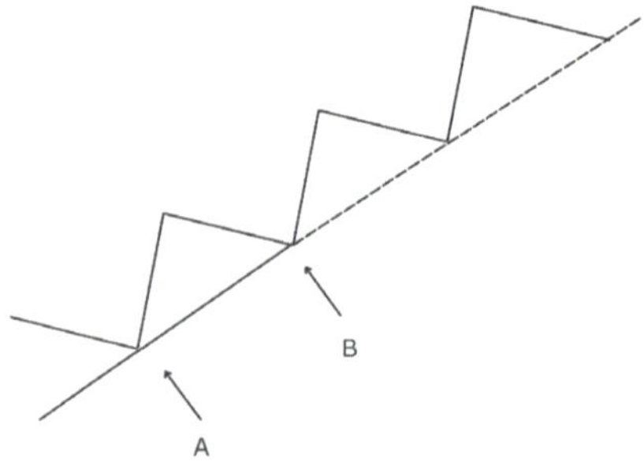

When is a trendline good to use?

A trendline becomes reliable when it has been touched by the price of a stock or asset at least three times without crossing over it. The more times it gets touched, the more powerful and important it becomes. A good trendline can work like a barrier, either stopping prices from going too high (resistance) or preventing them from falling too low (support). For traders, it's a useful tool to spot potential times to buy or sell.

In the example shown above, the lows at points A and B are linked together and extended. You might observe that as this line continues, it acts as support in the future.

Similarly, in the illustration below, points A and B are connected and extended. The subsequent peaks now encounter resistance along this line, indicating a downtrend.

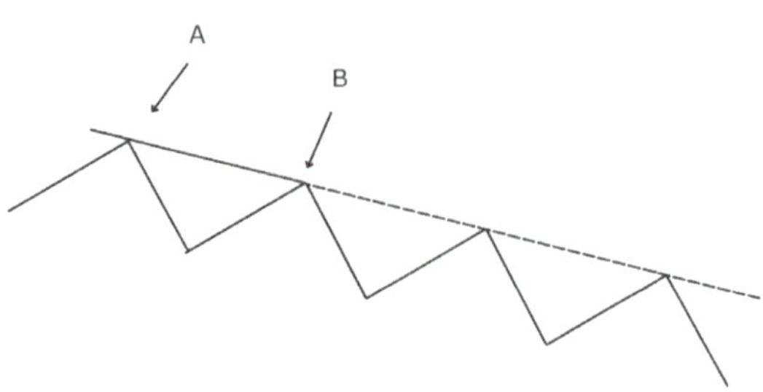

Different Types of Trendlines: Up, Down, and Sideways

1. **Upward Trend:** When a security's price is mostly going up, it's called an uptrend. In this case, we draw a line below the price to provide support, like a safety net.

2. **Downward Trend:** When the price of a security is generally going down, it's known as a downtrend. Here, we draw a line above the price to create resistance, like a barrier to stop it from going higher.

3. **Sideways Trend:** When a security's price moves neither up nor down, it's in a sideways trend. In this situation, the trendline can act as both support and resistance at different times, like a versatile tool.

Now, let's take a step back and remember the trading stages we discussed when reading Dow Theory. Let's connect those stages with the information in the paragraph above.

When we encounter an uptrending line, it's like the participation phase (Mark Up) we talked about earlier. When we come across sideways lines, it's a bit like a non-participating phase (Accumulation). And when we find a downtrending line, it's akin to participating for short sellers (Mark Down). We're connecting the dots to understand it better!

In the chart provided above, we've indicated the different phases using trendlines to make it easier to grasp. The Down phase is identified by a downtrending line, where the peaks are connected, and you can observe how this line functions as resistance.

Similarly, in the Up phase, where prices are consistently rising, forming higher peaks and troughs, we connect the troughs to create an uptrending trendline, which serves as support as the trend continues.

During the Accumulation phase, the tops and bottoms are nearly equal, leading to the formation of horizontal trendlines.

How to Create a Trendline

Drawing a trendline is simple. Begin on the left side of the chart and move your line to the right. Remember, for it to count, a trendline should pass through at least three price swings.

For an upward trendline, begin with a low point on the left and connect it to a higher low.

For a downward trendline, start with a high point on the left and connect it to a lower high.

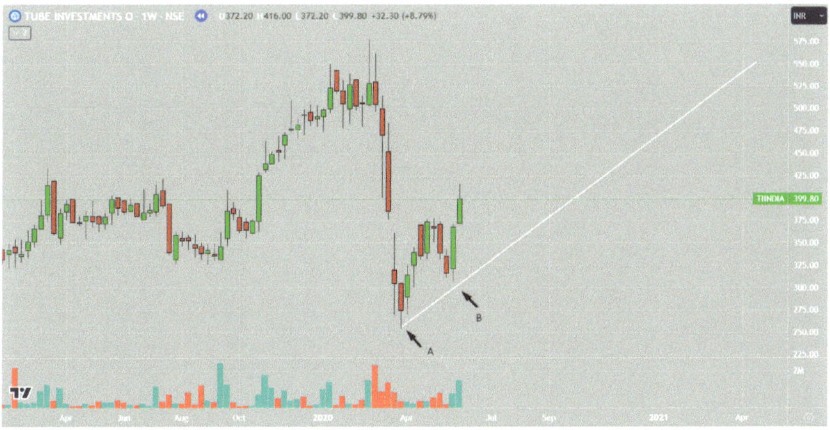

In the chart shown above, we'll link points A and B to create an upward trendline. Afterward, we'll extend this line so that it can provide support in the future.

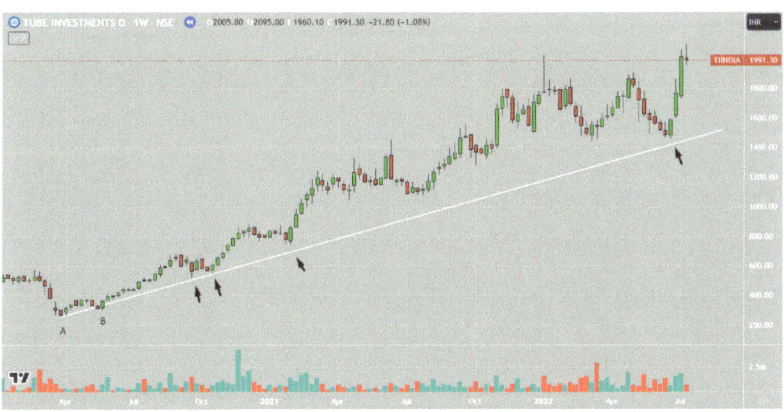

You might observe that as the main trend continued, the trendline drawn from reference points A and B acted as a support area for any "secondary" corrections.

I want to draw your attention to the two words I've used here: "primary" and "secondary." I'm using them to bring us back to Dow Theory, as it forms the basis for everything we do in Technical Analysis.

The chart above illustrates a downtrend line formed by connecting two lower peaks and extending the line to the right. Take a moment to notice how prices respond to this line in the upcoming periods.

One challenge I've noticed when using trendlines is their subjectivity. Different traders may draw different trendlines when analyzing the same chart. Furthermore, trendlines are not always precise. Occasionally, prices can break a trendline temporarily, only to revert to the original trend later on.

In the chart below, you'll notice two trendlines: one in red and another in violet. Following the violet trendline might suggest that the uptrend has concluded, while adhering to the red line would imply that the uptrend is still intact. Both lines are valid since they have numerous touch points. However, determining which one is correct isn't straightforward. It depends on your trading timeframe and the amount of data you consider.

To address this subjectivity, it's advisable not to rely solely on these lines. Instead, use multiple levels of confirmation, such as swing levels, moving averages, and other indicators (which we will discuss later in this book). This approach can provide a more comprehensive and reliable understanding of market trends and potential entry or exit points.

Now, let's delve into some intricacies of this tool. These observations stem from my nearly 15 years of experience using trendlines. Hopefully, you'll gain insights that you haven't encountered elsewhere!

Is there really a trend?

One crucial mistake beginners often make when using trendlines is applying them when there is no actual trend. The clue is right in the name!

Examining the chart below, it's evident that the market is simply moving sideways. Consequently, it's unsurprising that none of these trendlines are effective in this situation.

Avoid forcing the lines onto the prices; I've observed people overcrowding price action with trendlines. This issue is particularly common among traders who adhere to wave theory, where they strive to count every swing on the charts.

Take a glance at the chart below; it appears that trendlines have been applied forcefully to every swing.

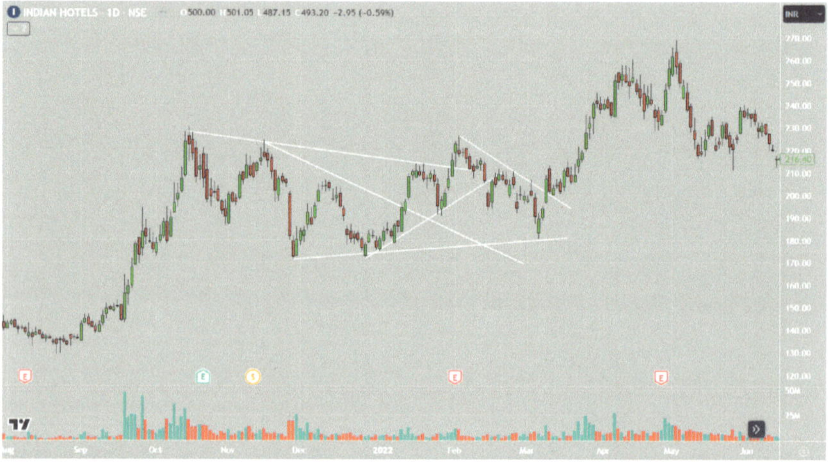

The reality is, this is a sideways zone, devoid of any discernible trend. Drawing slanted lines in this area lacks logic. The term "trendline" inherently implies the presence of a "trend," with the first four letters of the word emphasizing exactly that.

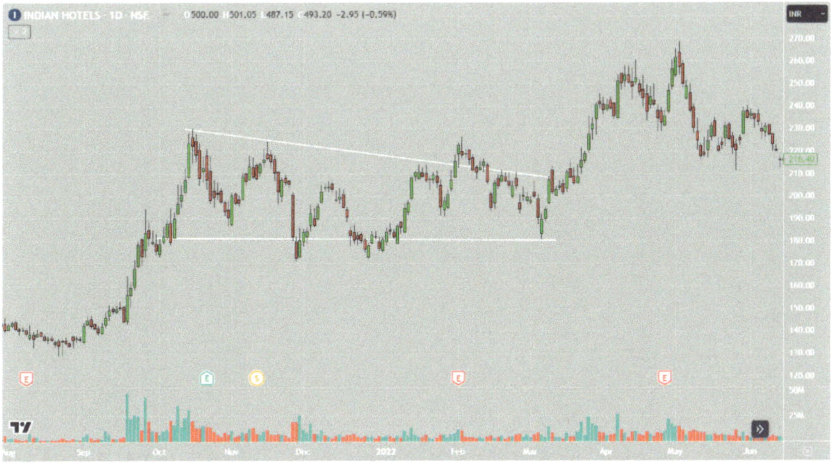

Now, examine the same chart above. When we draw only two lines, they neatly encompass the price movement. It appears straightforward and uncluttered. Rest assured, you'll hone these skills through consistent practice.

Trendline Angles

An ideal trendline typically forms at around a 40 to 45 degree angle. If it's steeper than 45 degrees, the price is climbing too rapidly (momentum is accelerating), and the trendline is prone to breaking, even if the trend persists. Conversely, if the angle is less than 45 degrees, it signifies a weaker trend, almost resembling sideways trading.

Examine the chart above, where we've identified a 45-degree trendline that beautifully captured the entire upswing, sustaining for over three months.

Now, on the same chart, take a closer look at the period when the trend was advancing swiftly. Here, we identified a trendline with an angle exceeding 70 degrees! This line remained intact for 10 sessions, indicating an exceptionally strong momentum move. The crucial lesson here is that steeper trendlines can be instrumental in capitalizing on rapid price movements, allowing you to secure gains without risking much capital.

Number of Touches

A trendline gains strength as it touches it creating more swing points, making it more noticeable to a broader spectrum of traders. However, this phenomenon has its limits. The more a trendline is touched, the more it absorbs the interest of buyers or sellers in that trend. In many instances, once a trendline is touched five times, the likelihood of it 'breaking' or being breached increases significantly.

In the chart below, we connected the lower peaks using a trendline. Notice that after five touches, the prices broke out of the line. What occurs with each touch? Supply is absorbed. During the initial touch, the maximum supply is encountered. As the trend continues, sellers gradually exhaust their resources, and ultimately, buyers take control.

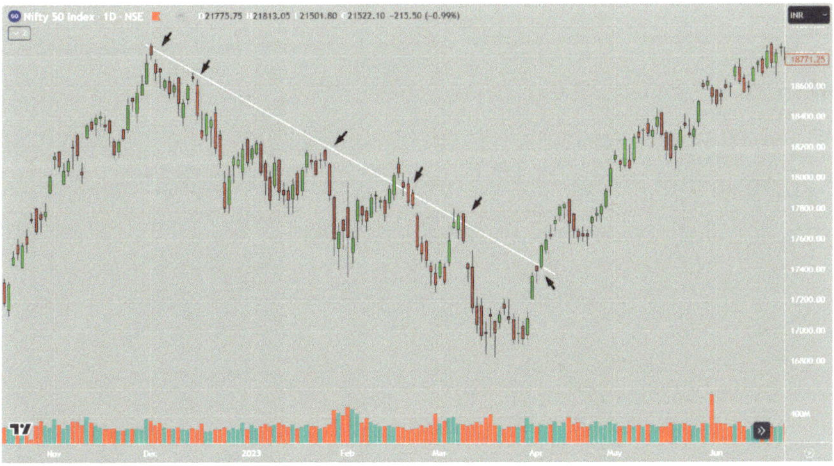

Trendline Data

I faced a common challenge during my early days of learning and trading - how much data should be considered when drawing a trendline. When we zoom in and out of charts, we come across numerous swings that could potentially serve as reference points for trendline drawing. The key to this question lies in what you're trading or analyzing.

If you're trading or analyzing shorter-term swings, then around 3 months of data is likely sufficient. Strong swings, whether up or down, may last for 3-4 months with minor corrections in between. On the other hand, if your goal is long-term trend trading, you might want to consider 1-3 years of data. Additionally, exploring higher time frame charts can also be beneficial in gaining a more comprehensive perspective.

In the chart below, I'm focusing on the upward movement that occurred from late March 2023 to late July 2023, spanning a period of 4 months. During this time, there was a primary upward move with minor intermediate corrections. You might be curious about why I've drawn double trendlines. Not to worry, we'll discuss that in detail shortly!

However, if our aim is to grasp the broader trend, I've extended my data selection back to June 2022, covering almost 19 months of price action! (Refer the chart below)

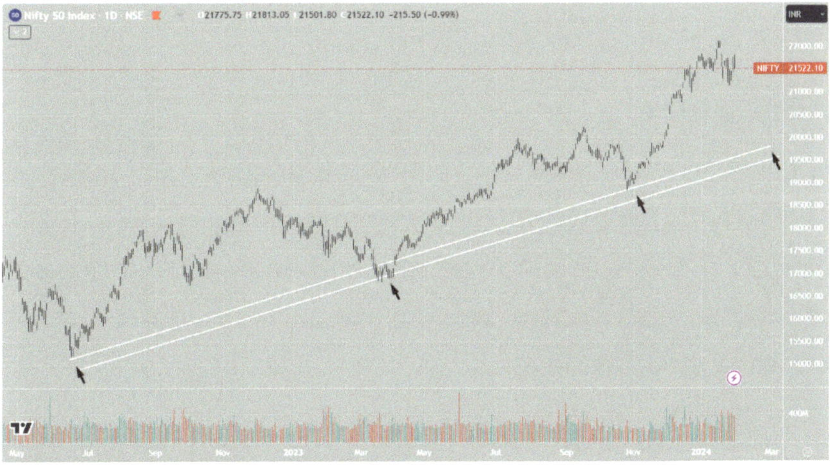

Similarly, for those of us who are committed to strong trend-following strategies and aren't concerned with daily price fluctuations, larger time frames like monthly and weekly charts become valuable tools. Take a look at the Nifty's chart below – we've gathered data dating all the way back to 2003, encompassing almost 18 years of information. Notice how this trendline from 2003 provided critical support during the Covid crash of 2020, with prices rebounding precisely from that point. It almost appears like a form of witchcraft, doesn't it?

Trendline zones

Trendlines do not follow strict rules! It is uncommon for the price to perfectly touch a trendline and immediately reverse. Instead, think of trendlines as a 'range' rather than an exact price point. Recognizing this concept aids in establishing your entry price and setting stop-loss levels.

I hope it's clearer now why I've incorporated double trendlines in some of the charts above. We should allow the price some flexibility to fluctuate.

Take a look at the chart below. We've drawn a trendline from point A to point B, and it works wonderfully at point C &

F. However, what about points D and E? Important entry points could have been planned there, but we missed them because there was no trendline support.

Now, I've drawn a parallel line to the initial trendline to accommodate more touch points. You can see how this becomes a more viable approach, as it now touches points D and E as well.

Trendline Breakouts and Breakdowns

A trendline breakout takes place when a security's price surpasses an declining (downward sloping) trendline, signifying a bullish signal, or falls below a rising trendline, signaling a bearish trend. Refer charts below:

Wrapping Up

Keep in mind that all support and resistance rules also apply to trendlines, given their subjective nature. To enhance their effectiveness, it's advisable to use trendlines in conjunction with other confirmations and confluences.

Drop VIII

The Power of Humility: Embracing Growth in Trading

In trading, managing ego is crucial. A balanced self-confidence aids success, but an unchecked ego can lead to mistakes. Embracing humility helps traders recognize their limits and stay open to learning. Ego-driven decisions often backfire, so maintaining self-awareness and humility is key for rational, market-driven choices. Success comes from humility, curiosity, and learning from all experiences, allowing traders to transcend ego and unlock their potential.

Chapter 8

The Larger Patterns (Classical Chart Patterns)

I hope you recall from our previous discussions that chart patterns can be categorized into two types: shorter chart patterns involving candles and larger chart patterns. We initially covered candles, and you might be wondering why we shifted to discussing trendlines. The reason is that trendlines serve as the foundation for these larger chart patterns, making it crucial to address them first.

Classical chart patterns are readily identifiable shapes and structures present in price charts, which traders utilize to identify potential trading opportunities and make well-informed decisions.

These patterns, grounded in the principles of technical analysis, rely on historical price movements and are among the most widely recognized tools in a trader's toolkit.

Similar to candlestick patterns, there are numerous classical chart patterns that have been identified, with some given fancy names. In this discussion, we will focus on the significant ones. Just like with candle patterns, it's crucial to comprehend the underlying dynamics when these patterns emerge.

Certain patterns tend to appear more frequently on trading charts because of their geometric configurations and the repetitive nature of financial markets.

One of the remarkable aspects of chart patterns is their ability to offer us entry points, stop-loss levels, and target prices.

Therefore, we are taking into account some of the most prevalent classical chart patterns:

- Double Top & Double Bottom,
- Head & Shoulders,
- Triangles,
- Flags & Pennants,
- Cup & handles,
- Wedges.

Continuation, Reversal, or Both?

Based on the shapes and locations of these patterns on the chart, they are typically classified as "continuation" or "reversal" patterns. However, let me share an insight from my 15-plus years in this market: patterns can manifest anywhere on the chart and can act as triggers for both continuation and reversal (there is one exception to it). Hence, we won't distinguish these patterns solely based on their appearance and indications. Instead, we will concentrate on their practical utility and approach when they appear on a chart.

Moving forward, whenever we delve into a chart pattern, we'll consider a set of questions:

1. Is the chart pattern a continuation pattern or a reversal pattern? (This will be determined by the pattern's location within the trend.)
2. Where is the optimal entry point for the trade?
3. What is the appropriate stop-loss level in case the market doesn't validate the pattern?
4. What are the potential target levels and price targets for the pattern's momentum?

We will frequently utilize two key terms throughout this section:

1. Breakout
2. Breakdown

Let's swiftly grasp their meanings.

A breakout occurs when the price of a security surpasses a resistance level, suggesting the possibility of an upward trend. Traders often consider entering buy orders above the breakout level. Conversely, a breakdown takes place when the price drops below a support level, indicating the potential onset of a downward trend. When we engage in trading chart patterns, we are actively participating in breakout and breakdown trading strategies.

Now, let's begin by exploring the initial set of chart patterns: Double Top and Double Bottom.

Double Bottom

Let's focus on the underlying process that led to the formation of a double bottom. Initially, the markets were in a corrective or downtrending mode, characterized by the creation of lower highs and lower lows. Each rally in prices was met with selling pressure, pushing prices below the previous swing lows.

However, at a certain point, the formation of lower lows ceased, and instead, equal lows began to emerge. This shift indicates that the sellers might have weakened, or some level of demand emerged, preventing the creation of new swing lows. Finally, the prices break out from the last swing high (resistance) level, completing the double bottom pattern.

Now, let's connect this with Dow Theory. Does the markdown phase also conclude in a similar manner? Ah, you've got it now!

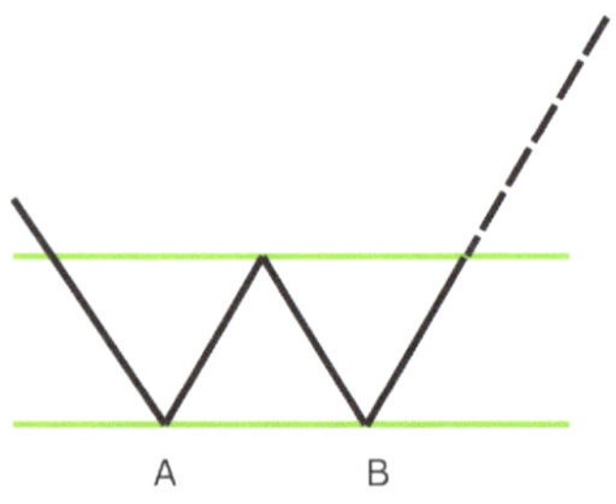

The double bottom pattern is a bullish reversal chart pattern that typically emerges at the conclusion of a downtrend, indicating a potential trend reversal. Alternatively, it may manifest as a continuation pattern following a secondary correction.

The double bottom pattern can be categorized as either a trend reversal pattern or a continuation pattern. In this pattern, two nearly identical bottom levels form near the same **support line** before the price rebounds, signaling the beginning of a new bullish uptrend. The highest point between these two bottom levels is referred to as the neckline. This bullish reversal pattern is often observed at the conclusion of a downtrend or a secondary correction and is confirmed by the occurrence of two final attempts to break the support level.

In essence, recognizing a double bottom pattern on a trading chart is quite straightforward. This pattern becomes evident when the price revisits the support line and subsequently rises above the neckline. As a helpful tip, you can often identify this pattern by its resemblance to the letter "W."

Below, we've outlined the steps to help you identify and trade the double bottom chart pattern effectively in the market:

1. Look for a retest of the first bottom and draw a support line connecting the price levels of both the first and second bottoms.
2. Identify the first and second tops and draw the neckline, connecting these levels.
3. Exercise patience and wait for the completion of the first candle after the price breaks above the neckline.
4. Initiate a long buying position while setting a tight stop-loss order either at or just below the neckline.

In the chart above, I've identified a double bottom reversal pattern as it marks a reversal from a preceding downtrend. Points A and B represent the two bottoms, with the highest point between them forming the neckline. After the breakout above the neckline, you can observe prices starting to advance.

You might be noticing that the pattern doesn't precisely resemble a letter "W." Indeed, this deliberate choice was made because I could have handpicked a flawless double bottom chart and presented it here. However, it's essential to acknowledge that real market scenarios often deviate from textbook-perfect patterns.

The chart above illustrates a continuation double bottom pattern. The trend was already established, and after an initial upward move, it experienced a temporary pause or secondary correction. During this phase, a double bottom pattern formed, and ultimately, the price broke out in the same direction as the existing trend.

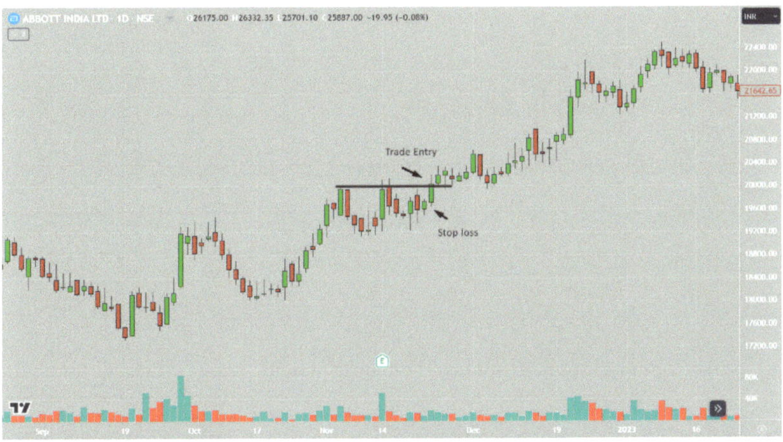

In the chart above, I've indicated both the entry point and the stop-loss level. The stop-loss level represents the point where we need to exit the trade if it moves against us.

Now, do you recall that we mentioned classical chart patterns can be either a reversal, continuation, or both? This principle applies to all chart patterns. Take a look at the chart below: initially, it appeared that a reversal double bottom pattern was forming, and upon completion, prices were expected to rise. However, it failed to do so, with the failure point being a close below point "B." As a result, what was initially perceived as a Bullish Reversal pattern has now transformed into a Bearish Continuation pattern!

The optimal approach to trade the double bottom pattern is to exercise patience and wait for the price to break above the neckline. At that point, consider placing a stop-loss order and determining an appropriate risk-reward ratio, which we will delve into in our upcoming discussion.

Double Top

Just as the name suggests, the double top chart pattern involves the presence of two distinct tops. In essence, it signifies a retest and subsequent failure to surpass the previous highest price point.

This pattern typically emerges following a bullish trend, wherein a stock reaches two consecutive peaks, essentially forming the shape of the letter "M." Its formation serves as an indicator of a potential trend reversal, which is confirmed once the asset's price breaks below the support neckline.

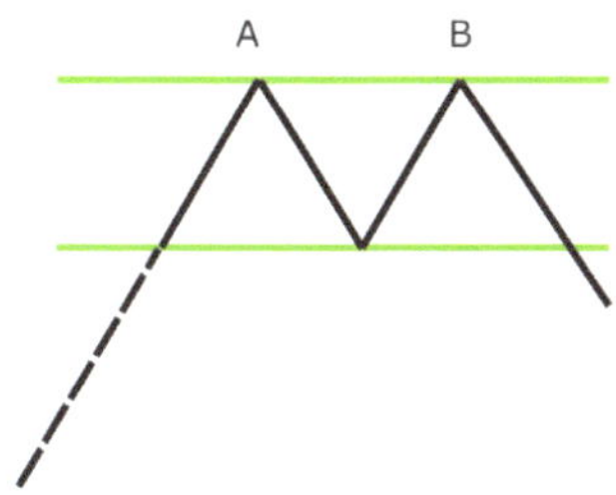

Given that we've thoroughly examined the factors influencing the pattern's formation and its connection with Dow Theory when we discussed the Double Bottom formation, let's shift our focus in this section. I am looking forward to you to construct a thought process to understand the driving forces behind the formation of the double top pattern and explore its correlation with Dow Theory.

Spotting a Double Top Pattern on the Charts:

With the above considerations, here's a step-by-step guide to assist you in recognizing and utilizing the double top pattern in your trading strategy:

1. Identify the first (A) This swing high "may " now act as a resistance line if a new higher top is not formed. Soon we get equal tops (A&B) now we can draw the neckline, aligning it with the bottoms of A & B
2. Exercise patience, waiting for the completion of the first candle following the price's breach below the neckline.
3. Initiate a short-selling position while implementing a close stop-loss order, either at or just above the neckline.

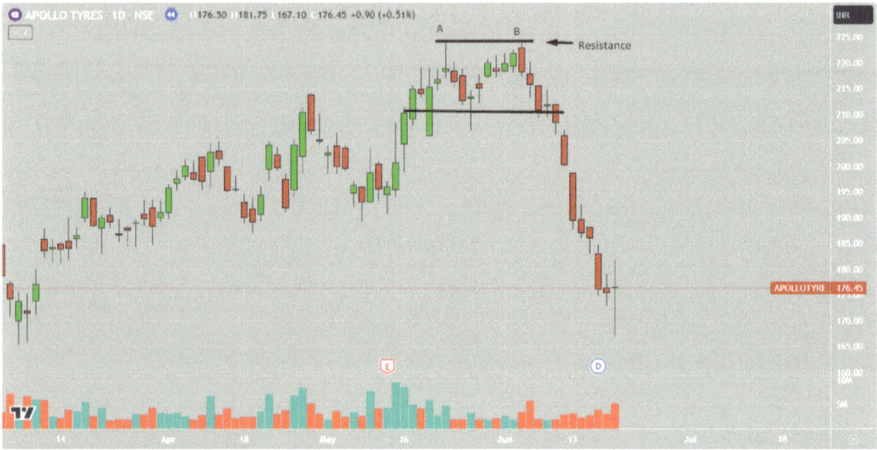

Examining the chart above, can you discern any early signals indicating a potential weakening of momentum?

Observe the candle formed at peak A – it's characterized by a long upper wick and a small body, resembling a shooting star pattern. What does this pattern typically signify?

Now, shift your attention to peak B. As prices approach B, notice how the candle bodies gradually shrink, culminating in a substantial red candle that engulfs the preceding small candles – a bearish engulfing pattern. What does this sequence of candlestick patterns suggest?

It appears that the prices are struggling to maintain upward momentum, resulting in the failure to establish a higher high formation (resistance). These candle signals serve as accompanying indicators of this price action.

Now, we can observe candles, Dow Theory, and the patterns all harmoniously aligning! Isn't it a fascinating synergy?

Now, let's introduce another layer of elegance: the trendlines.

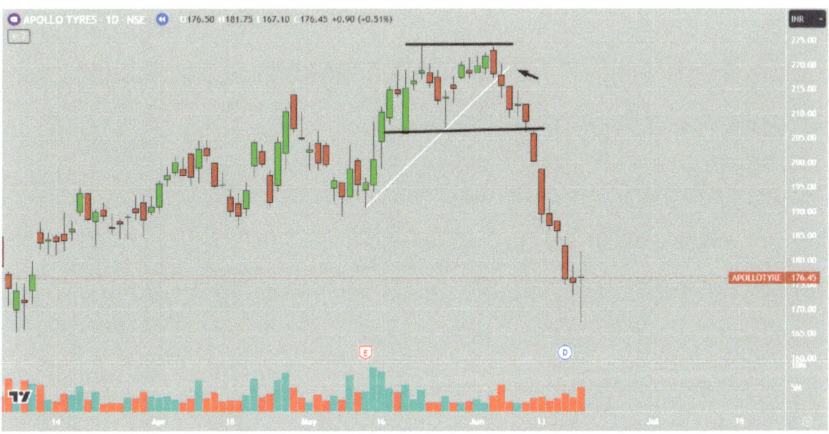

Do you see how all the dots are coming together to create a beautiful picture?

Head & Shoulder

The head and shoulders pattern is a bearish formation that emerges at the end of an uptrend, signifying a potential trend reversal. It serves as an indicator that the preceding upward trend could be reaching its conclusion. Traders often employ this pattern as a signal to consider initiating a short-selling position or exiting a long-position trade.

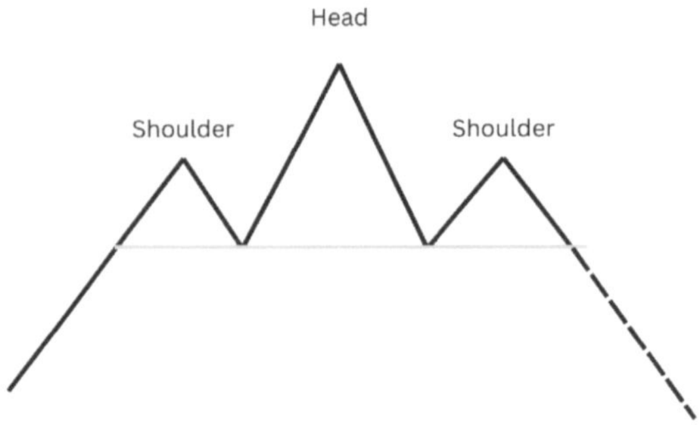

In the above illustration you can see the head and shoulders pattern features three distinct peaks, forming the shape of the head in the center, along with two shoulders – one on the left and one on the right. Additionally, it exhibits a neckline, which functions as a critical support level.

When identifying a head and shoulders pattern on trading charts, it's essential to pay attention to specific characteristics. Initially, this pattern typically occurs following a bullish uptrend when the buying pressure is waning.

Next, you'll notice the formation of a left shoulder, succeeded by a central peak that rises higher than the initial top. Subsequently, another right shoulder takes shape, typically aligning with the level of the first left shoulder (or close to it). Lastly, a well-defined neckline should be present, serving as a crucial support level within the pattern.

Before delving into how to trade it, it's important to grasp the dynamics at play when a head and shoulders pattern is in the process of formation.

In the chart below, you can observe that the stock experienced a strong uptrend starting from February 2016, characterized by the formation of higher highs and higher lows, in line with Dow's definition of a perfect uptrend. However, pay close attention to what transpired when the trend established a higher low in March 2019 and moved upward. It failed in creating a higher high and, instead, formed a lower high in May 2018.

This marked a critical transition within the trend, shifting from a pattern of higher highs and higher lows to one of lower highs. This transition served as an early warning that the trend might be undergoing a change, as buyers were unable to generate enough momentum to sustain the previous trajectory. Finally, in July 2018, a lower low was established, completing the shift from a pattern of higher highs and higher lows (bullish) to one characterized by lower highs and lower lows (bearish).

This transition in the trend, which we have thoroughly explored in our study of Dow Theory, was later identified as the Head and Shoulders pattern.

Even without prior knowledge of pattern recognition, a solid understanding of market structure through Dow Theory would have allowed us to readily identify the transition in the trend.

In the chart below, I've intentionally removed the context of the Head and Shoulders pattern, focusing solely on marking the transition in the trend using Dow Theory. Take a moment to examine it and consider how this context might be constructed.

Entry into the pattern occurs when the neckline is breached. To manage risk, a stop-loss is placed either just above the trendline or above the right shoulder, provided it doesn't significantly distort the risk-reward ratio.

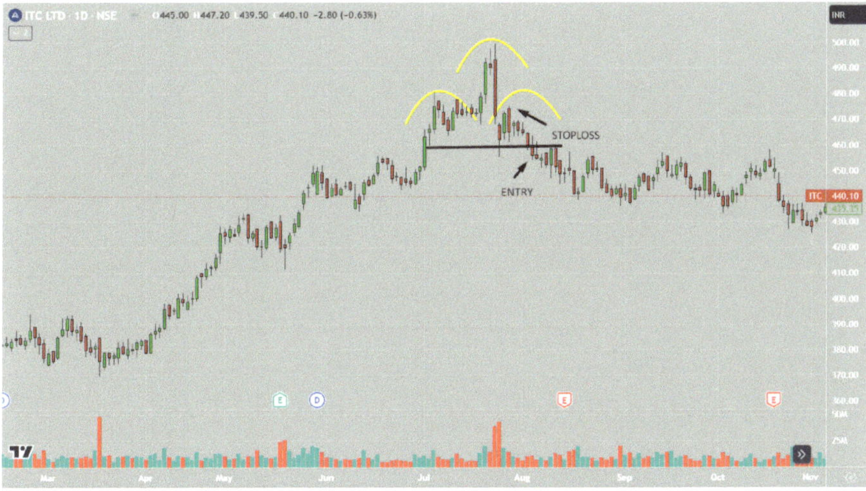

Now, let's conduct a critical assessment of the chart below, by employing candlestick analysis and trendlines. What becomes apparent is that there was a break in the trendline on July 25, 2023, preceding the breach of the neckline on August 3, 2023. Additionally, if you observe closely, there were early signs of exhaustion signaled by the candlesticks within the head of the pattern.

The head is composed of three candles: first, a wide green candle, typically appearing after a significant upward move, indicating late buying. Next is a small-bodied candle, suggesting waning momentum and a lack of follow-through after the wide green candle. Finally, there is a wide red candle that engulfs both the small candle and the preceding wide green candle.

Upon analyzing the pattern alongside price action, it becomes evident that there is strong confirmation in the formation of the head and shoulders pattern.

At times, the head and shoulders pattern can also manifest as a continuation pattern. Refer to the chart below.

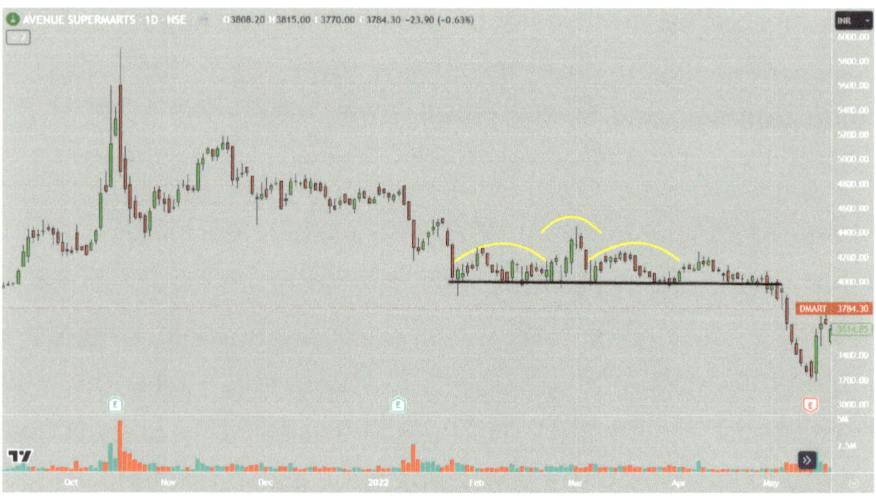

Inverse Head & Shoulder

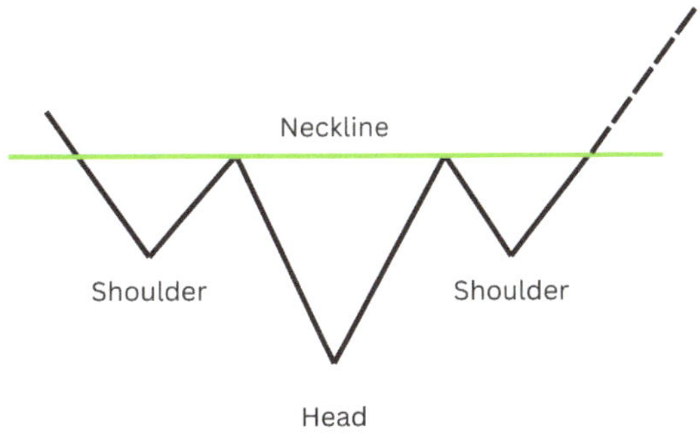

The inverse head and shoulders is a classical chart pattern that typically emerges at the conclusion of a downtrend, signaling an impending reversal of the prior trend. This pattern is frequently linked with bullish price reversals, indicating the potential for an upward trend reversal.

The inverse head and shoulders pattern is a bullish candlestick formation that materializes at the conclusion of a downward trend, suggesting the possible termination of the prevailing trend and the initiation of a new upward trend. This pattern serves as the reverse counterpart of the standard head and shoulders pattern.

In its structure, the inverse head and shoulders pattern consists of three troughs, with the central trough situated lower than the first and third troughs (which represent the two shoulders). Consequently, it forms the distinctive shape of an inverse head and shoulders.

In the chart provided below, you can observe the formation of the inverse head and shoulders pattern following a bearish trend. This pattern encompasses both the left and right shoulders, as well as the bottom level representing the head. Once the price surpasses the neckline level, it triggers the onset of a fresh bullish trend.

Now, let's delve into the dynamics that were unfolding within the price action as this pattern was developing. We'll combine insights from candlestick analysis, Dow Theory, and our trendline concepts to gain a comprehensive understanding.

Refer to the chart below. The prevailing trend was characterized by a series of lower highs and lower lows, aligning with Dow's definition of a downtrend. However, an interesting development occurred on June 15, 2022, when a conspicuous wide red candle materialized, despite the ongoing downtrend. This can be seen as a form of exhaustion in the selling pressure. Following this, there was a notable absence of further downside momentum, and smaller red candles began to appear, suggesting that sellers were losing their grip.

Subsequently, a sequence of green candles emerged, marking a shift as the stock commenced forming higher highs and higher lows, which, according to Dow Theory, signaled a change in trend. Additionally, a downtrending trendline was breached during this transition. The culmination of these factors collectively resulted in the formation of an inverse head and shoulders pattern.

We've examined the favorable outcomes of both patterns, but it's essential to acknowledge that these patterns are not infallible. There are instances where they falter, and when they do, many traders find themselves on the wrong side of the trade. Interestingly, the market's response to failed patterns tends to be more pronounced and intense compared to the reactions to successful ones. Let's take a closer look.

The failure point for a Head and Shoulders pattern occurs when prices move above the right shoulder and close above it. Conversely, for an Inverse Head and Shoulders pattern, the failure point is when the price closes below the low of the right shoulder.

Cup & Handles

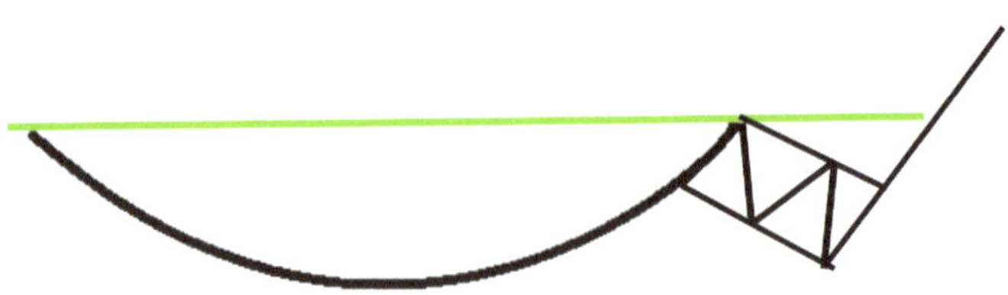

Rounding Bottom

A cup and handle pattern is a chart formation that resembles a U-shape with a flat, often slightly descending, horizontal line, resembling the shape of a teacup. This pattern is typically bullish, suggesting a potential price increase upon its completion. To execute successful trades utilizing the cup and handle chart pattern, it's essential to accurately identify the pattern, enter at a logical entry point, establish a stop-loss to manage risk, and determine a price target for exiting a profitable trade.

Similar to the rounding bottom, the reversal formation of a cup and handle pattern may take several months to develop and reverse the price trend. However, the continuation pattern of a cup and handle tends to be more efficient, effective, and faster in generating trading opportunities.

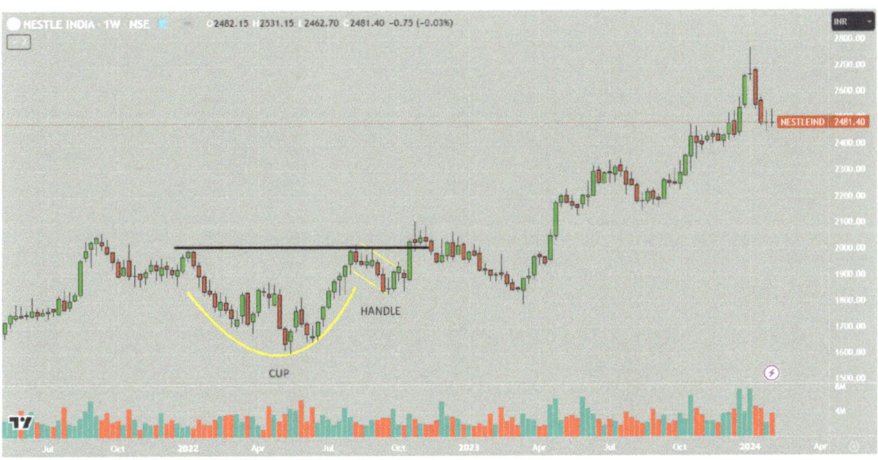

In the chart above, you'll observe the formation of the cup and handle pattern, which took a span of 6 months to fully develop. Subsequently, a handle formation ensued, requiring an additional 6 weeks before a breakout occurred. As previously discussed, these patterns often hold more analytical value than immediate trading potential, given their tendency to take a considerable amount of time to complete.

An important aspect to note about the handle is its size relative to the cup. The handle should be smaller in scale compared to the cup. This implies that while the stock's price forms the handle, it should not descend to the level of the lower half of the cup. Ideally, the price should remain within the upper one-third of the cup's height.

The chart above serves as a solid and exemplary illustration of the cup and handle relationship, with the handle occupying less than one-third of the cup's depth. In contrast, the chart below does not exhibit a cup and handle pattern, as the handle has retraced the entire body of the cup.

Let's examine smaller continuation cup and handle formations.

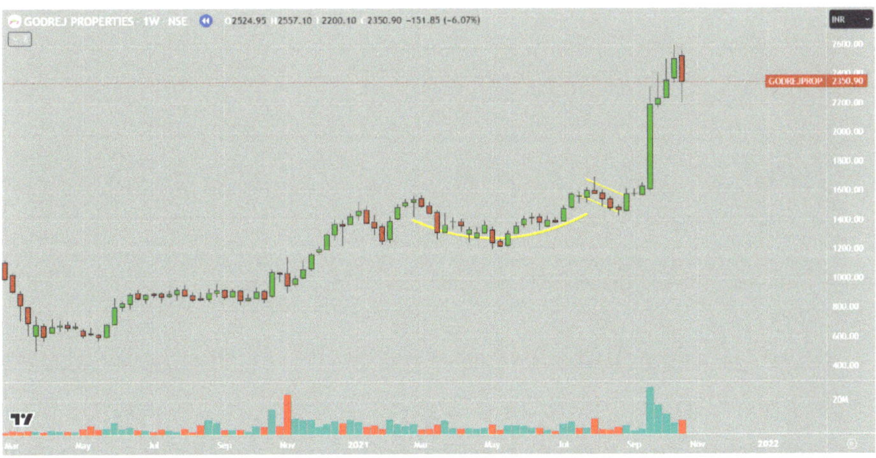

Analyze the chart presented below, where the cup and handle pattern emerged amidst an ongoing trend. Take note of the pace of the price movement following the breakout. The cup took shape over the course of 25 trading sessions.

Never underestimate the possibility of pattern failures. Although a cup and handle pattern typically anticipates a price rise, there are no certainties in the market. The price might experience a modest increase and then decline, remain in a sideways movement, or even drop immediately after entry. To mitigate risk, it's imperative to implement a stop-loss strategy. Refer to the chart above.

Have you noticed a particularly noteworthy observation among the patterns we've just discussed? It's quite striking. These more extended patterns, which require time to develop, tend to represent Dow's Accumulation Zone when they form following a bear market and Dow's Distribution Zone when they form after a bull market! Now, let's revisit all the above charts from the perspective of accumulation and distribution.

Furthermore, it's important to note that not all of these patterns assist in determining price targets once they break out in the anticipated direction. In technical analysis terminology, this concept is referred to as the "measured move."

The depth of the pattern is added into the breakout point to provide a rough estimate of the potential move. However, it's crucial to remember that these are not definitive targets; they represent the anticipated pattern targets. The actual move can reach, exceed, or fall short of these levels. Because these targets are not particularly definitive, I did not place a strong emphasis on discussing them individually when going over the patterns. Refer some charts below to get clarity.

Triangle Patterns

A triangle chart pattern occurs when the price gradually narrows within a tighter range over time, visually representing a struggle between bullish and bearish forces.

This pattern is typically classified as a “continuation pattern,” implying that once the pattern concludes, it is expected that the price will resume its previous trend direction.

Three primary types of triangle chart formations include the symmetrical triangle, ascending triangle, and descending triangle.

Symmetrical Triangle

The symmetrical triangle is a chart pattern characterized by the convergence of the price's high and low slopes, forming a triangle-like shape.

During this formation, the market is creating lower highs and higher lows, indicating a lack of decisive action from both buyers and sellers. In essence, it resembles a draw in a battle between these two forces. This pattern is also a form of consolidation.

The breakout direction remains uncertain, but it is highly probable that the market will experience a breakout. Eventually, either the buyers or sellers will win.

How can we capitalize on this situation?

It's straightforward.

We can set entry orders above the declining highs' slope and below the ascending lows' slope of the symmetrical triangle. Given our anticipation of an imminent breakout, we can position ourselves to follow the market in the direction it decides to move.

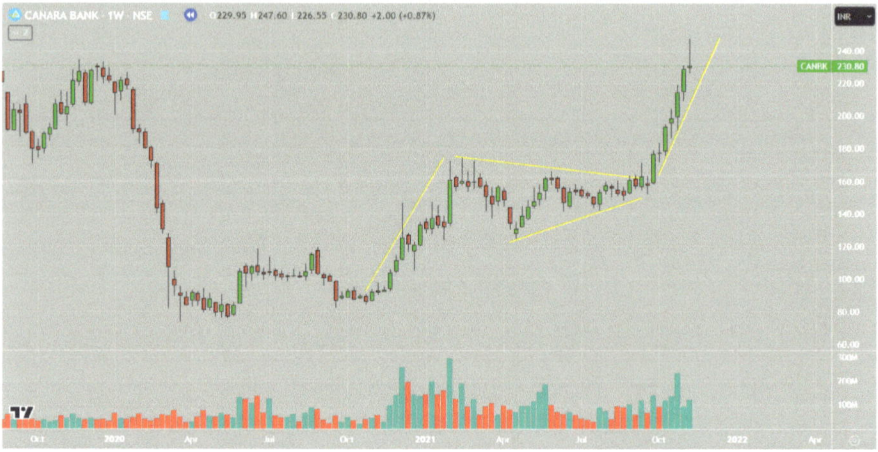

In this instance, had we positioned an entry order above the descending highs' slope, we would have enjoyed a profitable upward journey.

Ascending Triangle

An ascending triangle is a specific type of triangle chart pattern formed when there's an identifiable resistance level alongside a sequence of ascending lows.

In this scenario, buyers encounter a particular price level they struggle to surpass. Nevertheless, they progressively raise the price, demonstrated by the series of higher lows. When analyzing an ascending triangle, we infer that buyers are gaining strength since they consistently establish higher lows.

Their continued pressure on the resistance level eventually leads to an anticipated breakout.

Many books on chart analysis often say that when prices are stuck between two lines (like a ceiling and a rising floor), they expect prices to break through the ceiling. But, from our experience, it's not always that simple. Sometimes, the ceiling is too strong, and there aren't enough buyers to push prices through it.

While most of the time, prices do go up, the important thing to remember is that you should be ready for prices to go in either direction. Triangles on charts can be quite tricky!

Now, take a look at the chart below. In this situation, the buyers didn't win the fight, and as a result, the price dropped significantly!

Descending Triangle

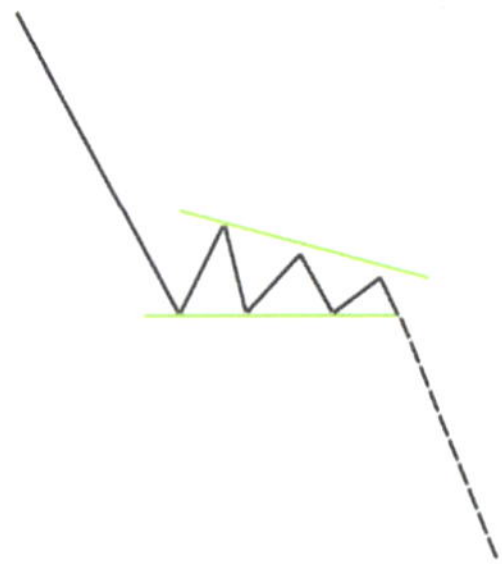

Descending triangles are like the opposite of ascending triangles (we thought you might have guessed that, you're smart!).

In descending triangle patterns on charts, you'll see a series of peaks getting lower and forming the top line. The bottom line is like a support level where the price just can't seem to go below.

In the chart above, you can see that the price is gradually forming lower peaks, which indicates that the sellers are starting to gain an advantage over the buyers.

Now, most of the time (and we really mean MOST), the price will eventually break through the support line and keep falling. But sometimes, that support line can be quite sturdy, causing the price to bounce off it and make a strong move upwards.

The good news is we're not fixated on where the price ends up. We just know it's about to make a move. In this case, we'd place orders to enter trades above the upper line (the lower peaks) and below the support line, so we're ready for whichever way the price decides to go. No need to concern yourself with the entry and exit aspects at this moment; we'll delve into those details as we progress.

Triangles can help predict where prices might go after they break out. To figure out a potential target, you measure how tall the triangle is and then add that distance to the breakout point. But remember, this is just a minimum target, and prices could go even further.

Wedges

In a Wedge chart pattern, you'll see two trend lines coming together, like two lines meeting at a point. This means that the size of the price changes is getting smaller inside the Wedge.

Wedges basically tell us that the current trend is taking a break. When you spot this pattern, it means that traders are uncertain about which way the price will go next.

Now, there are two types of Wedges:

1. A Falling Wedge is a positive sign when you're in an upward trend. The lines inside it slant downward, suggesting that prices might rise soon.

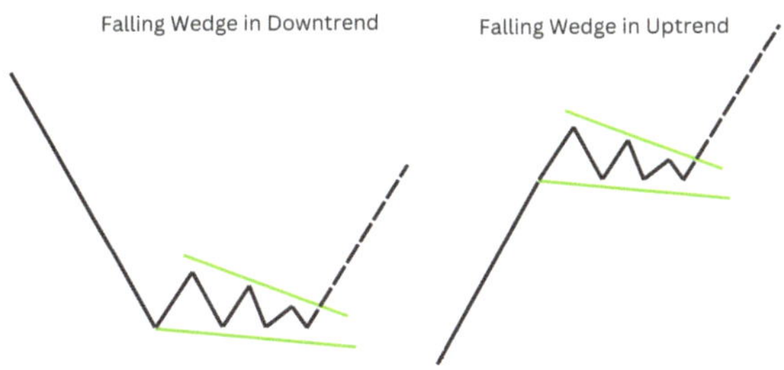

Falling wedges are usually seen as good signs for traders. They happen when a trading range gets narrower, but this time it's sloping downward. Imagine a triangle with the top side slanting down.

Here's the important part: in a falling wedge, the prices move down creating lower tops & lower bottoms & the price action in the pattern gets narrower as the trend progresses down.

Usually, when you spot a falling wedge, it's a hint that a strong downtrend might be coming to an end, and the price could start going up. It's like a green light for a potential trend reversal.

But, there's a twist sometimes: falling wedges can also show up in the middle of a strong uptrend. In that case, they're basically going along with the flow. So, if you see a falling wedge during an uptrend, it's likely that the price will keep going up even after the wedge forms.

Think about how confusing it can be for someone who doesn't understand how technical analysis works. When the prices suddenly break out of the wedge in a way that's the opposite of what they expected, it can really catch them off guard!

2. On the flip side, a Rising Wedge is a bit of a downer in a downward trend. The lines in this one slant upward, hinting that prices could drop further.

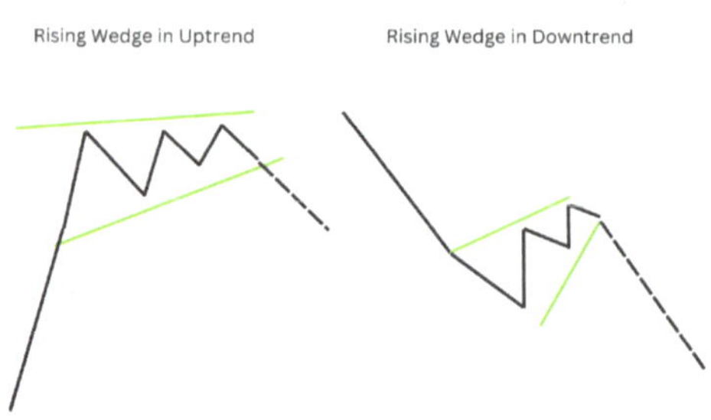

Rising wedges are like warning signs in trading. They happen when a trading range starts to get narrower, but the important thing is that it's sloping upwards.

Now, what's key here is that both the lowest points and the highest points in this pattern are going up as it gets narrower.

This is different from some other patterns where they might be going in different directions.

When you see a rising wedge, it's often a sign that a strong uptrend might be running out of steam and could be about to change direction, going down instead. It's like a caution light telling you to be prepared for a potential reversal.

But here's the twist: sometimes rising wedges can show up in the middle of a strong downtrend. In that case, they're kind of going against the flow. So, if you see a rising wedge during a downtrend, it's likely that the price will keep going down even after the wedge forms.

Think about someone who doesn't know much about technical analysis. They might look at this pattern and think it means the price will keep going up. What makes it tricky is that even in this rising wedge, you'll see higher highs and higher lows. It looks like a recipe to trap traders.

The only way to tell the difference between a rising wedge and an uptrend is that as the wedge goes on, the price action gets squeezed between the converging trend lines. That's the telltale sign that things might turn around and head down.

The way wedges can trick traders actually makes them one of the best patterns to trade in the stock markets. These patterns have incredibly high success rates. In bull markets, the falling wedge pattern succeeds about 74% of the time, while in bear markets, the rising wedge pattern has a strong success rate of 81%.

In the previous example, you might have observed that the prices were consistently rising, forming higher peaks and higher troughs. There weren't any clear indications of a trend reversal, but starting from early December 2020, the prices began to form a rising wedge pattern. This wedge pattern eventually broke in January 2021, leading to a correction in the trend.

Likewise, in the chart below, you'll observe that the downturn (covid crack) came to an end when a falling wedge began to take shape in the final phase of the trend. This falling wedge pattern emerged, and prices eventually broke out of it in late May 2020, thereby reversing the trend.

Simply try to grasp what's happening behind the charts. A trap is slowly being set where traders are caught off guard. Notice the rapid price reaction after the breakout; it's swift and decisive in both cases! This characteristic makes this pattern a high-probability one with minimal risk.

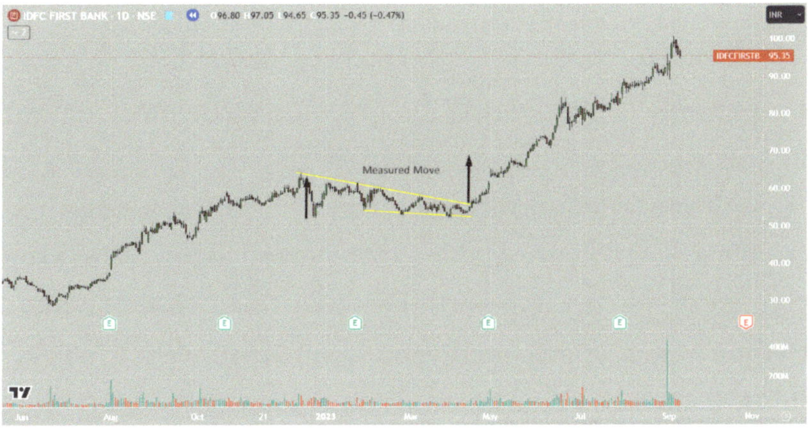

In the chart above, we observe a continuation falling wedge, or a falling wedge within an uptrend. I've also highlighted how we can determine targets from the pattern; we add the widest part of the pattern to the breakout levels to get the minimum target. But, do you truly believe this measured move is beneficial in your trading? It often creates an anchor bias, where we fixate on the targets and prematurely book profits before the trend fully develops.

In the chart above, you can observe a rising wedge within a downtrend.

I was really intrigued and caught off guard when I stumbled upon this pattern. I started wondering why technicians make things seem so fancy and complicated. This simple wedge pattern is actually called "diagonals" in Elliot Wave Theory. When there's a rising wedge in an uptrend, they call it an "ending diagonal," and when it's a falling wedge in a downtrend, it's called the "leading diagonal." The continuous wedges are referred to as "complex" corrections.

I've always believed that unless you simplify your process, you won't succeed in this profession. Wave theory often involves looking at past price movements and trying to predict what might happen in the future. But let me tell you something, everyone seems smart when looking back in hindsight, and no matter how hard you try, you can't predict the future!

Flags & Pennants

These patterns are known as short-term continuation patterns and are commonly observed. They often take the form of wedges, rectangles, or triangles, but they are much smaller in size and their shapes may not be perfectly defined. Despite this, both formations indicate a period of consolidation in the market, suggesting that the previous trend is still strong. During this time, most market participants maintain their positions, and there are very few exits from the market, which encourages more traders to join in the direction of the prevailing trend.

Once a breakout occurs in either direction, the price action typically moves swiftly, with minimal pullbacks or throwbacks. Many traders favor flags and pennants because of this characteristic, as it allows for quick and decisive trading opportunities.

This pattern stands out as one of the most successful and offers a remarkably high reward-to-risk ratio. Its beauty lies in its ability to allow traders to enter positions in line with the prevailing trend. Based on our understanding of Dow Theory, trading in the direction of the trend consistently carries a high probability of success.

Bullish & Bearish Flags

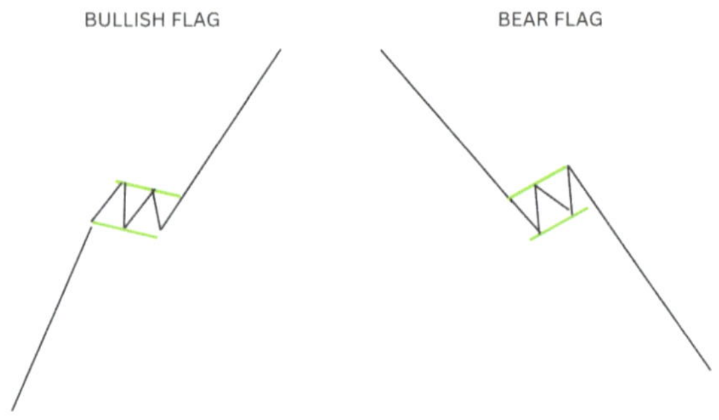

Flags are indicative of short channels, characterized by their slope in the opposite direction of the prior trend. Occasionally, their slope aligns with the trend direction, indicating potentially stronger momentum in that trend.

During the formation of flags, volume typically declines. These patterns emerge over relatively brief periods, spanning from several days to a few weeks. Flags commonly follow steep price movements.

In the chart below, you'll notice a significant upward momentum that began in late October 2023, resulting in a 20% rally in the stock. Following this surge, the stock paused for four days, forming a pattern resembling a flag. During this pause, volumes dwindled, indicating that the major players driving the trend were taking a breather, deliberating their next move for the stock.

This pattern suggests a temporary halt in the trend, with market participants assessing whether to continue pushing the stock higher or to exit their positions. Eventually, a breakout from the pattern occurs, propelling the stock even higher.

Although flags are relatively small patterns, they hold significant power. They signify strong buying pressure, with stockholders showing reluctance to sell, leading to minimal corrections during the pause. In essence, they are eager to accumulate more shares within a short timeframe.

The same holds true for downtrends. Following a significant selloff, there's often a pause lasting from three to seven sessions before the selling resumes. A flag formation in a downtrend suggests a significant change in the company's circumstances, such as poor earnings or regulatory bans. Regardless of the reason, it's crucial to pay attention to the price action. A bearish flag indicates that the stock is continuing its downward trajectory and may only be halfway through its downtrend journey.

Pennants

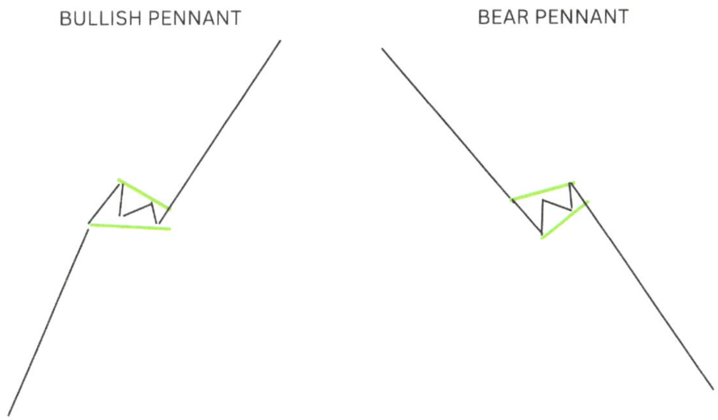

Pennants share many similarities with flags. The primary distinction lies in how their trend lines behave. Pennants feature trend lines that ultimately converge, forming a miniature triangle, while flags typically have parallel trend lines. Additionally, the slope of pennants often runs counter to the prior trend, although it may occasionally be horizontal or align with the major trend direction.

Unlike wedges, which develop over longer periods and are preceded by significant price trends, pennants form relatively quickly. During the formation of a pennant, volume tends to decrease. However, when the breakout occurs, volume typically surges.

In the chart below, you'll observe a significant upward movement in the stock during late March 2023. Following this sharp rise, the stock paused in May 2023, forming a pennant pattern. Subsequently, it broke out of the pennant pattern and continued its upward trajectory. It's worth noting that the volumes decreased during the formation of the pennant.

Unlike other patterns where measuring moves are determined by adding the height of the pattern to the breakout levels, flags and pennants present a unique challenge. Due to their small size, the width of these patterns cannot be used for target measurement. Instead, the preceding move or advance, also known as the pole of the flag/pennant, is utilized for target determination. This move is added to the breakout zone to ascertain the target. Have a look at the chart below.

A key insight from the above paragraph is that a smaller depth of the pattern is preferred. Typically, the most effective flag and pennant patterns fall within the 8% range.

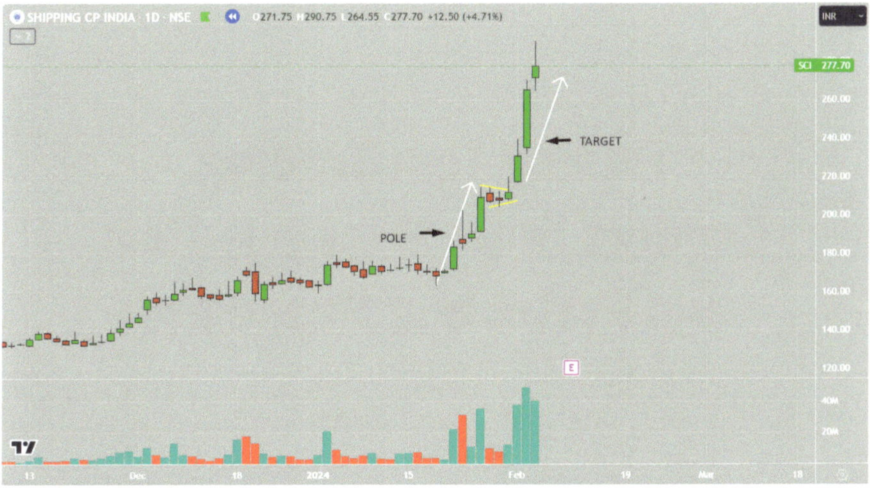

Wrapping Up:

Classical chart patterns are widely recognized in technical analysis. However, like any market analysis approach, they should not be relied upon in isolation. It's advisable to seek confirmation before making any trading decisions. As demonstrated, we've incorporated everything we've learned about these patterns thus far. Moving forward, we'll continue to refine our understanding of these patterns and strive to produce actionable outcomes.

Drop IX

Finding Your Trading Comfort Zone: Managing Pain and Protecting Happiness

Successful trading isn't just about market knowledge; it's also handling the psychological and financial ups and downs. Knowing your limits—financially and emotionally—helps tailor a strategy that minimizes stress. The right approach fits your risk tolerance and lifestyle, ensuring trading enhances rather than depletes your life. A well-crafted trading plan considers worst-case scenarios, empowering you to trade with confidence. Success comes from aligning strategy with personal well-being, making trading a rewarding part of your life.

Chapter 9

Indicators

Technical indicators are tools that translate past price, volume, and open interest data into patterns. Traders who specialize in technical analysis use these patterns to anticipate potential price movements and make informed trading decisions.

Technical analysis is the study of past **price** movement and **volume** to identify trading opportunities and predict future market trends.

While indicators can be useful tools, it's crucial to remember that they are ultimately derived from price and volume data. True market insights come from developing a deep understanding of how price and volume interact. Indicators should be used to support your analysis, not replace your ability to read the core market data directly.

Absolutely! Here's a rephrased version that improves clarity and presents the information in a more visually appealing way:

Types of Indicators

Technical indicators fall into two main categories:

- **Overlays:** These indicators are plotted directly on top of the price chart, using the same scale as the price data. Examples include:
    - Moving Averages
    - Bollinger Bands
- **Oscillators:** These indicators move within a set range (oscillate) and are plotted separately from the price chart, often below it. Examples include:
    - Stochastic Oscillator
    - MACD
    - RSI

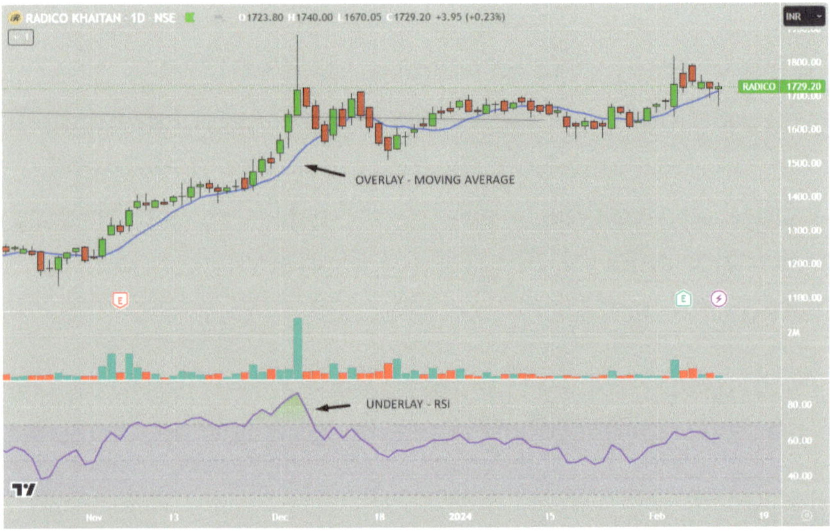

Before we proceed, let me caution you about the abundance of indicators available. As a novice trader, it's easy to see them as pathways to wealth in the stock market. However, they can actually hinder your decision-making process. It's crucial to understand three things:

1. Traders should select indicators that suit them and understand their functionality.
2. Indicators should be used alongside price studies, not in isolation.
3. Remember, price action holds the utmost importance, and indicators are merely signals, not final confirmations!

For the sake of simplicity and to maintain focus on delivering effective strategies, we'll concentrate on two widely used indicators: one overlay and one underlay. These are Moving Averages and RSI (Relative Strength Index). Let's begin with moving averages, which are often the first indicators every aspiring technical analyst encounters.

Moving Averages

A moving average calculates the average price of a trading instrument over a specified time frame. It helps to smooth out price fluctuations and highlights the trend direction in relation to an average price over the trader's chosen time period. Moving averages are valuable technical tools utilized on charts to identify trends effectively.

There are numerous types of moving averages, such as Simple Moving Averages (SMA), Exponential Moving Averages (EMA), Weighted Moving Averages (WMA), and the list fancy continues. However, to maintain simplicity, I'll solely focus on

Simple Moving Averages (SMA) & Exponential Moving Averages (EMA).

So, what sets EMA apart from SMA? I could delve into the intricacies of their calculations and the mathematical functions behind them to showcase my intellect. However, that's not our focus here. Many resources provide detailed calculations. Our emphasis lies solely on practical application.

We need to know only this - A simple moving average treats all prices in the price data equally. On the other hand, an exponential moving average (EMA) assigns more weight to recent prices. This makes EMA more responsive and quicker to adapt to price changes. It adjusts faster to recent price movements, providing traders with quicker entry and exit signals compared to a simple moving average.

When analyzing shorter-term trends, it's crucial to prioritize recent data, whereas for longer-term trends, a broader set of data is essential. Hence, we opt for EMA for shorter lookback periods (10, 20) and SMA for larger lookback periods (50, 200).

Uses of Moving Averages

Moving averages assist traders in:

1. Identifying market trends.
2. Offering support and resistance levels in a trending market.
3. Determining whether the market is overextended in a particular direction or not.

Many traders utilize moving averages for trading signals, often relying on crossover signals. However, it's essential to note that crossover signals are generally ineffective for trading. In fact, moving averages are not primarily intended to provide trading signals at all.

Many traders utilize moving averages for trading signals, often relying on crossover signals. However, it's essential to note that crossover signals are generally ineffective for trading. In fact, moving averages are not primarily intended to provide trading signals at all.

Take a glance at the chart below. I've highlighted the 50-200 SMA crossover. This "BUY" signal emerges after the stock has surged over 28.5% following a bottom formation. Additionally, observe that after the buy signal, the stock only experienced a modest 4.5% increase before correcting by over 17.2%.

Likewise, in the chart below, you'll observe that the sell signal occurred after the stock had already corrected by 32%. Subsequently, it reversed, offering minimal gains to short sellers.

Therefore, it should be abundantly clear by now that moving averages are not suitable for generating Buy and Sell signals.

Let's explore the application of moving averages step by step, as we've discussed earlier. First, we'll delve into how moving averages can help identify market trends.

Two features of moving averages determine the price trend: 1) The sequence of the moving averages, and 2) The slope of the moving averages.

The sequence implies that the moving averages must be arranged correctly for trend analysis. For example, in an uptrend, the price should be above the shorter moving averages, and the shortest moving average should be above the larger moving averages. Using 10, 20, 50, and 200-day moving averages, for an uptrend, prices should be above the 10-day moving average, the 10-day moving average above the 20-day, the 20-day above the 50-day, and the 50-day above the 200-day for a valid uptrend. Conversely, for a downtrend, the opposite sequence applies.

In the chart below, observe how the prices align with the moving averages. The prices remain above the 10 EMA (orange line), the 10 EMA is above the 20 EMA (green line), and both are above the 50 SMA (blue line). Furthermore, the 10, 20, and 50 moving averages are all above the 200 SMA (red line). This alignment indicates a phased uptrend, highlighting the importance of the correct sequence of moving averages.

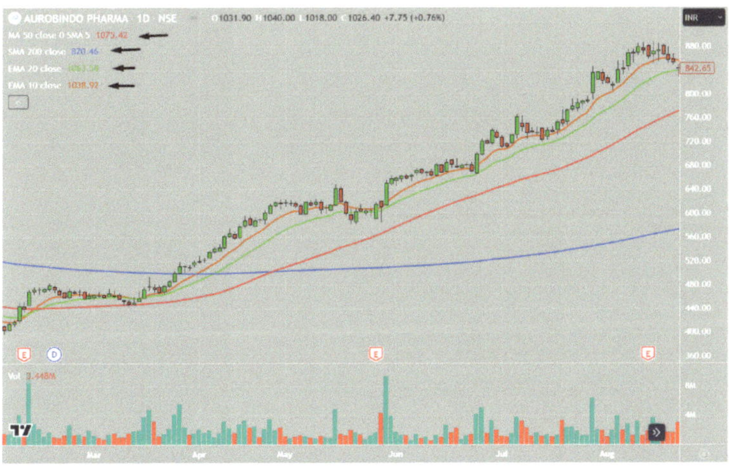

Let's connect this observation with Dow Theory. In an uptrend, prices typically form higher highs and higher lows. This aligns with the concept of an uptrend in Dow Theory, where each upward movement is followed by a higher pullback, signifying strength and continuation of the trend. So, when we see higher tops and higher bottoms in price action, it reflects the underlying bullish sentiment and supports the idea of an ongoing uptrend.

Now, let's shift our focus to the chart below. Here, we can observe a distinct downtrend characterized by prices trading below the shorter moving averages, with the shorter moving averages positioned beneath the larger ones. Applying Dow Theory principles, downtrends are often marked by the formation of lower highs and lower lows. This reinforces the notion that the market is in a downward trajectory, as indicated by the price action.

Now think of a scenario where all the moving averages are converging without following a proper sequence. What does that market resemble? A trendless and sideways market. Take a glance at the chart provided below.

Take a look at the chart below. You'll notice that the moving averages are all mixed up, and it's hard to figure out their order. This means the trend is choppy, which isn't ideal for traders.

When trends aren't clear, trading can be risky. Successful trading strategies rely on clear trends. Moving averages are great for spotting trends, but when they're all tangled up, it's tough to make informed decisions.

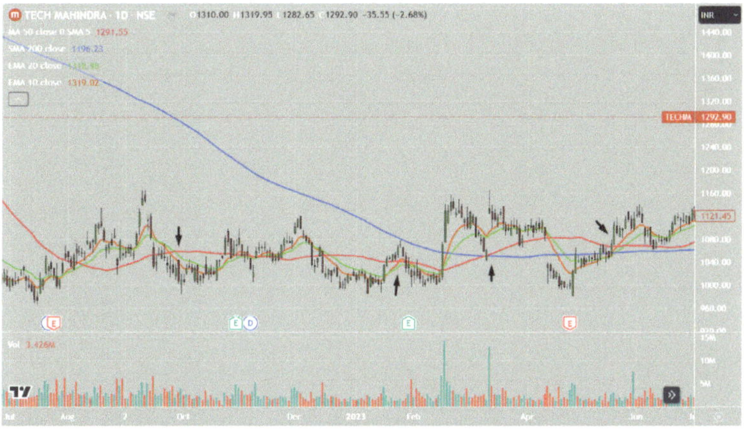

Another significant insight to consider when analyzing trends with moving averages is the slope of the moving average. Maintaining a consistent upward sequence is crucial, and the slope of the moving averages serves as an indicator of the momentum within the trend. A proper sequence should correspond with an appropriate slope. In bullish markets, the slope of the moving averages should be upward, and conversely, in bearish markets, it should be downward.

In the example below, you can observe that the stock is experiencing a strong uptrend. Pay attention to the upward slope of the moving average; it signifies strong momentum within the trend. Additionally, any bending or deviation in the slope could serve as an early indication of a potential shift in momentum for the trend.

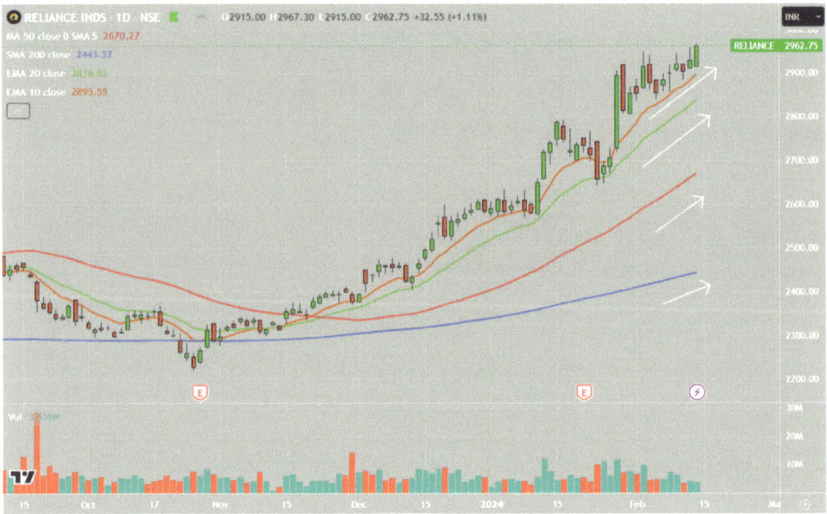

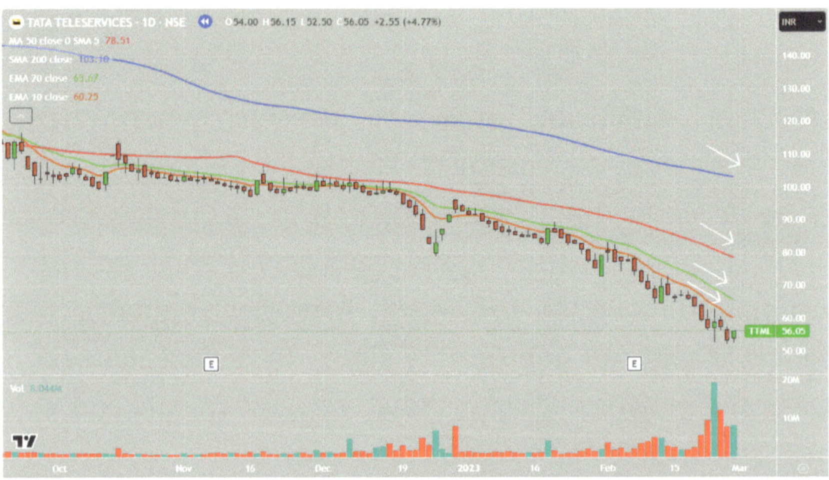

Now, observe the chart above; the trend is downward. This downtrend can be confirmed by the sequence: the price is below the 10 DMA, the 10 DMA is below the 20 DMA, the 20 DMA is below the 50 DMA, and the 50 DMA is below the 200 DMA. The momentum can be assessed by examining the slope of the averages. Take note of the downward slope of all the averages, indicating that the downtrend possesses both momentum and strength.

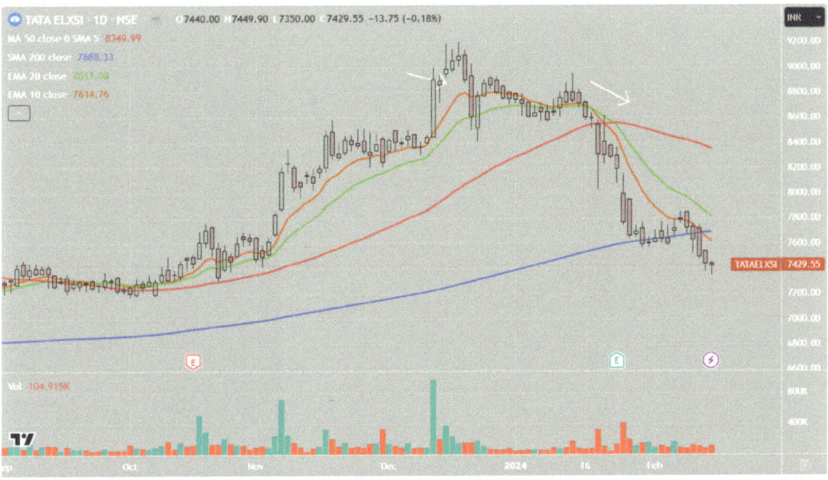

Take a look at the chart above. Up until mid-December 2023, the trend was upwards, and the sequence of moving averages was consistent. However, after mid-December, you might notice that the slope of the moving averages started to flatten out a bit. Even though the sequence remained unchanged, the falling slope suggested a potential loss of momentum in the upward trend. This eventually disrupted the sequence, and the trend corrected itself. The slope provided an early warning sign of a possible upcoming trend change!

In the chart below, you might see that in late October 2023 (highlighted with a yellow semi circle), the slope of the moving averages (10, 20, and 50) started to turn upwards, even though the sequence still suggested a downward trend. This rising slope of the moving averages hinted at a potential loss of momentum in the downtrend. It suggested that the sellers might be losing strength. This was confirmed when the sequence of the price and moving average changed, followed by a change in slope.

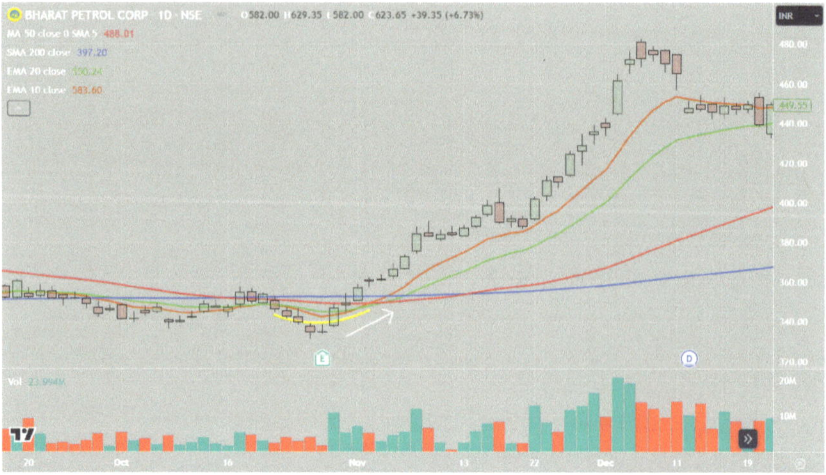

The slope gives us a heads-up about a possible shift in the trend or a likely correction in the current trend. When the slope changes and is backed up by a sequence switch, it means the trend change is confirmed.

Now that we grasp how to analyze trends using moving averages, let's explore how moving averages provide **support and resistance** levels in a trending market.

Just like we've learned before, previous swings and trendlines can act as support and resistance for the price. Moving averages work similarly as support and resistance, but with a dynamic twist. As the trend continues, the moving averages move along with it. This dynamic nature allows moving averages to be used as dynamic levels of support and resistance.

We've been employing various sets of moving averages such as 10, 20, 50, and 200. Each of these serves different purposes and is used to determine support and resistance levels and assess market activity. Let's take a closer look at each one individually.

The 10 Day Moving Average

The 10-day EMA (Exponential Moving Average) tells you the short-term trend on a chart. It can help you stay on the right side of a market trend for days, weeks, or even months.

Keeping your position long when the price is above the 10-day EMA, and short when it's below, can help avoid a lot of trading difficulties. However, the 10-day EMA doesn't work well in volatile or range-bound markets. It's also ineffective if the price stays within its range for several days in a row. You're looking for momentum in the price movement that consistently closes on one side or the other of the 10-day EMA for multiple days.

Starting a position when there's a momentum breakout over key long-term moving averages can be a good strategy, with the 10-day EMA serving as a filter for the trend.

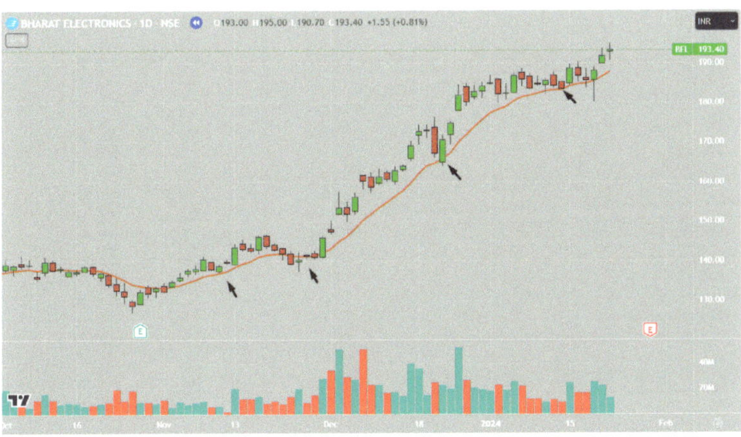

Take a glance at the chart above. The red line represents the 10 EMA (Exponential Moving Average). Notice how the stock is experiencing a strong uptrend. Every time there's a pullback, it tends to pause or bounce off the 10 EMA. Therefore, it's a strategic point to plan entry positions to align with the trend. As long as the prices remain above the 10 EMA, it suggests that the price has the strength to continue moving upwards with strong momentum. Whenever the price has touched the 10 EMA line, it has bounced back, forming a strong bullish candle pattern (as indicated by the arrows for reference).

Likewise, in a downtrend, the 10 EMA serves as a resistance, with strong downward swings less frequently breaking above the 10 EMA line. For swing traders, the 10 EMA can function as a trailing stop-loss, while for intraday traders, it serves as a decision line for entering long or short trades. For instance, an intraday trader would typically opt to go long when daily prices are above the 10 EMA, and vice versa.

The chart below illustrates how the 10 EMA acts as resistance during a strong downward move. Pay attention to the candlestick patterns when the price touches the 10 EMA and then moves downward again.

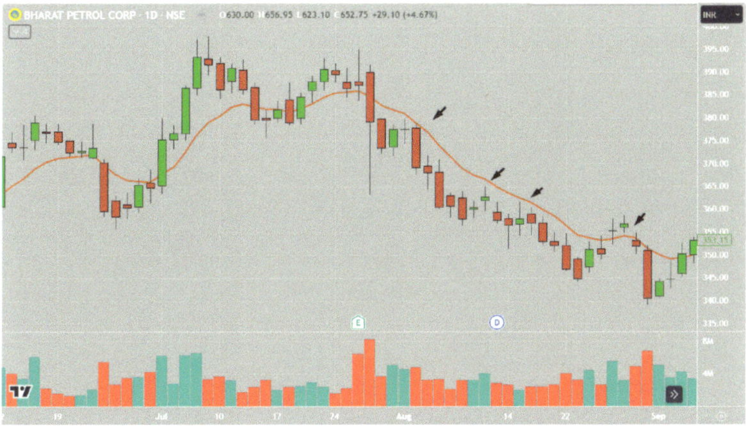

The 20 Day Moving Average

The 20-day EMA (Exponential Moving Average) is a responsive technical tool used to identify the intermediate trend. It captures trends by trading based on whether the price is trending above or below the moving average.

Traders can utilize the 20-day EMA as an entry signal for trades and combine it with oscillators to signal exits, maximizing potential gains. When prices consistently close below the 20-day EMA, it indicates an intermediate downtrend. Conversely, prices consistently closing above the 20-day EMA define an intermediate uptrend.The 20 EMA is really important because traders all over the world use it a lot - probably the most used average!

Check out the chart below. Prices respond really well to the 20 EMA. Every time prices drop back to the 20 EMA, it reacts and moves up again, forming a bullish candle pattern. Sometimes, the 10 EMA might not work well for certain stocks, causing lots of whipsaws. In that case, the 20 EMA comes in handy, and it's the most trusted average. So, for any swing trader, the 20 EMA is definitely seen as a very important average.

As mentioned earlier, there are times when a 10 EMA might be too narrow for a trend to develop fully. That's when a 20 EMA becomes useful. It's important to remember that one size doesn't fit all. Just like clothes, different stocks might need different EMAs to work effectively.

Take a look at the chart above. The stock has broken through the 10 EMA several times, but it has consistently held onto the 20 EMA (marked by arrows for reference).

The best approach is to use both the 10 EMA and 20 EMA together. The space between these two averages is where we find high value. As long as prices test this area and bounce back, the trend looks promising. However, if we start seeing breaks below this area, we need to be cautious because corrections might become more significant.

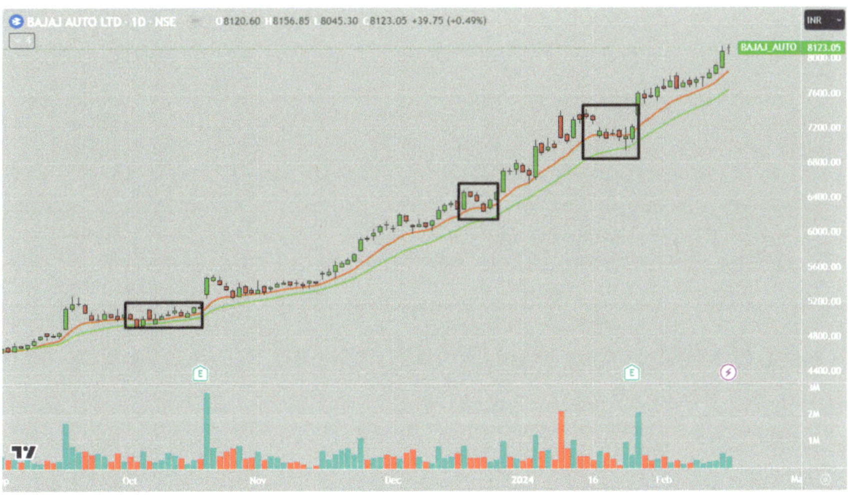

Take a look at the chart above. There were times when the stock dipped below the 10 EMA (marked in the boxes), but the combination of the 10 EMA and 20 EMA helped prevent sudden changes or shakeouts. The space between the 10 EMA and 20 EMA acts as crucial support, pushing the price back in line with the main trend.

Similarly, observe the chart below to see how the area between the 10 EMA and 20 EMA acted as resistance during a downtrend.

Another important takeaway is that all the smaller classical chart patterns we discussed earlier, such as flags and pennants, are best traded when they form in the 10-20 EMA zone. You'll find the best ones in this zone.

Check out the chart below, where a triangle forms as prices find support at the 10-20 EMA levels. Afterward, there's a strong move following the breakout.

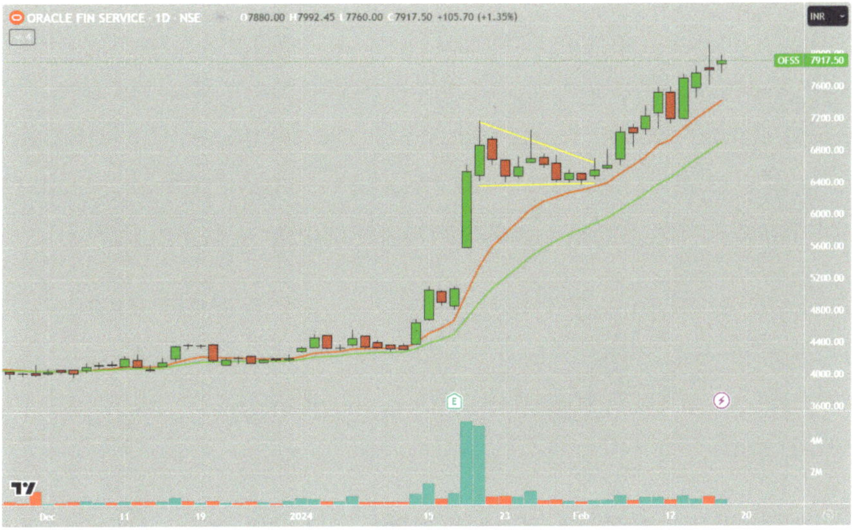

The 50 Day Moving Average

The 50-day Moving Average is like the final defense for the trend. If the price breaks below the 50-day moving average, it's a big deal. It means there's a serious shift in the existing trend and a change in how the market feels about things.

In the strongest of stocks, the 50-day moving average can be a powerful indicator on its own. Staying in a long position as long as the price remains above the 50-day line and exiting if it drops below can help capture longer-term trends.

During a strong bull market trend, the 50-day Simple Moving Average (SMA) often acts as reliable support, holding up the price multiple times before potentially failing.

The 50-day SMA is crucial during a strong market as it often serves as a key support/resistance level.

As long as markets are trading above the 50-day SMA, traders should consider "buying the dip" because selling a strong market trading above this line isn't where the easy money lies. The easiest profits come from following the trend on the long side. Many of the classic chart patterns we've discussed earlier in the book tend to form near the 50-day Moving Average (DMA).

At the start of a downtrend, prices often break through the 50-day SMA and then become resistance. Attempts to rally back to the 50-day SMA may fall short, signaling the beginning of a downtrend.

In a stock or market undergoing distribution, the 50-day SMA can act as resistance for an extended period, even signaling a short trade until the line is broken and the price can sustainably stay above it.

For a market trending lower and lower below the 50-day SMA, selling short may become the direction of least resistance.

In the chart above, you can see how significant corrections find support at the 50-day Moving Average (DMA) and bounce back. It's like the last line of defense for traders! Also, pay attention to how when prices stay close to the 50 DMA, they tend to respect the support of the 10-20 EMA. But when prices move away from the 50 DMA, they often break through the 10-20 DMA and head towards the 50 DMA for support. Pretty interesting, right?

Likewise, during a downtrend, traders aiming for larger short swings find that prices resisting at the 50 DMA become an ideal place to initiate short trades!

Check out the chart. The bold red line represents the 50 DMA. When prices approach the 50 DMA and then drop back down, we often see significant price reactions on the downside. Also, pay attention to the bearish candle patterns that form at the 50 DMA when prices touch it.

As mentioned before, the 50 DMA is where you should focus on larger chart patterns forming. Take a look at the chart above, where a very nice cup and handle formation is observed at the 50 DMA level!

The 200 Day Moving Average

It's often seen as the last line of defense between bulls and bears.

In simple terms, when the price breaks and stays above the 200-day Simple Moving Average (SMA), it often marks the beginning of uptrends and bull markets. On the flip side, the first sign of a downtrend or bear market is when the price breaks and stays below the 200-day SMA.

The 200-day SMA is a common setting in charting software and is used by many traders. Some traders buy when the price breaks above this line and sell short when it breaks below. Others may wait for confirmation the next day.

Since the 200-day SMA signals whether the market is in a long-term uptrend or downtrend, buying weakness on pullbacks above it and selling short on strength below it helps swing traders stay on the right side of the market's movement.

Being under the 200-day SMA can spell trouble for long positions.

In the chart above, you can see that on January 1st, 2024, the prices closed above the 200-day DMA. Following this, there was a strong rally, and the stock shifted its trend from downward to upward.

Likewise, in the chart below, you can observe what occurred in March 2020. The prices broke below the 200 DMA, leading to a strong downward move. The 200 DMA acts as an important decision line. It's crucial to ensure that prices are above the 200 DMA when entering a bullish setup and vice versa.

Typically, larger basing patterns like accumulation and distribution patterns tend to form near the 200 DMA lines. Take a look at the chart below for reference.

Determining whether the market is overextended in a particular direction or not

Apart from determining trends and acting as support and resistance levels, another crucial function of moving averages is indicating whether current prices are excessively distant from the mean. If prices are too far above the moving averages, they're considered overbought, while if they're too far below, they're deemed oversold. This suggests that if prices are significantly away from the averages, there's a strong likelihood of an impending correction, with prices retracing back to their mean position.

If you remember, I briefly mentioned this concept when we were discussing the 50 DMA.

If prices stray too far from the 50 DMA, there's likelihood that they'll find support at the 10-20 DMA. there are chances they may retrace back to the 50 DMA again.

Take a look at the chart below. The stock was in a downtrend, forming lower highs and lower lows, and it was trading below the moving averages. Notice that whenever the stock stayed within a range of 5 - 7% of the 50 DMA, the retracement tended to move towards the 10-20 DMA. This indicated that the trend was in a normal mode, as it found support at the 10-20 DMA.

However, when the trend accelerated and moved beyond the normal 5-7% correction, correcting more than 14% in March 2023, this was not normal. The stock almost doubled its previous correction, making it unlikely for the stock to hold at the 10-20

DMA when retracing back. As a result, we saw the stock pull back deeply towards the 50 DMA.

Likewise, in the chart above, you'll notice that whenever the stock moved 14 - 15% away from the 50 DMA, it corrected back to the 10-20 DMA levels. As the trend continued, this gap widened, and the stock started moving 25% away from the 50 DMA, resulting in a correction towards the averages.

Now, two questions should arise in your mind:

1. How can we determine whether the stock will correct to the 10-20 DMA or the 50 DMA?
2. How can we know at what percentage beyond the 50 DMA there will be a pullback?

The answer to the first question is that we need to use other technical trend measuring tools like trendlines along with the moving averages to determine the same. Additionally, it's often observed that young trends, which have started recently, tend to correct to the 10-20 DMA, while mature trends may sometimes correct to the 50 DMA. The best alternative is to use additional technical analysis tools on the charts.

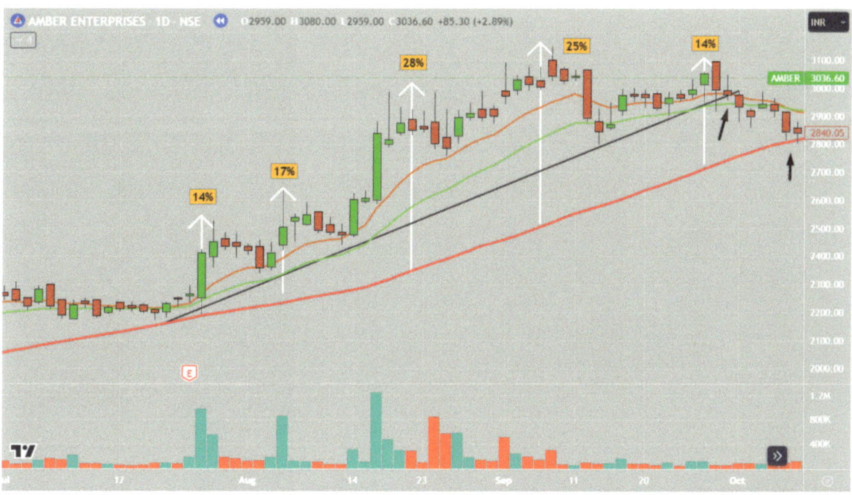

Take a look at the chart above, where I've included a trendline to track the movement. You'll notice that when prices correct to the 10-20 DMA, it coincides with the trendline as well. Once the prices breach the trendline, they correct a bit deeper to the 50 DMA, indicating that the trend has matured a bit.

Additionally, if you observe closely, you'll see correlations with Dow Theory and moving average slope analysis.

The answer to the second question is a bit tricky, as this number varies for each stock. You need to backtest to determine the mean percentage that may lead to a reversal far from the 50 DMA. In general, it's around 10% for large caps and around 15-25% for small and midcaps. The best approach is to correlate this overbought and oversold signal with other technical studies.

Wrapping Up

In general, technical analysis and specifically moving averages are valuable tools for investors, but they alone **may not provide a complete picture of a stock's overall performance.** Moving averages help smooth out price data and identify points of support or resistance in a security's price, offering valuable insights to traders.

Drop X

Mastering the Art of Staying Calm: How to Navigate Losing Trades in Trading

In trading, resilience in handling losses distinguishes the successful. To manage losses effectively:

1. 1. **Balance Time and Money**: Quickly cut losses to safeguard capital, learning from each setback to refine strategies.
2. 2. **Respect Market Trends**: Align strategies with market conditions to avoid repeated losses.
3. 3. **Harmonize with Market Movements**: Adapt to ensure timely entries and avoid premature exits.
4. **4.Cultivate Emotional Resilience**: Embrace a "lose fast, win slow" mindset, focusing on disciplined progress.

Trading is a long-term journey. Embracing these principles fosters stability and improves prospects for enduring success. Stay disciplined, emotionally balanced, and aligned with market dynamics to navigate trading challenges.

Chapter 10

RSI (Relative Strength Index)

Trading the financial markets can seem daunting for beginners. Making sense of RSI charts and indicators is key to finding profitable opportunities. One of the most useful yet confusing tools for new stock traders is the Relative Strength Index RSI. This momentum indicator tracks recent price action to spot overbought and oversold conditions. Understanding RSI signals can help new traders better time entries and exits.

This chapter will explain RSI in simple terms. We'll go over how RSI works, the best RSI settings, and tips for integrating RSI analysis into a trading plan. With the right guidance, even stock beginners can leverage RSI to boost their chances of success. By understanding the context around RSI signals, novice traders can make more informed decisions around position sizing, risk management, and developing a strong trading strategy.

The Relative Strength Index RSI is a popular momentum indicator used by many stock traders. It was created in 1978 by an American technical analyst named J. Welles Wilder.

While J. Welles Wilder initially created this tool, Andrew Cardwell further developed many unconventional uses of RSI. He presented a different perspective on RSI altogether. I had been associated with Andrew since 2011 until 2023 (when he passed away). Today, many RSI learners know me because of my skills in RSI, which I honed through my collaboration with Andrew.

If I were to cover RSI in detail, it would require a completely different edition. So for now, let's keep things light. However, I promise that if this current book attracts learners, I will definitely release a book on RSI later on.

The main goal of RSI is to help traders identify market conditions where a stock has become overbought or oversold. An overbought stock may be ready for a downward correction, while an oversold one could see a bounce upwards.

In simple terms, RSI looks at recent price movements to see if gains or losses happened too quickly. It measures momentum by comparing the size and speed of recent gains versus recent losses in a stock price.

This comparison results in a number between 0 to 100. Traders mainly watch for high and low RSI readings to predict potential trend reversals. Values above 70 suggest overbought conditions, while values below 30 indicate oversold conditions.

By recognizing these extreme momentum situations, RSI strategies have become a helpful tool for stock traders looking to enter or exit positions. When combined with other analysis methods, it can offer additional insights for trading decisions.

RSI is an underlay indicator, which means it is plotted below the price, unlike the moving average, which was plotted on the price.

All indicators serve two fundamental purposes: 1) to help us determine if the trend is stretched in a particular direction (overbought or oversold) and 2) to detect any loss of momentum in the existing trend, which could disrupt the ongoing trend (divergence). Traders primarily use RSI for these two purposes!

In this book, we won't delve into the calculations of the RSI. As a beginner trader, simply understand that higher RSI readings indicate faster uptrends, while lower RSI suggests faster downtrends.

Most trading platforms display RSI as a separate line chart below the main price chart.

The RSI line shows momentum on a scale from 0 to 100. Readings above 70 mean the asset is overbought, while readings below 30 mean it's oversold.

Trading platforms also have horizontal lines at the 70 and 30 levels. These lines indicate overbought and oversold conditions, which can help traders anticipate potential reversals.

By paying attention to these signals, traders can identify when price movements may be reaching their limits. Combining this analysis with your overall strategy can improve decision-making.

In the chart below, you'll notice that the RSI is displayed in a separate window below the price chart. It appears as a line that fluctuates between 100 and 0. Many platforms also automatically mark the levels of 70 and 30.

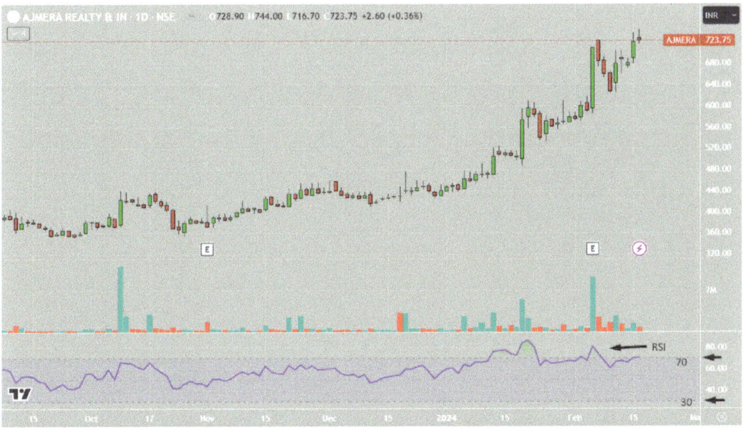

Before we dive into the concepts, let me offer a word of caution. Remember that indicators are derived from the price, so they can't replace price action. Also, have you ever wondered why they're called indicators? It's because they only signal something impending; they don't confirm it. Whenever we use an indicator, we need the price to confirm the signal it's showing. This fact is crucial to understand.

Let's begin by understanding the functions of RSI one by one. We'll start with the **overbought and oversold** functions of RSI.

An overbought reading above 70 tells traders that recent gains happened too quickly. It means the upward momentum probably reached its peak, increasing the chance of a price pullback or consolidation. On the other hand, an oversold reading below 30 indicates that recent losses happened too fast. This extreme negativity suggests panic selling rather than thoughtful decision-making. As a result, an oversold bounce becomes more likely as buyers look for bargains.

Take a look at the chart below. There was a rapid and powerful move, causing RSI to climb above 70. It remained there for a few days, indicating that the trend had become extended. Soon after, the price reversed and corrected. When RSI is above 70, it suggests the market is in an extended condition.

Similarly, observe the chart below. The stock corrected rapidly, causing the RSI to drop below 30. Afterward, the stock rebounded, indicating that the correction had been excessively prolonged and the trend required a breather.

Now it might seem like controlling the markets and making money is simple—just follow the 70-30 levels and start printing cash! But it's much easier said than done.

However, new traders shouldn't rush to sell when conditions are overbought. Strong uptrends can keep overbought readings high for a long time before reversing. Similarly, traders shouldn't immediately buy when RSI values are oversold. In strong downtrends, RSI may stay below 30 for a while before momentum shifts.

Take a glance at the chart above. There was a rapid price move that pushed RSI above 70 on August 5, 2022, marked with a green vertical line. Afterward, RSI remained above 70 until September 16, 2022. During this period, the price surged by more than 30%. Now, just imagine exiting the trend when it's at its peak—it's painful, right? Or consider the worst-case scenario: someone shorting the stock at this point!

Now, take a glance at the chart below. The RSI was pushed below 30 after a strong downward move. From April 18, 2022, to

May 16, 2022, the RSI remained below 30, and the prices further corrected by more than 15%. Just imagine if you had followed the textbook and bought at the oversold levels—your account would have been down by 15% straight in just one month.

So, how should we utilize these overbought and oversold levels? The answer lies in combining the 70-30 levels with other technical tools such as moving averages and trendlines to confirm reversals from the overbought and oversold levels.

Take a glance at the chart above. On November 29th, 2023, the RSI climbed above 70 and remained there until December 20th, 2023. Throughout this period, the price surged by over 20%, and there were no indications of a trend reversal. Prices consistently found support at the 10/20 EMA, and the trendline remained unbroken. Therefore, there was no reason to consider booking profits or selling.

Now, consider something unconventional! When the RSI moves above 70 and the price is in a strong uptrend, could it be advantageous to consider buying on dips at every support level?

Likewise, examine the chart below: on December 22nd, 2022, the RSI dipped below 30. Following this, all the rallies were merely weak pullbacks that encountered resistance at the 10/20 EMA. Therefore, rather than going long below 30, it would be prudent to wait for the price to pull back to resistance and consider taking a short trade if the price action and risk allow for it.

Therefore, we've observed an unconventional application of RSI.

To summarize, when RSI surpasses 70, it's not a signal to sell; instead, it's an opportunity to seek support levels to initiate new positions or add to existing ones (Buy on Dips). Similarly, when RSI drops below 30, one should be prepared to take short positions at resistance levels (Sell on Rise).

These overbought and oversold levels also assist in identifying trend transition points, indicating when there's a likelihood of a trend change. This aspect is referred to as Rejection Swings of RSI.

We've observed that during a strong uptrend, RSI tends to remain overbought, consistently above 70, while in a strong downtrend, it tends to stay oversold, consistently below 30. But what happens when this pattern shifts? Let's explore!

Imagine a scenario where RSI was consistently in overbought territory during a strong bull market. However, a significant correction caused RSI to drop deep below 70 levels (towards 30). Now, as RSI attempts to rebound, it fails to surpass the 70 mark, stopping somewhere between 60-65. This suggests a significant loss of momentum in the trend, signaling a potential change from bullish to sideways or even bearish. However, it's crucial to note that these observations must be cross-referenced with price action tools. Relying solely on RSI without considering other factors may not provide a complete picture.

We've observed that in trending markets, the Relative Strength Index (RSI) can linger above or below the typical overbought and oversold levels for quite some time. In strong bull markets, it may persist above 70, while in strong bear phases, it may linger below 30 for extended periods. However, there's another intriguing aspect of RSI behavior during these phases: it often exhibits a "shift" in the overbought and oversold levels. Instead of adhering strictly to the conventional 70-30 levels, RSI tends to deviate from these norms during strong trends. In an exceptionally strong trending market, the fixed levels of 70-30 often yield unsatisfactory outcomes.

Andrew Cardwell discovered this aspect of RSI, which he termed as "Range Shifts." In strong uptrends, the overbought and oversold levels shift to 75-80 and 40-45 respectively, while in downtrends, they shift to 60-65 and 20-25 respectively.

Simply put, during uptrends, when prices retrace to support levels, the RSI is expected to settle in the 40-45 zone. Similarly, during downtrends, when there is a pullback towards resistance, the RSI is expected to reach the 60-65 zones.

In the chart below, I've marked the upper extreme with a dotted line at 75 and the lower extreme with two dotted lines at 40 and 45. We can observe a strong momentum initiating, with the RSI surpassing 70 and remaining there. As we aim to seize opportunities to buy on dips at support levels in an ongoing uptrend, I've employed trendlines and the 10-20 EMA to identify potential entry points. Additionally, as discussed earlier, during uptrends, the RSI range shifts upward and doesn't typically reach oversold territory at 30. Notice how whenever prices retraced to the EMA or trendline, the RSI settled in the 40-45 range. Thus, we utilize the RSI for confirmation that the trend, which was overextended in one direction, has cooled off as the RSI found support in the 40-45 range. Importantly, this indicates that bullish momentum remains strong as the RSI doesn't dip below these levels!

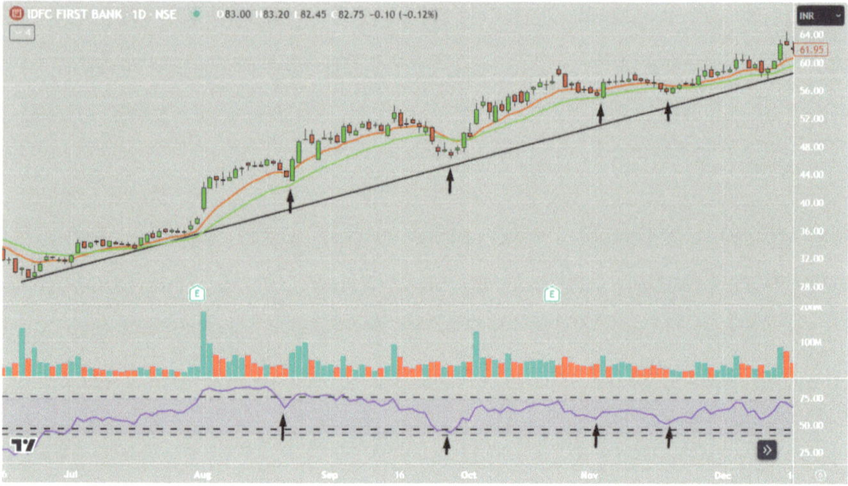

Now, examine the chart above. It's the same chart where the trend shifted from forming higher highs and higher lows to lower highs and lower lows. The RSI also shifted its zone; previously, it followed the 70-75 zone, but now it's hitting overbought levels in the 60-65 zone. Additionally, observe that each pullback towards the 60-65 zone coincided with the price hitting the descending trendline. You can see how beautifully they complement each other.

Now, for the million-dollar question: where did the transition from a bull to a bear trend occur?

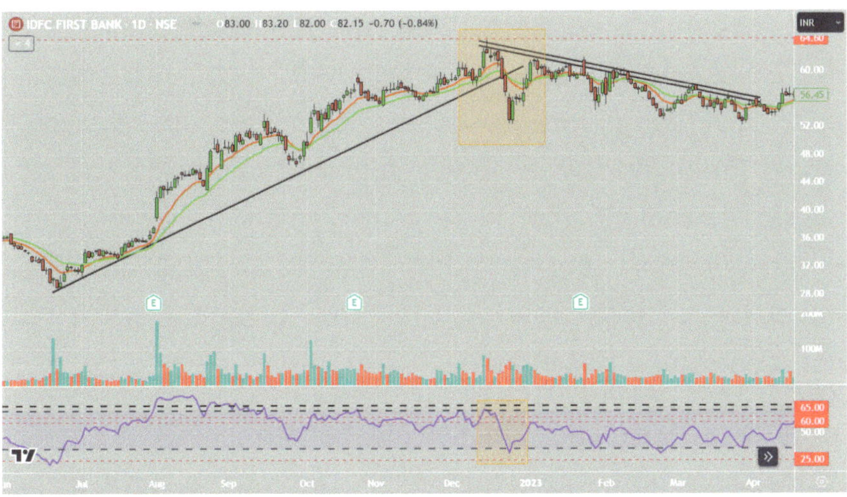

Take a look at the price action around December 20th, 2022. There was a rapid decline where prices dropped over 16% in just four trading sessions. If you observe the RSI during this period (both price and RSI highlighted), you'll notice that the RSI dropped below the 30 level for the first time. However, it failed to reach the 70-75 zone afterward. Instead, it began hitting the ceiling around the 60-65 levels, departing from the bullish overbought levels and starting to follow the bearish overbought levels. The uptrending trendline was last breached on the price. This zone, where the RSI transitioned from the bullish to the bearish zone, marked the trend transition zone!

Traders can utilize RSI to time retracement entries, continuation entries, or reversals. By focusing on momentum, trading actions are aligned with the directional edge.

Now, let's shift our focus to another crucial use of RSI, which involves understanding **divergences**.

RSI Divergence happens when the Relative Strength Index indicator begins changing direction before the price does. A bearish divergence occurs when RSI shows an **overbought reading**, followed by a lower high. Meanwhile, the price continues to make higher highs during this time. Conversely, in a bullish divergence scenario, RSI indicates **oversold conditions**, followed by a higher low. At the same time, the price forms lower lows during this phase.

Another perspective on RSI divergence is that it signals a shift in price momentum before it becomes evident in price movements. It serves as an early indication or warning signal, allowing traders to anticipate potential price reversals.

In the illustration above, you'll notice that the prices were on an upward trend, forming higher highs and higher lows, and the RSI was tracking this movement accordingly. However, a change occurred during the formation of the last higher high. While the price continued to make higher highs, the RSI failed to do so and instead formed a lower high. This scenario is referred to as Bearish Divergence. It suggests that the upward momentum is weakening, signaling a potential downward move in the near future.

Likewise, observe the illustration below, where you'll see a downtrend characterized by lower highs and lower lows, with the RSI tracking this trend. This pattern persisted until the last lower high and lower low were formed in the price. However, at this point, the RSI diverged from the price action by forming a higher low instead. This phenomenon is known as Bullish Divergence.

As anticipated, bullish divergence is essentially the opposite of bearish divergence. It indicates that the downward momentum is losing strength, hinting at a possible upward movement soon.

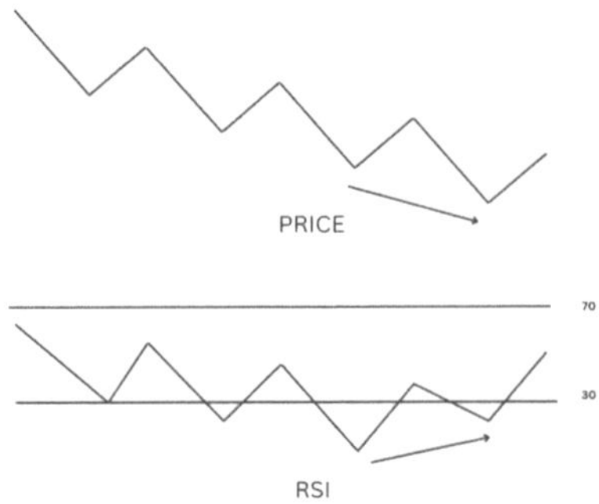

Make sure to confirm that you're dealing with a genuine divergence trading signal before jumping into a trade.

Thankfully, there are only a few factors to consider for a valid divergence signal.

Firstly, check if RSI is in an overbought or oversold state. This indicates an extreme movement, suggesting that the price is likely to rebound from that level.

Then, observe the following scenario:

For oversold conditions: Price creates a lower low, but RSI forms a higher low.

For overbought conditions: Price forms a higher high, but RSI forms a lower high.

Also, keep in mind that the candle needs to close to validate the RSI divergence signal (as RSI is based on Price Close, so it's very important to get the closing price in before taking any RSI signal into consideration).

In the chart above, you'll see that the RSI entered the overbought territory above 70, suggesting the trend was a bit stretched. Soon after, a bearish divergence emerged, signaling a possible trend reversal or cooling off. Subsequently, the price underwent a correction.

Similarly, in the chart above, you'll observe a downtrend with lower highs and lower lows. However, in March 2023, the RSI deviated from this pattern by forming a higher low instead of following the price to a lower low. This created a bullish divergence, indicating a softening bearish momentum and suggesting a potential pullback or reversal.

A big caution to all divergence enthusiasts! Divergence must be identified correctly. As mentioned earlier, only the "closing" price is used to calculate the RSI, so it's crucial to consider the close to pinpoint divergence. The highs and lows of the price don't constitute divergence. Sometimes, candlesticks can camouflage the price action, so it's essential to sharpen your skills through practice.

Observe the chart below. A new learner might easily identify a higher top in price with a lower top in RSI as divergence and feel that divergence didn't work, as the price didn't even budge and continued its uptrend!

The truth becomes clear when the candle chart is changed to a line chart! We may notice that the close was in tandem with the RSI; the price didn't close higher than its previous peak! So, there is no chance of divergence here! Be very careful about this fact.

Look at the chart below.

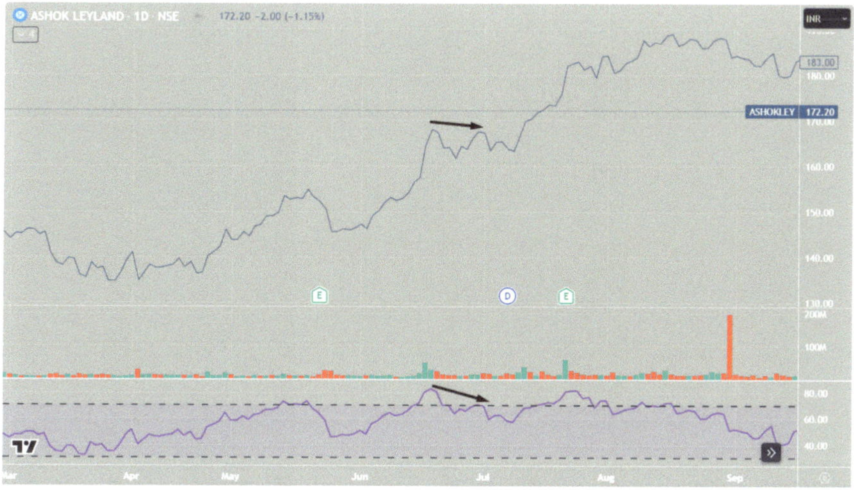

Divergence can be categorized into two types: 1) Wide Divergence and 2) Tight Divergence. Let's delve into each of these in detail.

When the swings on both price and RSI are wide enough that the divergence is easily visible, it is termed as a **wide divergence**.

Take a look at the two charts below where we've highlighted bullish and bearish divergences. You can observe that these divergences are easily visible without any additional effort, with sufficient space between the two peaks and troughs when RSI divergence is forming. This type of divergence is known as wide divergence. Additionally, note that we've marked divergences occurring either in the overbought or oversold zone, or close to it.

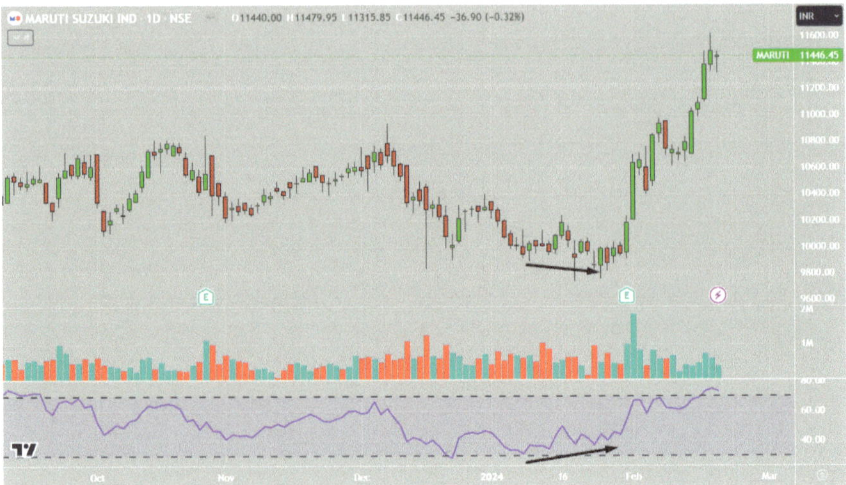

Tight divergence, on the other hand, poses a challenge for new RSI practitioners as it occurs within a shorter timeframe, typically between 3 to 7 price candles.

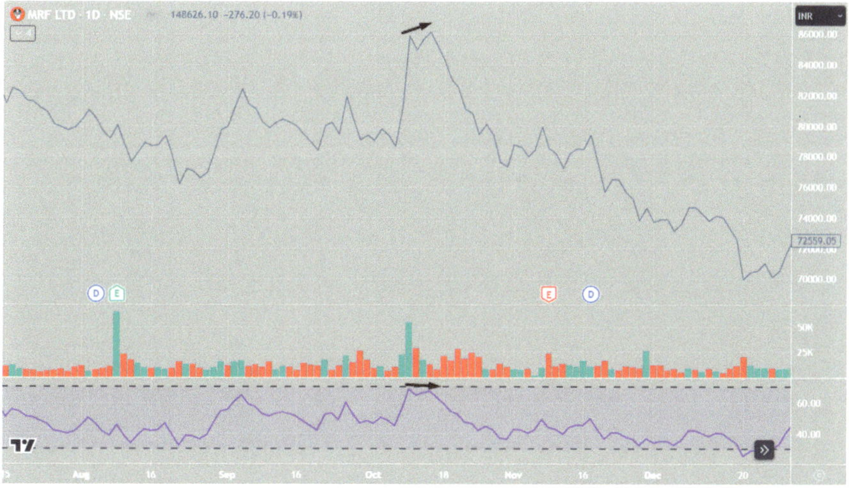

From the chart above, you can distinguish between the two types of divergences. A tight divergence triggers a faster reaction in the trend compared to a wide divergence. It's crucial to remember that while RSI signals act as indicators, the ultimate confirmation comes from observing price action. Therefore, it's essential to verify RSI divergence signals with the price action techniques we've previously discussed!

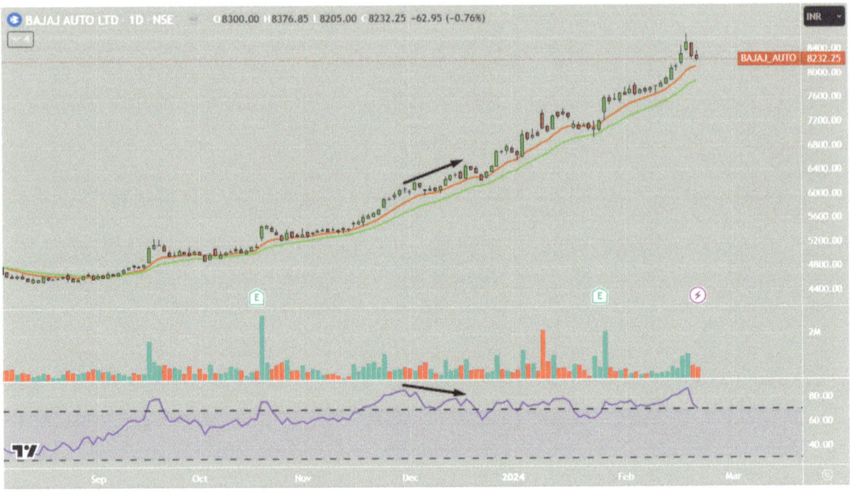

In the chart above, you'll observe a bearish divergence emerging in the overbought zone of the RSI. Despite this divergence, the prevailing trend remained strong, rendering the divergence ineffective. The price maintained support at the 10-20 EMA and proceeded to ascend, indicating an "unconfirmed" divergence.

Likewise, in the chart below, you'll observe a bearish divergence between the price and RSI. Following the emergence of this divergence, the price broke down from the trend line and the moving average, leading to a correction. This constitutes a confirmed divergence.

Divergence should not be considered as the ultimate signal; rather, it serves as a warning sign of a potential impending correction.

Another unique application of divergence is its indication of significant areas of support and resistance on the price chart. These areas where divergence occurs can act as crucial reaction points for price movements in the future. Let's examine the chart below for a clearer understanding.

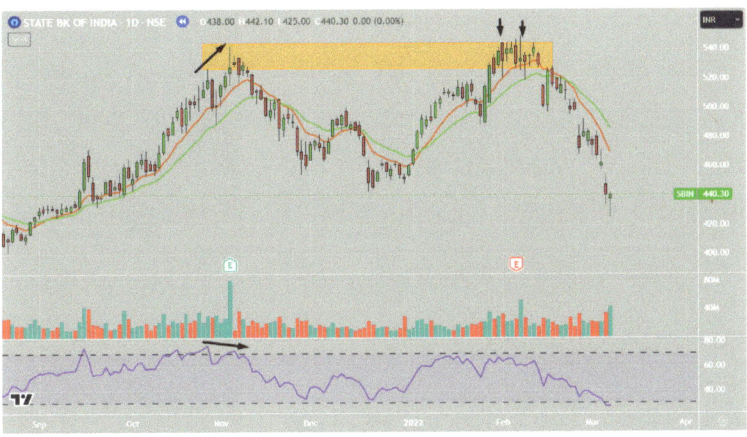

Another important aspect to remember when trading divergence is that it doesn't always guarantee a trend reversal, even after confirmation. Divergence might simply serve to cool down an overextended trend and bring the price back towards its mean. For instance, if a stock is trading significantly away from its 50-day moving average (DMA) and a divergence appears on the chart, there's a high probability that the trend will ease off, and prices might retest the 50 DMA before resuming their upward movement.

In the above chart, you can observe a divergence in the price when it was 30% away from the 50-day moving average (DMA). This divergence acted as a cooling mechanism for the price, bringing it back towards the mean represented by the 50 DMA. Consequently, the price resumed its trend from the 50 DMA line.

At times, multiple divergences may appear within an ongoing trend. However, it's crucial to understand that multiple divergences don't necessarily mean the trend is weakening with each rise. Rather, they suggest that the acceleration of the trend is slowing down, but this could pick up again at any moment. It's important not to take any trading action unless the divergence is confirmed by the price action itself. Let's take a look at the chart below:

Where to look for divergences?

Identifying divergence at significant levels holds more significance than randomly trading them anywhere on the charts. For instance, if we spot bullish divergence at a support level, the likelihood of the trend reacting to that support level increases. This is because we receive two signals: the price signal and the bullish momentum signal.

Examine the chart below, where I've highlighted two instances of divergence during price corrections. The first divergence, marked as "1," occurred without any notable support level nearby. Although prices reacted briefly, they ultimately found resistance at the 50 DMA and retreated. Contrastingly, divergence "2" formed at a longer-term support zone, resulting in a more significant price retracement. This divergence was also confirmed when the 50 DMA was breached. Additionally, we can enhance confirmation by incorporating trendlines. The greater the confirmation we receive, the stronger the signal becomes.

Did you notice another signal within the divergence here? Take a closer look at the type of divergence: the first is a wide divergence, while the second is a tight divergence. As we've discussed, tight divergences have greater potential, as prices tend to react more swiftly to tight divergences compared to wider ones. We'll delve deeper into the practical application of RSI in the upcoming chapters.

Wrapping Up

The RSI serves as a gauge of market strength, offering traders a versatile tool applicable across various markets. Its diverse applications empower traders to adapt their strategies as needed. However, it's crucial to remember that relying solely on RSI signals without proper confirmation can prove futile for traders.

Drop: XI

Understanding Emotions in Trading: Fear, Greed, and Hope

In trading, emotions significantly affect our choices and outcomes, particularly fear, greed, and hope.

1. **Greed:** drives the quest for large profits, prompting undue risk. Combatting greed involves adhering to risk management principles, ensuring disciplined trading.
2. **Fear:** can freeze decision-making, leading to hasty choices. Confidence in a well-tested trading system mitigates fear, encouraging reliance on proven strategies.
3. **Hope:** may keep traders in losing positions, expecting a turnaround. Employing a strict stop-loss strategy curtails this, allowing traders to cut losses and move forward.

Mastering these emotions through disciplined risk management, confidence in your strategies, and clear exit plans is key to trading success. Managing emotions is as crucial as mastering technical analysis for long-term achievement in trading.

Chapter 11

Risk Management

Stop Losses

A stop-loss order is a tool used in trading to minimize potential losses. Let's say you buy a stock at ₹50, but you're worried it might drop. To protect yourself, you can set a stop-loss order at ₹47. If the stock price falls to ₹47 or below, the order automatically sells the stock, preventing further losses. This strategy helps traders limit their risk and avoid losing more than they're comfortable with.

Why Stop Losses?

Every trader operates within finite capital, making the protection of that capital the paramount goal of trading. This safeguarding is best achieved through the concept of stop losses.

Implementing stop losses fosters discipline in trading. It ensures traders have a clear understanding of the risk-return trade-off in each trade by establishing predetermined stop loss and profit target levels.

Stop losses serve as a vital defense mechanism against market volatility. In a volatile market, it's essential to mitigate downside risk by setting appropriate stop losses while trading.

Calculating potential losses based on stop loss levels provides traders with insight into the amount of capital at risk in all open trades. This knowledge serves as a prompt to adjust positions accordingly, reducing overall risk.

Furthermore, stop losses facilitate the efficient churn of capital. Traders aim to continuously compound returns by actively managing their capital. Stop losses prevent capital from being tied up in unproductive trades, ensuring funds remain available for more lucrative opportunities.

Take a glance at the chart below, where you'll observe the stock exhibiting an uptrend, forming higher highs and higher lows, and consistently reacting positively with the 50-day moving average (DMA). Now, you're considering entering a trade on this stock at the next retest of the trendline and 50 DMA (POINT A). You patiently await a price action formation, and a hammer pattern emerges, indicating the presence of strong market participants. With this confirmation, you decide to enter the trade on the hammer pattern, expecting it to yield similar results to previous instances. (I've highlighted the potential entry point on the chart for your reference.)

However, the market didn't align with your anticipation, as is often the case. It's crucial to recognize that the market frequently behaves differently from what you expect. In this instance, the stock declined by over 15% from the entry point. Now, consider whether you're willing to risk a 15% loss on a single trade. This substantial loss could have been limited to just 3% from your entry point, emphasizing the importance of implementing risk management strategies.

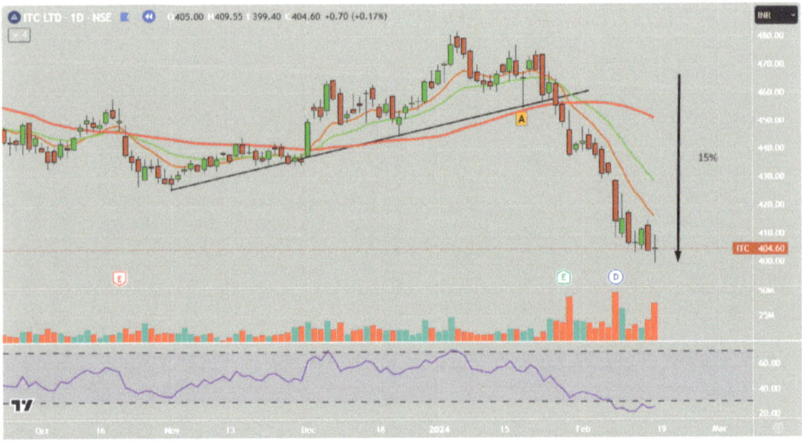

In the previous paragraph, I mentioned the possibility of curtailing your loss to 3%. Now, let's delve into the rationale behind this idea.

Have a look at the chart below.

We need to strategize our exit strategy just below the hammer candlestick, which coincides with the 50 DMA. But why? The primary reason is that the initial premise for entering the trade is no longer valid. The setup has become distorted, signaling the importance of exiting the trade. Otherwise, the trade could move significantly against us, as it did in this case. From a technical perspective, several factors support this decision. Firstly, the price broke below the low of the hammer candlestick. Secondly, it fell below the trend line, indicating a shift in momentum. Lastly, it breached the 50 DMA, further reinforcing the bearish sentiment. These multiple rejections to the trade suggest that the strong bullish evidence we relied upon while entering the trade is diminishing. Therefore, it's prudent to exit the trade to mitigate potential losses.

Consider the scenario where you incur a 15% loss on five consecutive trades. Now, envision if you had implemented a 5% stop loss to safeguard your positions. Let's examine the table to grasp the significance of this approach.

INITIAL CAPITAL	15% LOSS	CAPITAL	5% STOP LOSS	CAPITAL
100000	15000	85000	5000	95000
	15000	70000	5000	90000
	15000	55000	5000	85000
	15000	40000	5000	80000
	15000	**25000**	5000	**75000**

Henceforth, it becomes evident that a stop loss represents the maximum risk you are willing to undertake in a single trade. Stop losses form an integral component of your trading plan, ensuring disciplined risk management.

Risk

Now, let's delve into the concept of risk and accepted risk, and perhaps more crucially, determine the appropriate level of accepted risk for each trade.

Accepted risk represents the level of capital you are willing to lose on a single trade if it moves against you. Now, the crucial question arises: How do you determine your accepted risk?

How much of your capital should be allocated at once, and what portion should you risk on an individual trade? Let's delve into this critical aspect.

For instance, suppose you've determined that you don't want to risk more than 20% of your trading capital. This decision reserves 80% of your base for future trading to potentially offset any losses. But how do you allocate risk per trade? That's another factor to consider. Let's say you opt not to risk more than 5% of your trading capital on any single trade. This approach allows for approximately four trades, each risking 5% of your capital, while maintaining a maximum overall risk of 20%.

It's advisable to adhere to a simple guideline: your risk per trade should ideally remain in single digits, with a maximum of 9%. The rationale behind this figure is crucial. Loss and recovery dynamics operate differently in trading scenarios. Allow me to explain further.

LOSS INCURRED	RECOVERY REQUIRED TO MAKE UP THE LOSS
1%	1.01%
3%	3.09%
5%	5.26%
7%	7.53%
9%	9.89%
10%	11.11%

LOSS INCURRED	RECOVERY REQUIRED TO MAKE UP THE LOSS
15%	17.65%
20%	25%
40%	66.67%
50%	100%
75%	300%
90%	900%
99%	9900%

Now, take a look at the table above. On the left column, we've listed the potential losses from a single trade, while on the right side, it's the amount of recovery needed to offset that loss. Notice how as the losses increase, the pressure to recover also escalates.

With a maximum threshold of single-digit stop losses, the recovery needed is also confined within single digits. For instance, a 9% loss would necessitate a 9.89% gain to regain balance. However, once losses escalate into double digits, each subsequent recovery to offset that loss increases proportionally. As losses widen, the magnitude of recovery required grows exponentially.

Let's simplify this. If we set a 5% stop loss, the subsequent recovery needed in the next trade will be 5.26%. This appears quite achievable within a single trade. However, if we incur a

20% loss in one trade, the recovery would demand a 25% move! How frequently do we witness a 25% move in a single trade? It's rare. We might need at least 3-4 trades to recuperate from a single 20% loss. This illustrates the dynamics of trading.

The accepted risk shouldn't be arbitrary. For novices, it's advisable to limit risk to the 7-9% range. With experience, aiming for a maximum risk of 5% per trade becomes a good practice.

Avoid trades with a risk exceeding 7-9%. If a setup suggests a stop loss risk of over 9%, it's best to pass on it. Remember, there will always be numerous other trading opportunities available.

In the chart provided, the prices were poised to break out from the 52-week high level, indicating a potential trade opportunity. The entry point was set at 10935, with a stop loss positioned at the low of the previous swing, which was at 10400. Consequently, the total risk associated with this trade amounted to 535 rupees. In percentage terms, the risk stood at (535/10935)*100 = 4.89%. This falls below the 9% threshold, making it a suitable entry for us as traders.

Consider another example illustrated in the chart below, where a trade opportunity emerged as the stock was preparing to break out from a small rounding bottom pattern. The planned entry point was set at Rs 9, with the stop loss positioned at the low of the swing at Rs 7.40. Calculating the total risk in this trade in rupee terms, it amounts to (9 - 7.40) Rs 1.60, which may seem relatively small. However, evaluating it in percentage terms, (1.60/9)*100 = 17.77%, reveals a risk exceeding the recommended threshold. Despite the seemingly insignificant rupee value, the percentage-based risk exceeds the acceptable limit, emphasizing the importance of evaluating risk in relation to the entry and stop loss levels.

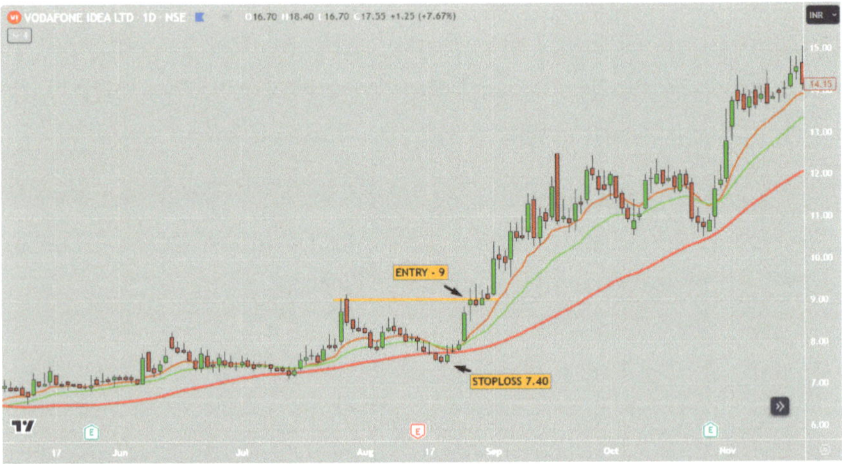

In both scenarios, the trades resulted in success. However, consider the potential outcome if the trades had gone against you. In the first trade, with a 4.89% loss, you would have needed to make a 5.14% gain in the next trade to recover, which seems feasible within a single trade. Conversely, if the second trade, with a 17.77% risk, had hit the stop loss, you would have needed a 21.61% gain to recuperate. Now, which of these scenarios do you think is more achievable: a 5.14% gain or a 21.61% gain? It becomes evident that smaller percentage losses are easier to recover from than larger ones, underscoring the importance of controlling risk and adhering to predefined risk management strategies.

So, we've grasped the concept of maximum risk permissible in a single trade. Now, it's crucial to note that this risk figure shouldn't be arbitrary. There must be a rationale behind your stop-loss placement. Typically, stop-losses are set at points where the pattern is invalidated, not randomly selected just to fit within single-digit percentages. Your stop-loss shouldn't be a rigid percentage without any valid justification. It should be strategically placed based on technical analysis, support and resistance levels, or other pertinent factors relevant to your trading strategy. This ensures that your risk management is purposeful and aligned with the dynamics of the market and your trading plan.

In the chart below, you'll notice the formation of a symmetrical triangle, signaling a potential trade opportunity above the breakout point. Now, when measuring the stop-loss from the breakout zone, the actual stop-loss should be set at the last completed swing. However, this places the stop-loss at 12.7%, which could be heavy on the portfolio. To mitigate this risk, some traders may opt to force the stop-loss at 5%, even though it may not align with technical analysis principles. Unfortunately, in the next chart, you'll observe that while the "technical" stop-loss wasn't hit, the forced stop-loss was triggered. So, what should be done in such a trading situation? The answer is to simply move on and look for another trade opportunity. It's crucial to adhere to your risk management principles and not let emotions dictate your trading decisions, even if it means passing up on a trade that doesn't meet your risk criteria.

Stop-losses are a critical component of any trading system, serving as a safeguard against excessive losses. However, they shouldn't be arbitrary; rather, they should be driven by sound reasoning and analysis. Each stop-loss level should be carefully determined based on technical indicators, market conditions, and risk tolerance. By setting stop-loss orders strategically, traders can protect their capital while allowing for potential profit opportunities. It's essential to avoid placing stop-loss levels randomly or based solely on emotions. Instead, traders should adhere to their trading plan and adjust stop-loss levels as needed based on market developments and price action. Ultimately, the goal of setting stop-loss orders is to manage risk effectively and preserve capital in the face of market volatility.

Win Rate

Let's delve into the concept of the win rate of a trading system: The win rate represents the percentage of winning trades out of the total number of trades executed. For instance, winning 5 out of 10 trades equates to a 50% win rate, while winning 30 out of 100 results in a 30% win rate. It's noteworthy that many professional traders maintain a win rate close to 50% or even lower. However, their profitability stems from the fact that they generate more profits from winning trades than losses incurred from losing trades. In essence, the win rate alone doesn't dictate a trader's success; rather, it's the ability to maximize gains relative to losses that ultimately determines profitability in the market.

Risk & Reward

Risk/reward is a comparison of the gains from winning trades to the losses from losing trades. For example, if you lose ₹100 on a losing trade but make ₹200 on a winning trade, your risk/reward ratio is 100/200 = 0.5. Alternatively, you can view it as reward/risk = 200/100 = 2. This means that your winnings are twice as much as your losses. By analyzing this ratio across numerous trades, you can determine your average risk/reward. Many experienced traders earn more from their winning trades than they lose on their losing trades. This approach allows them to maintain profitability even if they win only 50% or less of their trades.

The Right Balance

When I began my trading journey, I had lofty aspirations and dreams. However, as time passed and my hair turned gray, I started to grasp the intricacies of trading mathematics. Many of us enter the trading world aiming for a high win rate and substantial rewards. However, the reality is that neither of these is essential for success in trading. A modest reward-to-risk ratio of 2:1 and a system that is correct just 50% of the time are sufficient to earn a respectable living. Interestingly, many of the most successful traders worldwide also strive for this kind of payoff. So, while it's natural to dream big when starting out, understanding the importance of risk management and realistic expectations can lead to sustainable success in trading over the long term.

Now, let's delve into how the combination of a 50% win rate and a 2:1 reward-to-risk ratio plays out in practice.

Let's consider a scenario: You employ a trading strategy with a 50% accuracy rate. For each trade, you limit your risk to a maximum of 5%. Additionally, your target reward-to-risk ratio is set at 2:1.

Let's embark on our trading journey with Rs 100,000.00 (One Lakh Rupees). The maximum risk per trade in rupee terms will be 5% of Rs 100,000, which equals Rs 5,000. The reward we are aiming for will be 2:1, meaning 10% of Rs 100,000, which translates to Rs 10,000 in rupee terms.

TRADE	R:R	OUTCOME	LOSS	CAPITAL
1	2:1	LOSS	-5000	95000
2	2:1	LOSS	-5000	90000
3	2:1	LOSS	-5000	85000
4	2:1	LOSS	-5000	80000
5	2:1	LOSS	-5000	75000
6	2:1	PROFIT	+10000	85000
7	2:1	PROFIT	+10000	95000
8	2:1	PROFIT	+10000	105000
9	2:1	PROFIT	+10000	115000
10	2:1	PROFIT	+10000	125000

From the table above, you can observe that the journey began with a series of losses. We encountered five stop-losses back-to-back. However, following that, we experienced five consecutive profitable trades. At the end of these ten trades, we managed to achieve a profit of 25%. This demonstrates that with a modest expectation of a 50% win rate and a 2:1 reward-to-risk ratio, it's feasible to attain a 25% annual profit.

When engaging in trading, it's crucial to recognize that while the reward is not within our control, the risk is. Therefore, our focus should be on managing the aspects we can control, rather than chasing after elements beyond our influence.

As you embark on your trading journey, you'll discover that the 2:1 reward ratio isn't always consistent. Instead, you'll encounter a variety of outcomes. In my experience, the distribution of rewards tends to look something like this: out of 10 trades, 5 will hit the stop-loss, 1 will be exceptional, 1 will be good, 2 will be normal, and 1 may underperform. Let's delve into an example to illustrate this.

TRADE	R:R	OUTCOME	LOSS	CAPITAL
1	2:1	LOSS	-5000	95000
2	2:1	LOSS	-5000	90000
3	2:1	LOSS	-5000	85000
4	2:1	LOSS	-5000	80000
5	2:1	LOSS	-5000	75000
6	1:1	UNDERPER-FORMED	5000	80000
7	2:1	NORMAL	10000	90000
8	2:1	NORMAL	10000	100000

TRADE	R:R	OUTCOME	LOSS	CAPITAL
9	3:1	BETTER	15000	115000
10	5:1	EXCEPTIONAL	250000	140000

Examining the table above, we notice that with a fixed risk and a varied reward spread, we can achieve exceptional returns, particularly in favorable market conditions where exceptional rewards are more prevalent than normal ones. Trading under the right conditions with a controlled and predictable risk is the key to achieving outstanding performance in trading, and this is the secret behind the success of super performing traders.

As our win rate increases, we'll need lower-risk reward payoffs to remain profitable.

Take a look at the table below, showcasing different risk-reward payoffs with varying win rates of a trading system.

	20% WIN RATE	**30% WIN RATE**	**40% WIN RATE**	**50% WIN RATE**	**60% WIN RATE**
1:1	LOSS	LOSS	LOSS	BREAKEVEN	PROFIT
2:1	LOSS	LOSS	PROFIT	PROFIT	PROFIT
3:1	LOSS	PROFIT	PROFIT	PROFIT	PROFIT
4:1	BREAKEVEN	PROFIT	PROFIT	PROFIT	PROFIT
5:1	PROFIT	PROFIT	PROFIT	PROFIT	PROFIT

There are five scenarios presented in the table above. Let's delve into three of them: the 20%, 50%, and 60% win rate cases.

When dealing with a trading system boasting a mere 20% win rate, achieving profitability necessitates exceedingly lucrative trades. Each trade would ideally yield a minimum of 5% return to offset the 1% risk. For instance, if a trade carries a 4% risk, a whopping 20% return is required for profitability. To sustain profitability over 10 trades, at least two of these trades must yield a 5:1 reward-to-risk ratio. However, ponder the feasibility of attaining such substantial rewards. Additionally, consider the mental fortitude required to weather eight consecutive losses out of ten trades.

Now, consider a scenario where our success rate stands at 50%, indicating that half of our trades end in a stop loss. With this hit rate, achieving breakeven on our account is feasible if we aim for a 1:1 risk-to-reward ratio. However, profitability enters the picture when we set our sights on a 2:1 risk-to-reward ratio, as demonstrated in the table above.

With a system boasting a 60% success rate, even a 1:1 risk-to-reward trade payoff can render a trader profitable.

As traders, our aim should ideally fall within the range of a 50% to 60% success rate coupled with a 2:1 reward-to-risk ratio. This combination ensures that we avoid loss-making situations. Achieving such a reward-risk ratio is feasible, especially in favorable trending markets. It's crucial to steer clear of exotic systems promising unrealistically high success rates of 80% to 100%, or trading on leverage to amplify payoffs. Additionally, returns can be further enhanced by implementing advanced position sizing and position management techniques. By focusing on a balanced approach and building a system with a respectable hit rate, traders can establish a solid foundation for consistent profitability in the world of trading.

Getting Started with Trading

So far, we've covered a comprehensive array of tools and techniques to kickstart our trading journey. We delved into the Dow Theory, offering insights into market phases and indicating when to initiate long, short, or sideline positions. We explored price patterns, equipping us with the knowledge of what to seek when trading within an ongoing trend. Candlestick analysis provided us with timely triggers, while understanding moving averages and RSI empowered us to refine our trading decisions further. Finally, we delved into the realm of risk management, crucial for minimizing losses should a trade move against us. With this arsenal of knowledge and strategies at our disposal, it's time to take action and step onto the trading field with confidence.

Before diving into real-world trading examples, there's another critical decision traders must make: selecting the appropriate time frame for their trades. There's considerable debate over which time frame yields the most profit, but the truth is, all time frames can be profitable if you understand the trading styles associated with them. Generally, traders fall into several categories, each corresponding to a specific time frame:

1. **Scalpers (Time Frame: Seconds to Minutes):** These traders aim to capitalize on small price movements and execute numerous trades within a short time frame.

2. **Day Traders (Time Frame: Minutes to Hours):** Day traders open and close positions within the same trading day, exploiting intraday price fluctuations.

3. **Swing Traders (Time Frame: Hours to Days):** Swing traders hold positions for several days to weeks, aiming to profit from medium-term price movements.

4. **Position Traders (Time Frame: Days to Months):** Position traders take a longer-term approach, holding positions for weeks to months to capitalize on significant market trends.

The key is to align your trading style and objectives with the appropriate time frame. Each time frame comes with its own set of challenges and opportunities, so it's essential to choose the one that best suits your personality, risk tolerance, and trading goals.

In my experience, as you gain more years in trading, you tend to gravitate towards longer time frames. Smaller time frames are often plagued by excessive noise, making it challenging to discern meaningful price action. Conversely, as you transition to larger time frames, the noise gets filtered out, offering clearer and more reliable price signals. This purity of price action on longer time frames allows for better decision-making and reduces the likelihood of being swayed by short-term fluctuations.

Here are some reasons why I opt for larger timeframes for positional trading over smaller ones:

1. Reduced Risk: Larger timeframes provide more space for price movements, allowing for lower risk exposure.
2. Increased Analysis Time: With larger timeframes, there's ample time to analyze price action, volume, and other relevant factors. Additionally, it allows for thorough intermarket and intramarket analysis.
3. Lower Involvement: In today's information-rich environment, active involvement in the market can lead to biases that impact trading decisions. Positional trading offers a more detached approach, enabling traders to interpret news and information more effectively.

The price action, regardless of the timeframe, provides the same signals. However, one personal recommendation is to avoid using indicators on time frames below the hourly interval, as they can significantly distort the price information.

For the purpose of this book, we won't delve into lower timeframes. Instead, we'll focus on weekly, daily, and occasionally hourly charts. (Multi timeframe Analysis)

Multiple time frame analysis means looking at the same currency pair but on different time frames. Typically, a bigger time frame is used to figure out the long-term trend, while a smaller time frame helps to find the best moments to enter the market.

In stock trading, it's a good idea to switch between different time frames using a ratio of 1:4. This means if you're looking at a longer time frame like a weekly chart, you might want to zoom in to a shorter time frame like a daily or hourly chart. The reason for this is to catch smaller price movements for better entry points into the market. However, focusing on very small time frames like 15 min etc can be stressful and may not provide much useful information for your trades. For example, if you're checking the trend on a daily chart, you can look at a 60-minute or a 240-min chart for potential entry points. The shorter time frames give you a sense of what's happening in the short term, while the daily chart helps you track the overall progress of your trade.

We'll delve deeper into this concept when we explore our case studies later on.

Chapter 12

Putting everything together: Case Studies

Now that we've covered all the essentials to begin trading, it's time to consolidate our knowledge and dive into case studies. In these real-world examples, we'll apply everything we've learned – from understanding trends and patterns to identifying triggers, setting stop losses, and booking profits.

Case Study 1: Zomato Limited

We've examined the weekly chart of Zomato for trend analysis. It's evident that the stock is currently in a downtrend, characterized by forming lower highs and lower lows on a weekly basis. To consider entering this stock, it's advisable to wait for the trend to show signs of reversal.

You may observe that the downward sloping trend line, along with the shorter-term moving average (MA) positioned below the longer-term MA, indicates a strong downward trend at present. Additionally, the downward slope of the MAs further reinforces the notion that the trend is firmly moving downwards, with no apparent signs of a reversal.

Now, examining the chart below on August 1, 2022, we observe several key points. Firstly, there is a bullish divergence developing in the Relative Strength Index (RSI), suggesting that the downward momentum may be weakening. Additionally, there are two significant candles worth noting. The first is a large red candle accompanied by strong volumes. However, this may not necessarily be the right candle at the right place. What does it signify when a bearish candle with extraordinary volume appears after a substantial decline? It's indicative of the wrong pattern at the wrong place. In the subsequent session, a large wide-range green candle emerges with strong volumes, signaling a resurgence of strong buying interest. Nevertheless, are we ready to initiate a buy position at this point? No, we must exercise patience and wait for an accumulation zone to form. We require a proper confluence of averages in place before considering entering the market.

Now, let's analyze the chart below. Following the bullish divergence, Zomato did not proceed to form another lower low. Instead, it formed an almost equal high. Additionally, take note that the Relative Strength Index (RSI) is now holding around the 40 levels. Moreover, the prices have broken the trendline, and the downtrend has transformed into a sideways accumulation zone. However, are we ready to enter the market at this point? Not yet. We still need the confluence of moving averages (the 10-day Simple Moving Average (SMA) above the 40-day SMA and price above both) and a proper series of higher tops and higher bottoms to be formed. According to Dow Theory, we are currently in the accumulation phase and not in an uptrend.

Another significant aspect of the accumulation phase is the volumes. Take a closer look at the volumes during this phase; they are trending upwards. There is a notable increase in activity in the stock during this time.

On the chart below, on April 24th, we observe a strong wide bullish candle accompanied by strong volumes. This marks the first instance post-accumulation where prices have sustained above the moving averages. Additionally, there appears to be a probable convergence of moving averages (COMA) in place. Pay attention to the cup and handle formation, signaling that the stock is poised for a potential trade opportunity. At this juncture, we will transition the chart to the daily timeframe to further refine our entry and determine the appropriate stop-loss level.

Now, let's examine the daily charts and build a case for entry. The trend is upward, characterized by higher highs and higher lows. The moving averages are aligned correctly, with the 10-period above the 20-period, the 20-period above the 50-period, and the 50-period above the 200-period, with the price trading above all of them. The slope of the moving averages is upward, indicating a positive trend. Turning our attention to the Relative Strength Index (RSI), it has entered the overbought zone, and during retracements, it is not reaching oversold levels. With these factors aligned, we are now prepared to enter the market above the swing high.

In the chart below, we observe that the swing high has been surpassed by a wide-ranging candle accompanied by strong volumes. Additionally, there is a formation of a small cup and handle pattern near the moving average, suggesting that prices are not overextended. An entry opportunity can be considered at the breakout point, with a stop-loss placement below the swing low.

The entry is initiated above the large wide candle accompanied by strong volume, with a stop-loss positioned below the swing low. As anticipated, the stock begins to move in the desired direction, gaining 35% from the breakout point. However, with the RSI at 80 and the appearance of an indecisive candle, caution is warranted. If the price exhibits any signs of weakness below the indecisive candle, it may be prudent to book profits. This precaution is necessary due to the excessive momentum and movement, indicating a potential correction ahead.

Now, observe the chart below. Exiting below the indecisive candle proved to be a wise decision as the stock subsequently experienced a correction. During this correction, the stock found support at the 10-20 moving averages. Additionally, notice the RSI remained above 40, indicating that the overall trend remained intact. This correction appeared to be a secondary one, characterized by low trading volumes. Eventually, the stock formed a triangle pattern and broke out once more, accompanied by significant trading volumes.

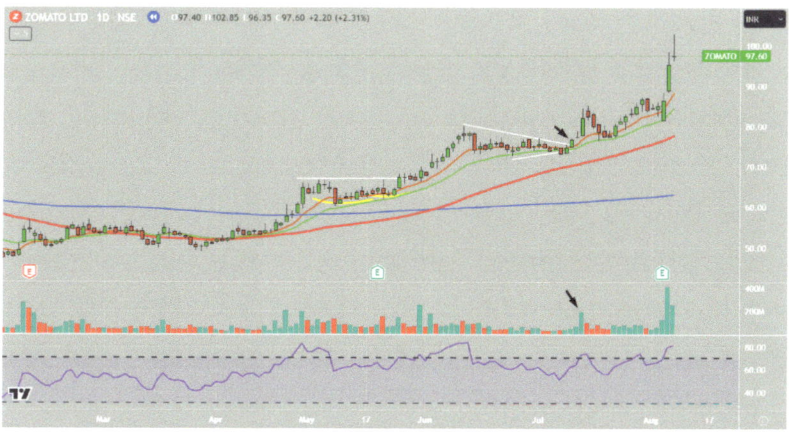

Take another look at the chart below. This time, we observe that the stock broke out of the triangle pattern, presenting an even more favorable risk-reward ratio as the trend strengthened. Subsequently, the stock formed a long-wick candle with high trading volumes. What does a long wick signify? Profit booking. Therefore, if prices dip below the long wick candle, it's prudent to book profits. Additionally, note that the RSI has reached 80 once again, and prices are considerably distant from the moving averages, suggesting that the trend is somewhat extended and could benefit from a cooling-off period.

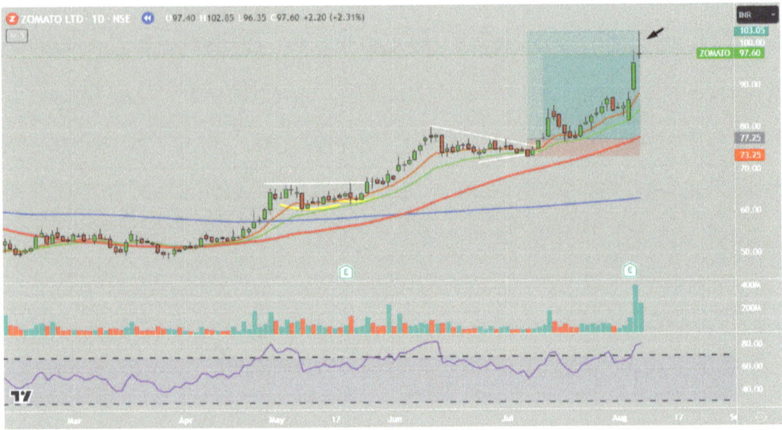

Take another look at the chart below. Following that long wick candle, the stock experienced another correction phase. This correction was marked by lower trading volumes. Finding support at the 10-20 DMA (Daily Moving Average), the stock began to form a "W" pattern. During this correction, the RSI (Relative Strength Index) remained in the bullish zone and did not become oversold. The breakout from the "W" pattern occurred on high trading volumes, accompanied by an upward turn in the RSI once again.

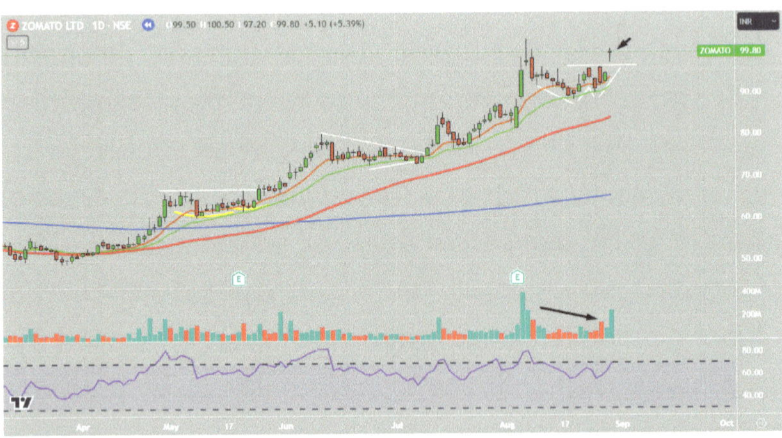

Now, take a look at the chart below. Throughout the trend progression, there were corrections whenever prices pulled away from the moving averages, and the RSI approached or exceeded 80. However, during the entire trending movement, the stock consistently remained above the moving averages. Pay attention to the price pattern it formed as it moved upward. Throughout the entire progression, Zomato created 7 distinct bases from which prices successfully broke out. A trend provides multiple entry opportunities, so we shouldn't chase entries if we miss them.

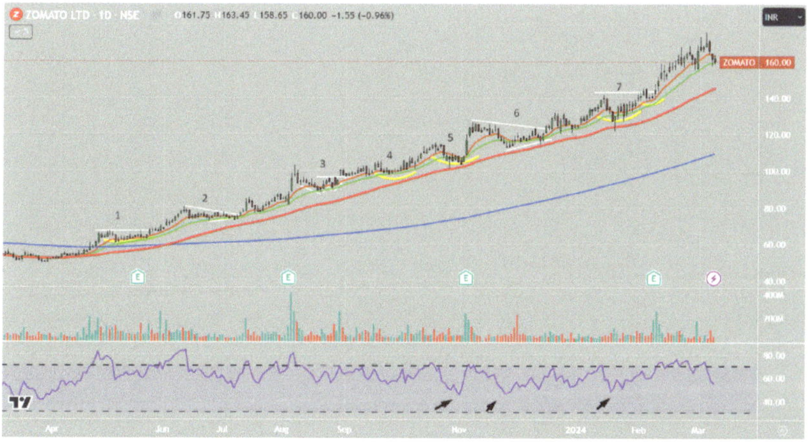

In the meantime, let's also take a look at the weekly chart below. Here, we observe that the trend is forming higher highs and higher lows, indicating an upward movement. The 10 SMA (Simple Moving Average) is providing strong support to the prices. This is a classical example of a Dow Theory uptrend. As long as the trend remains intact, particularly on the weekly swing lows, everything looks favorable. Take a look at the RSI (Relative Strength Index); it consistently oscillates between the

80 and 60 zones. As we shift to higher time frames, the purity of the price action becomes more pronounced.

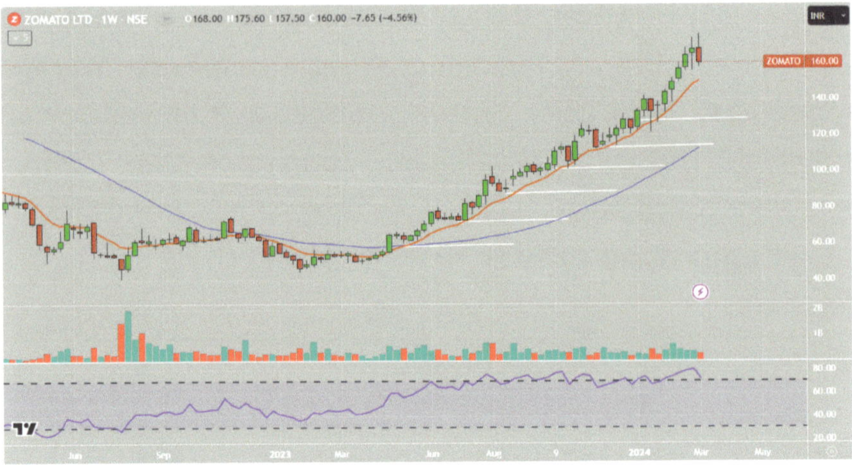

Case Study 2: NVDA

In this illustration, we will conduct the analysis progressively. Observing the chart, the initial observation is that NVDA exhibits a pattern of lower highs and lower lows, aligning with Dow Theory principles. This indicates that the 10-week moving average (WMA) has served as a resistance level, with the stock failing to maintain positions above it. Additionally, a trendline has been drawn, highlighting that it has effectively acted as a barrier, preventing the stock's price from ascending. Notably, the 10 WMA is positioned beneath the 40 WMA, with both exhibiting a downward trajectory. At this stage, initiating long positions is premature, as the duration of this trend of descending peaks and troughs remains uncertain.

Turning our attention to the chart presented below, a notable shift in dynamics has occurred. As prices neared a support zone, they retreated, but notably, they have now breached the trendline. Additionally, for the first time, the stock succeeded in closing above and sustaining its position over the 10-week moving average (WMA). Although it encountered resistance at the 40 WMA and declined, this pullback didn't result in the creation of a new lower low. Instead, it established a higher bottom. The Relative Strength Index (RSI) also made a significant move, crossing above 50, while the slope of the 10 WMA turned upward. What other patterns do you observe? Is there an inverted head and shoulders formation visible? At this juncture, it would be prudent to switch our analysis to a daily timeframe and strategize our positioning in anticipation of a breakout. Acting early is key, as waiting until the breakout occurs will likely find us competing with a rush of others looking to establish positions.

Observing the daily chart provided, an inverted head and shoulders pattern becomes apparent. Let's delve a bit deeper into the Relative Strength Index (RSI) analysis at this point. The recent market movements have propelled the RSI into overbought territory, with readings surpassing 70. This contrasts with earlier phases when the market was declining, and the RSI avoided reaching the 70 mark. Additionally, during each formation of a lower low, the RSI dipped below 30, but after climbing above 70, it has not entered the oversold zone. This behavior suggests that momentum is building, as it no longer dips into the oversold region. Currently, the prices are consolidating in a flag pattern above all moving averages, although the 10, 20, and 50-day moving averages remain beneath the 200-day moving average (DMA), which is quite typical when planning an entry before a breakout. The configuration of the moving averages (DMA) is expected to align post-breakout. Our next step involves timing our entry based on the breakout from this flag pattern. Let's take a closer look at the chart.

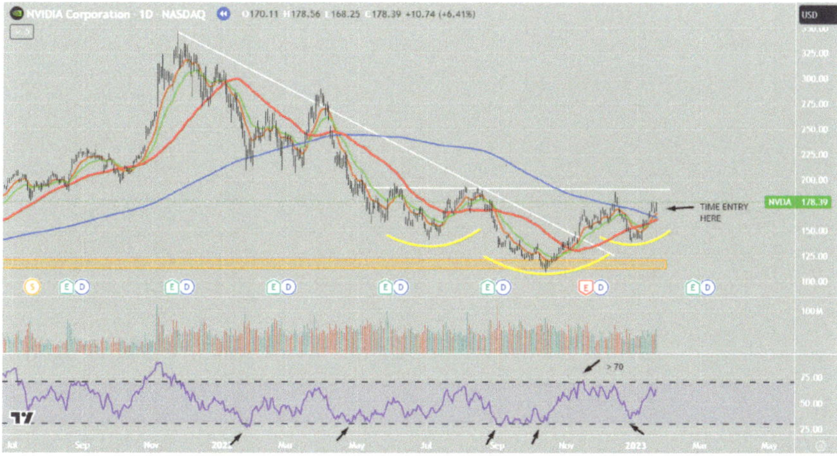

Examining the chart presented below, it's evident that a flag pattern has formed. The entry point will be set above the consolidation zone, with a stop loss positioned below it, entailing a total risk of 6.58% for this trade. In this instance, we will adjust our strategy for trailing stops and taking profits, offering an alternative approach that leans towards a more passive strategy. Instead of utilizing the 10-day and 20-day moving averages (DMA) for trailing our positions, we will shift to employing the 50 DMA. Hence, we will close our long positions when the prices fall below the 50 DMA. This strategy is ideal for traders seeking a more passive and less hands-on approach.

The entry was triggered, positioning us in the trade before the breakout occurred. Furthermore, the latest candle confirms the materialization of the head and shoulders breakout, and the moving averages are aligning in the correct sequence!

In the chart below, you can observe how our early entry strategy initiated and how others might enter the trade based on traditional knowledge after the breakout. We secured an early position with a risk of less than 7%, while a traditional breakout strategy typically involves a risk exceeding 15%.

However, there's an important consideration with this approach to early entry. It's advisable not to commit the full position size when making anticipatory trades, that is, entering before a breakout. It's prudent to start with a third of the intended position, with the option to add more as the trend develops.

In the chart below, you'll notice another opportunity for entry presented itself when the stock completed its breakout from the inverted head and shoulders pattern and retested the breakout zone. The total risk for this entry point was 8%, allowing for an additional third of the position to be taken. It's important to highlight the advantage of early entry: we are already up by 10% before the traditional entry signal is activated.

In the following chart, observe the effectiveness of utilizing a 50-day moving average (DMA) to trail our positions, which enables us to remain aligned with the trend. The price experienced a surge of over 140% from our initially planned entry point. This highlights a significant advantage of successfully identifying and properly trailing a trend.

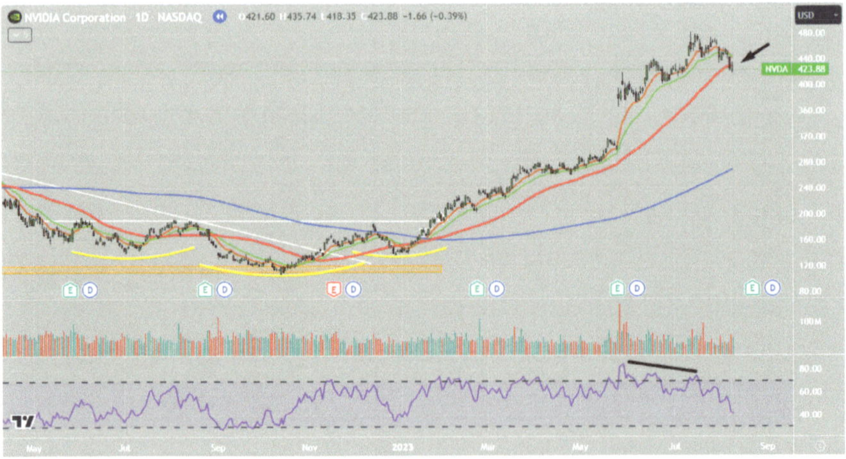

As the trend advanced, numerous opportunities arose to pilot the positions further.

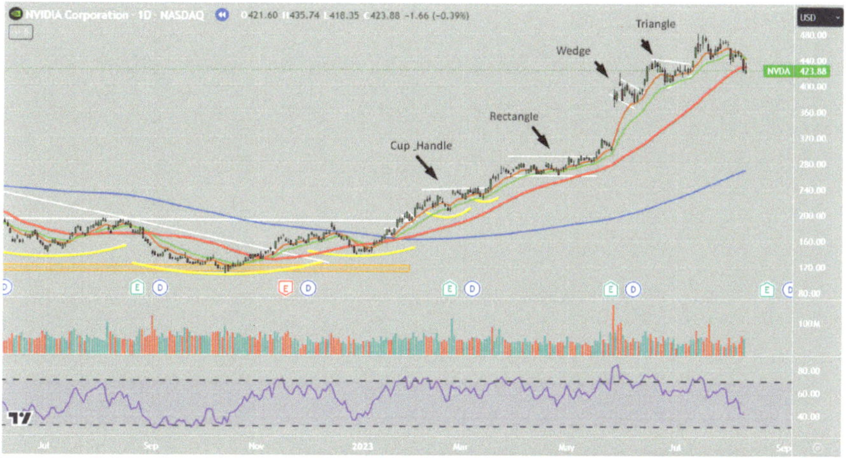

If you miss the initial entry, don't abandon the chart; keep it on your watchlist, as it will likely offer another opportunity to enter.

Case Study 3: Bitcoin

Notice the chart below, Bitcoin reached its peak in November 2021 and has been on a downward trajectory since, forming lower highs and lower lows. Throughout this period, the 10-week moving average and the trendline consistently served as resistance levels. Until January 2023, Bitcoin remained in a strong downtrend.

After January 2023, the trend shifted to a more sideways movement. The pattern of lower highs was broken, and in March 2023, the cryptocurrency formed a higher low accompanied by increased trading volumes. Notably, the downward-sloping trendline was breached, and prices surged above the moving averages, finding support at previously resistant moving averages (a Support and Resistance Flip). Additionally, an inverted head and shoulders pattern emerged. Another significant development was the Relative Strength Index (RSI) trading above 50 for the first time in a while. These signals collectively suggested a potential bottoming process underway.

At this point, we'll employ our multi-timeframe analysis technique and transition to the daily chart to identify an early entry opportunity. It's crucial because after a breakout, numerous traders will likely rush to establish positions in the cryptocurrency. Let's switch over to the daily chart and examine the developing trends there!

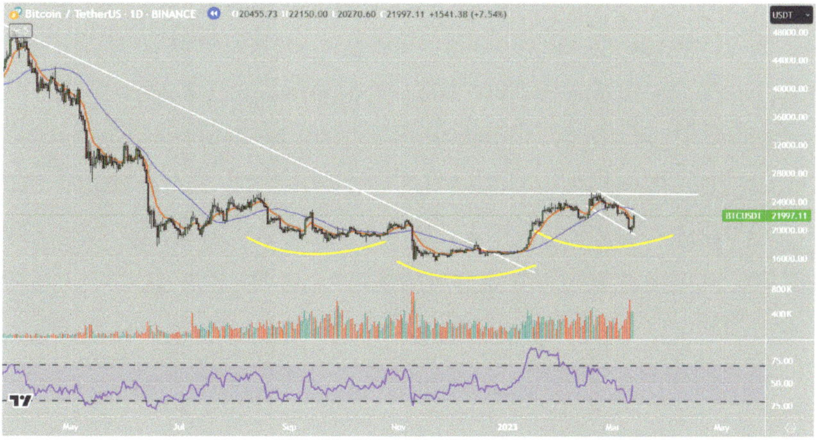

In the daily chart above, we observe that the right shoulder is forming within a falling channel. A breakout from this channel would offer an early entry point into the trend. Additionally, take note of the changing behavior of the RSI. It has begun to reach overbought levels and fails to dip into oversold territory below 30, signaling a significant shift in momentum. Our strategy will be to enter the market upon a breakout above the trendline. Refer to the chart below for further details.

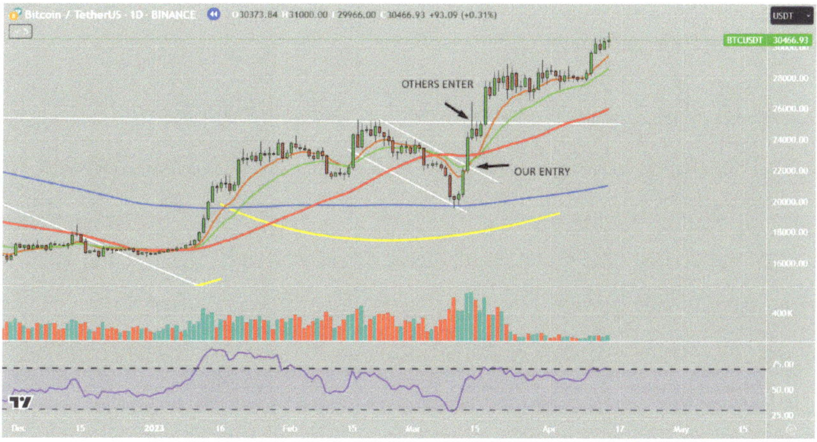

You may observe that we entered the market before the inverted head and shoulders pattern broke out. While others might have entered upon the breakout, let's examine what occurred at that point. There was a trap, as many traders rushed to enter, resulting in a shakeout designed to force them out of their positions. By entering earlier, we avoided this trap. Now, it would be wise to trail our stop loss with the 10-day moving average (DMA) to manage risk effectively.

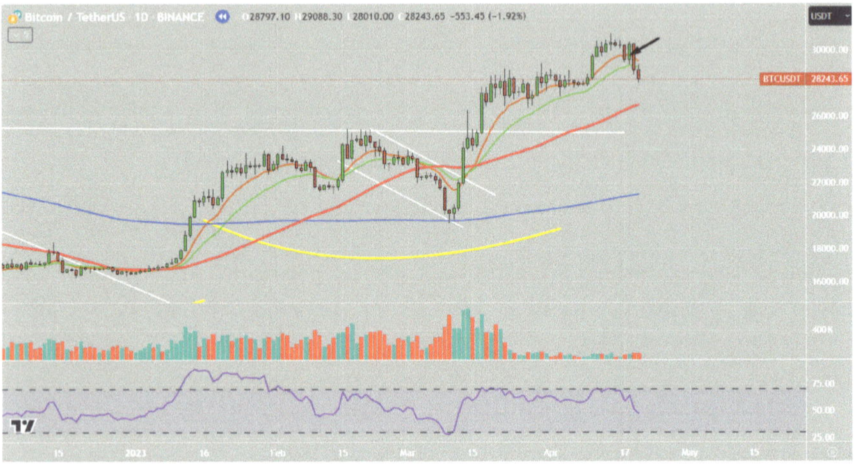

Ultimately, we were stopped out with a respectable 32% gain from our entry point.

One of the biggest mistakes I made when I started trading was removing a stock from my watchlist as soon as it gave me a profit or loss. This approach, however, was flawed. Take Bitcoin, for example. Its chart was in its infancy, and the move had just begun after recently bottoming out. If this signaled a trend change, there could be a much larger move to capitalize on. It's crucial to keep such stocks or instruments on our radar.

Let's revisit the weekly chart (below). After several weeks, we notice another pattern emerging—a double bottom. What makes this particularly significant is that it formed above the previous base, which was the inverted head and shoulders pattern. This is known as Base on Base, a powerful accumulation signal.

So, what's next? We switch to the daily timeframe to time our entry early, before others catch on.

On this daily chart (below), we observe a trendline break followed by a retest. A favorable move from this point onward will serve as the trigger for our entry, with a very tight stop. However, it's important to remember that timing our entry early may sometimes conflict with the moving average rule. There could be instances where the 50 and 200 DMA (Daily Moving Average) may not align with our trading decision.

On the chart above, we've strategized our entry at a trendline break, which also appears to be forming a falling wedge pattern. Once the prices break out, we'll enter the trade and manage our position by trailing it with the 10 DMA (Daily Moving Average). However, there's something that will always distinguish human decision-making from that of computers: the ability to go beyond the rules and assess the situation. Since we recognize this as a base on base formation, a strong bullish signal, can we consider using the 50 DMA to trail our position instead? This could potentially allow us to capture a larger portion of the market move.

In the chart above, we opted to trail our positions using the 50 DMA (50-Day Moving Average), which resulted in capturing a significant move of 56%. However, we were subsequently stopped out as prices closed below the 50 DMA. Now, observe the series of divergences on the RSI (Relative Strength Index) before the cryptocurrency closed below the 50 DMA. What do you interpret from this? Take a moment to think; after all, you're not a computer!

Although we experienced a stop-out on the daily chart below the 50 DMA, let's take a look at the weekly chart. There, we see the formation of a long upper wick candle, resembling a shooting star!

Isn't technical analysis a fascinating field of study?

As mentioned earlier, I won't remove Bitcoin from my watchlist; it's crucial to keep an eye on it. Later, we observe it forming a cup and handle pattern on the daily chart, with moving average confluences. Now, we'll transition to a 4-hour chart to pinpoint our entry. Once the entry is triggered, we'll revert to the daily chart to manage our position effectively.

On the four-hourly chart, we observe a symmetrical triangle formation within the daily handle. A breakout occurred, triggering our entry.

In the chart below, the position was closed at the 10-20 DMA, capturing a 50-point move. Subsequently, prices closed below the 10-20 DMA, prompting an exit. Take note of what formed on the RSI: a divergence.

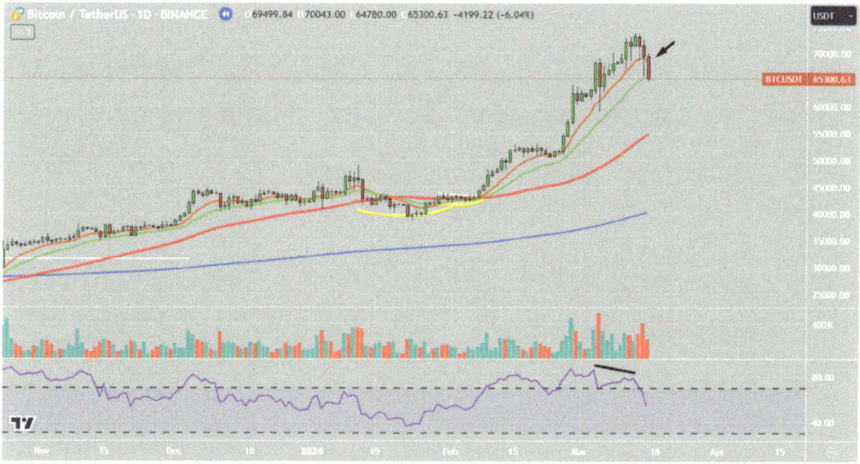

Case Study 4: Crash of 2008

Many of you may recall the 2008 financial crisis, while some may not have experienced it firsthand. Nevertheless, it remains one of the most significant crashes in stock market history, marking the end of numerous ventures in the financial world. Whether you lived through it or not, the charts from that period allow us to revisit the atmosphere and dynamics of the time. Regardless of the fundamental factors at play, focusing on technical analysis reveals an interesting story. For me, 2008 was a turning point as it spurred my decision to delve into understanding how markets function. Prior to that, charts and technical analysis were unfamiliar territory.

The bear market persisted for over 10 months, witnessing indices plummeting by more than 64% from their peaks. Now, let's put our technical analysis expertise to the test and examine whether we could have navigated through both the downturn and the subsequent recovery. It's important to acknowledge that discussing these scenarios in hindsight may seem straightforward, but it's essential to learn from historical data and truths that remain unchanged. After all, understanding past market movements can provide valuable insights into potential strategies for future endeavors.

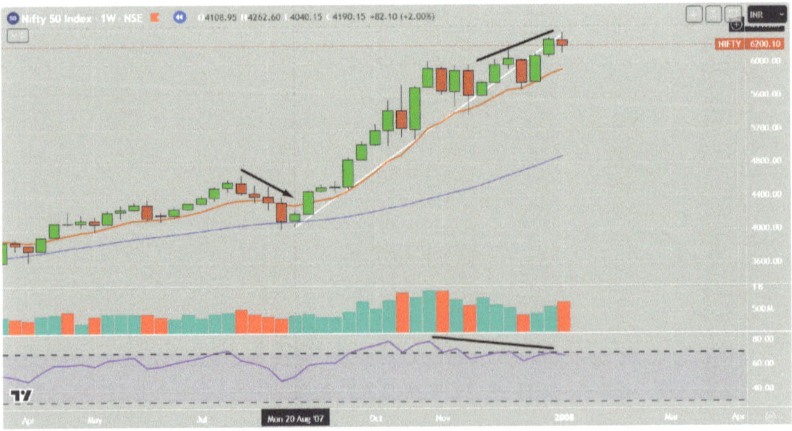

In the chart displayed above, following a four-week correction, the markets found a bottom in August 2007, marking the beginning of a strong uptrend. During this period, the Nifty index displayed a consistent pattern of advancing, characterized by higher highs and higher lows. The uptrend was accompanied by the formation of strong, wide green candles, punctuated by intermittent corrective phases. This price action aligns closely with the principles outlined in the Dow Theory, unfolding in a manner consistent with the classical teachings of this foundational concept in technical analysis.

Observing the highlighted phase in the chart above, several noteworthy developments become apparent following the correction in November 2007. Firstly, there was a distinct decline in trading volumes during this period, a phenomenon that holds significance according to Dow Theory's emphasis on the relationship between price and volume. Secondly, the uptrend was disrupted as the rising trendline was breached, with the once-supportive trendline transforming into a barrier of resistance. Thirdly, there was a notable shift in the frequency of candle colors, with an increase in the occurrence of red candles compared to green ones. Lastly, a divergence in the Relative Strength Index (RSI) prevented it from reaching overbought levels.

These collective observations point towards a loss of momentum in the uptrend. However, despite these indicators suggesting a weakening trend, it is important to note that the prices continued to form higher highs and higher lows. Loss of momentum serves as an early warning sign or evidence of a potential trend reversal, but the ultimate confirmation lies in the price action itself. Nonetheless, these clues provide valuable insight into the evolving dynamics of the market, highlighting the need for vigilance and cautious assessment of trend strength and momentum.

In the second week of January, a wide red candle appeared, breaching the 10-week moving average. This breach signaled market weakness and prompted an exit strategy, as the Nifty corrected by about 10% from its peak.

You may also observe that the previous swing support was breached at this juncture! Let's examine the daily chart to observe its progression.

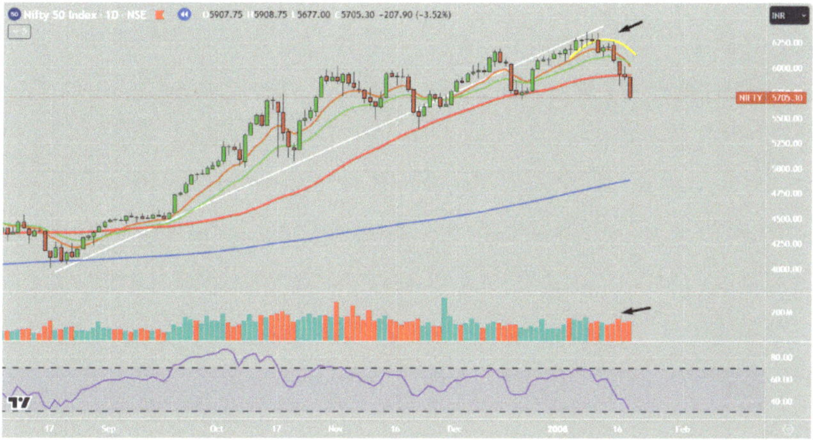

On the daily charts, we can observe a downturn in the slope of the moving averages. The prices have decisively fallen below the 50-day moving average, forming lower highs and lower lows accompanied by increasing volumes. These signs suggest that a significant correction may be imminent.

Over time, Nifty began to decline, breaching the 40-week moving average and forming distinct lower highs and lower lows. Upward movements encountered resistance at the 10-week moving averages and the downward-sloping trendline. Additionally, the slope of the moving averages shifted downwards. Also, take note of the RSI, which consistently remained below the 50 level throughout this fall. While technical analysis didn't signal the market peak, it did help mitigate potential losses for those holding long positions or attempting long-side trades. It's essential to remember that no analysis can consistently identify market tops and bottoms.

The Final Drop XII

All You Need Is...

The stock market's essence isn't just in strategy or tips; it's a mental arena. Success hinges on mindset, discipline, and emotional control, recognizing losses as part of the process.

Key Insights

- **Capital Mindset:** View your trading funds as tools, detaching from the emotional weight of gains and losses.
- **Learning from Losses:** Treat losses as educational, not emotional setbacks. Analyze, learn, and adapt without carrying past burdens into new trades.
- **Embrace Failures**: Failures are invaluable lessons. Reflect on mistakes, refine strategies, and approach the market with refreshed resolve.
- **Discipline Over Impulse:** Adhere to your trading plan as a guard against market-induced emotions.
- **Long-term Perspective:** Building a trading career is a gradual journey focused on strategic consistency and learning from every outcome.

Cultivating a resilient trading mindset requires ongoing effort and the discipline to remain rational amidst emotional turmoil.

www.ingramcontent.com/pod-product-compliance
Ingram Content Group UK Ltd.
Pitfield, Milton Keynes, MK11 3LW, UK
UKHW060007051026
15591UKWH00001B/80
9798893632866